Writers and Partisans

AMERICAN CULTURAL HISTORY SERIES

Editors:

Loren Baritz, University of Rochester
William R. Taylor, University of Wisconsin

Writers and Partisans:

A HISTORY OF LITERARY RADICALISM IN AMERICA,
James Burkhart Gilbert

Writers and Partisans:

A History of Literary Radicalism in America

JAMES BURKHART GILBERT

JOHN WILEY AND SONS, INC.
New York • *London* • *Sydney*

Library of Congress Catalog Card Number: 68-18485
GB 471 29892X
Printed in the United States of America

For Susan

Preface

When I first planned this book, I intended to write a history of the *Partisan Review,* dealing almost exclusively with events that occurred during the lifetime of the journal. I found very soon, however, that this could not simply be a history of another little magazine. The literary attitudes of the editors at the moment the magazine began in 1934 could be traced to a general set of ideas held by a number of other young writers, but this did not explain them. I could not agree with their assumption that radical literature or avant-garde literature had any necessary relationship to socialist politics. It seemed that this connection was an historic one, whose roots lay in earlier generations of writers and radicals; therefore, my research extended backward to ask a number of important questions. How did avant-garde literature become identified with radical politics? What was the meaning of avant-garde? Did the *Partisan Review* belong to any important tradition in American cultural history? What were the traditions that the *Partisan* opposed? How did the political and literary positions of the editors conform to those of their contemporaries?

The book that I have written tries to answer, at least in part, some of these questions, as well as a good many others. It does not evaluate the accomplishments of a group of astute critics, nor does it test the judiciousness of their taste in poetry or prose. It is not a history of ideas or the biography of an important group of men who eventually emerged at the core of the American intelligentsia, although it involves all these things. More accurately, it is a history of assumptions about literature and the role of the intellectual seen through an important institution, the little magazine.

As a vehicle for new movements in literature and politics, the little magazine has been of immense importance in the twentieth century. It has been at once the public birthplace, the homestead, the prison, and sometimes the rescue mission of many contemporary intellectuals. If that function is now somewhat less important, since many writers have joined the universities or found access to large circulation magazines, this development is in some sense due to the success of the little magazine in popularizing dissident intellectuals.

In my study of the *Partisan Review* I have examined the beginnings of literary radicalism in the twentieth century through the 1920s. After the onset of the Depression, I have focused almost exclusively on the *Partisan* as the best and most interesting example of literary radicalism. The discussion ends at two dates: at 1945 insofar as the editorial staff is concerned and at about 1952 regarding important intellectual trends. I do this for two reasons. I do not wish my history to converge or pass judgment upon the present. But more important, the subject itself ends with these dates. Literary radicalism loses many of its old meanings after World War II, just as the independent little magazine plays a somewhat different role after 1945. I have followed the history of literary radicalism to the point where it became possible to trade alienation and independence for academia.

In the research and writing of this book I owe many debts which are always easily acknowledged but often impossible to repay. For financial aid I wish to thank the Woodrow Wilson Foundation and the University of Wisconsin for providing support during the initial stages of research and writing.

I am indebted to William Phillips and Philip Rahv who allowed me to use the *Partisan Review* manuscript collection and who were very generous with their memories of the 1930s and 1940s. I am also grateful to Dwight Macdonald, Fred Dupee, and Nancy Macdonald who very kindly discussed with me the years of their work on the magazine, and to Franklin Folsom for making available his fascinating collection of the League of American Writers' papers. Acknowledgments are also due to Jack Conroy for the use of his private papers and especially for recreating the excitement of the first years of the "proletarian renaissance." I thank George Novack for his help in clarifying the very complex history of the American Trotskyist intelligentsia. Finally, I am grateful to the late Alexander Trachtenberg for his discussion of the 1930s.

Of those who have read the manuscript and criticized it, I am most indebted to William R. Taylor whose comments and general perceptiveness have helped me countless times. Loren Baritz suggested a number of helpful changes and tactfully showed me some weaknesses. I am grateful to Warren I. Susman who read one chapter and lent his enormous knowledge to correct some of my errors.

I am also indebted to the staff of the Newberry Library in Chicago for their assistance. Felix Pollack of the University of Wisconsin helped with the history of little magazines. I wish to thank James Weinstein for several discussions of early American socialism. To William Appleman Williams I wish to acknowledge a long-standing intellectual debt. And above all I thank my wife Susan for her fine editorial work, her criticism, and especially her patience.

JAMES BURKHART GILBERT

University of Maryland
College Park, Maryland
December 1967

Acknowledgments

I am grateful to the following publishers for permission to quote from works published or controlled by them:

The *Partisan Review:* The *Partisan Review* Papers, Rutgers University, and the *Partisan Review* (1934-1954).

E. P. Dutton & Co.: *World of Randolph Bourne,* edited by Lillian Schlissel, 1965.

Farrar, Straus & Giroux: *Sights and Spectacles,* by Mary McCarthy, 1956, and *Shores of Light,* by Edmund Wilson, 1952.

Harcourt, Brace & World: *Letters of Lincoln Steffens,* edited by Ella Winter and Granville Hicks, 1938, and *Movers and Shakers,* Volume III of *Intimate Memories,* by Mable Dodge Luhan, 1933.

Horizon Press: *Politics and the Novel,* by Irving Howe, 1957.

Charles Scribner's Sons: *Axel's Castle,* by Edmund Wilson, 1931, and *The Liberation of American Literature,* by V. F. Calverton, 1932.

The Viking Press: *Where We Came Out,* by Granville Hicks, 1954.

The following individuals have very kindly allowed me to quote from their private correspondence: Malcolm Cowley, Floyd Dell, Granville Hicks, Dwight Macdonald, William Phillips, and Philip Rahv.

Contents

Writers and Partisans

Introduction

Every new tendency in art has begun in rebellion.

  Leon Trotsky, *The Partisan Review*, 1938

The history of literary radicalism in the United States from the
founding of the *Masses* and the *Seven Arts* before World War
I to the 1950s is fascinating for its intellectual gyrations and
the causes it has favored. But it has also influenced and reflected intellectual developments that at first glance appear to
have little to do with political radicalism or Marxism. From the
association of radical politics with advanced art in Greenwich
Village before World War I to the presumed end of ideologies
in the 1950s, political radicalism has been an issue, if not always the primary issue, that confronted an important segment
of American writers and critics, exercising an influence disproportionate to its impact in other realms of American life. Despite
the fusion of literary radicalism to broader questions, it has, in
another sense, had a curiously sectarian history. Developments
before World War I have stretched across decades to affect
young intellectuals of the 1930s and 1940s; assumptions about
the nature of politics and literature have continued to be relevant to later generations; and the "radical tradition," whatever
it has meant to its various interpreters, has placed limits on the
present. In part, the isolation of literary radicalism has been a
function of its close identification with New York City and its
involvement in the rise of New York as a cultural center. The
radical tradition has lingered in that city while elsewhere it
has disappeared. Thus the history of literary radicalism must be
seen in the larger perspective of cultural history and the centralization of literary life in New York.

1

One of the most consistently articulate and long-lived centers for the discussion of literary radicalism has been the *Partisan Review*, founded in 1934 and still published by the original editors. Itself a part of the history of radicalism and responsive to its traditions, the *Partisan* provides a unique focus through which to examine the meeting of literary radicalism with issues going far beyond Marxism or literary criticism. Although the magazine after a few years became estranged from the dominant radical movement, that of the Communist party, it never entirely stretched beyond the influence of its origins in that tradition. And ultimately the magazine had an important effect on the course of literary radicalism. Its immersion in the issues of New York publishing and politics has made it extremely sensitive to major intellectual currents in that city.

Within the broad subject of literary radicalism three primary areas are most consistently illuminating for the history of the *Partisan Review*. The first of these is the history of the literary left written by its participants. The isolation of radicals has often encouraged them to nurture and preserve the obscure events of their own past when there was little more than a tradition in which to believe. To understand the most important decade of literary radicalism, the 1930s, it is necessary to trace the origins of the movement and the way in which habits of mind have been passed on and sometimes distorted by subsequent generations. The compulsion of the intellectual left to write about itself has made the memoirs of such figures as Max Eastman, Joseph Freeman, Granville Hicks, Floyd Dell, and others, as well as their criticism and even their poetry and prose, important documents in understanding the context of radical letters in America.

In addition to the Writers' Congresses and literary-political organizations, the history of the literary left is part of the broader history of little magazines in America and their role in shaping the literary and political tastes of the culture. For the entire period, from 1900 to the 1950s, radical intellectuals have often relied for publication of their work on small and occasionally obscure journals. The fluctuating fortunes of such magazines have been a decisive factor in the history of the literary left. The *Seven Arts*, the *Masses*, the *Dial*, the *Rebel Poet*, the *Symposium*, and countless others are the embodiment of the changing radical tradition.

A final broad source in the history of literary radicalism is the story of Marxist political organizations, specifically the Communist party and its relations with the Soviet Union. For some time the Communist party was the most relevant political party for a group of prominent intellectuals, and their attitudes toward it often expressed their more general political views. Because they felt that Communism was important to their lives and sometimes to their writing, intellectuals found themselves upon occasion in heated arguments that reflected the various splits within the international Communist movement.

The importance of political radicalism to American intellectuals, particularly writers and artists, has frequently been noted, but few historians have seen the 1930s, sometimes called the Red Decade, as an integral part of American cultural history, and not a momentary, mindless aberration. While it is common knowledge that radicalism, especially in its Marxian variety, has had a rather wide influence on certain intellectual groups, most significantly during this period, the impact of the reverse influence—of intellectuals on American radicalism—has rarely been discussed. The quite natural interchange between individual and movement has somehow been lost, smothered by the propensity to recount the oddities of the movement and the tragedies of lost causes. It is a truism to argue that Marxism is not the American intellectual's own, original response to reality; that, like so many other ideas, it is a migrant philosophy; that in the early twentieth century it came to America first to intellectual ghettos to await slow transformation and then assimilation. As a philosophy and a system of perceptions relative to the American environment, however, Marxism, by the many causes it has been made to serve, has been altered and sometimes entangled with other issues. If it was appealing as a "foreign ideology," it was often so because intellectuals wished for detachment from the native soil; if it has been confused at other times by its attachment to American liberalism, it is because some intellectuals wished the best of two worlds—an identity with profound political change and the security of an allegiance to that respected American philosophy. Immensely complicated, intellectual radicalism in this century has struck out in many directions. It has been forced to depend on foreign working-class movements, such as that in Soviet Russia, largely because its roots after World War I have not been in the working class, but in the intellectual community itself. Unlike European radicalism, it has been largely isolated from its traditional constituency, the proletariat, and, perhaps more importantly, from the working-class party. Thus isolation and the recurring attempt to end such estrangement became one of the characteristic sources of energy in literary-political movements.

The introspection of the radical intellectual movement, exemplified in the tendency to muse upon the private intellectual life, has been matched at times by an outwardness and a receptiveness to European ideas. Uniting these converse attitudes has often been the Bohemianism of the radical intellectual movement and, above all, the Bohemianism of Greenwich Village. The association of political radicalism, experimental art, and the Bohemian life in the early part of the century had a profound effect on the history of the 1930s. The free association of ideas, the intellectual inclusiveness of the Bohemian community, and its sensitivity to anything it considered new and modern made it an ideal medium for the growth of a peculiar sort of experimental culture. At times the American intellectual has been called homeless or a wanderer, even an exile, but often his real home has been Bohemia, whether in New York City, Paris, or elsewhere. The internationalization of culture, of which American literary radicalism was a part, made many writers aware, if they had not been before, that American culture was largely middle-class culture, although what was provincial or even rural was often dismissed as bourgeois. Somehow a way had to be found to bridge the enormous gap between modern European ideas and art (much of it opposed to bourgeois culture) and the culture of America, which continued to explain itself with ideas that seemed irrelevant at best to the young intellectuals of Greenwich Village before World War I. The artists and the intellectuals, because of the new discovery of Europe, became aware of a modern world that seemed to escape the mundane minds of their contemporaries. To preach, to proselytize was of the utmost importance, and the writer was encouraged to assume a role he had often played in the past—that of social critic.

In the early days before World War I when Bohemianism and radicalism met, the role of the intellectual as social critic was largely unquestioned. Even if one important group of New York radicals considered reform of the Progressive variety benign and middle-class, social change nevertheless seemed possible and probable: the power of ideas was not challenged, and the assumption reigned in Bohemia that modern political, scientific, and artistic discoveries were all revolutionary. Well aware of their own origins, for many had come from the Midwest or other provincial areas, Bohemian intellectuals tended to reject the America of the past and the backward areas that they had abandoned for Manhattan. But the America of their own generation and their newfound home in Greenwich Village seemed to present a great variety of possibilities.

The war and America's entry into the conflict suddenly burnt away the optimistic clouds that had hidden the future: to many writers and artists America became intolerably bourgeois and inhospitable. The role of the social critic remained; in fact, it sometimes overwhelmed other functions. Yet the image of America as a land of promise was retained even by many of the intellectuals who sought a new Bohemia in Europe. The domination of American culture in the 1920s by the middle class might not continue in the future. Even the political rebels who stayed in the United States to fan the faint hope for revolution shared many of the more optimistic assumptions of their exiled friends.

The Great Crash and the Depression touched off a new response among radical intellectuals. First, it increased their ranks and amplified their voice, making their predictions and criticisms audible to a much larger audience. More importantly, the economic crisis seemed to confirm what Marx had predicted in classical terms. The crisis created a new constituency, the working class, to replace the isolated intellectual community, thus initiating a reappraisal of the Bohemian and radical tradition. The role of the intellectual as social critic was at once greatly strengthened and undermined. Finally, the Depression inaugurated a new search for America that ended in the rediscovery and the ultimate acceptance in the 1940s and the 1950s of the old America. The generation that came to maturity at the beginning of the Depression, living at a time when advanced art, political radicalism, and the Bohemian life once more were joined, eventually began to suspect the validity of relating the three. In part, their doubts were simply the result of growing older. More fundamentally, after the 1930s there was a questioning of the old assumption that the intellectual must be a social critic, that the writer should remain detached from his environment, and that America was provincial and therefore an inferior culture. The former links between radical art and radical politics were eroded by the abrasive events of the 1930s, and this generation ultimately came to doubt that Bohemianism and radicalism should be joined. In post-World War II America both movements appeared to be dead.

The fissure between advanced art and radical politics was crucial to the intellectual history of the postwar period. One reason for the severity of this division was the debilitating failure of the radical movement and liberal politics in the 1930s—a failure of which the *Partisan Review* was well aware, a failure that, in fact, illuminates the existence of the magazine and its importance in American cultural history. Contrary to what some historians have written, the 1930s was not a period of successful social experimentation. It was a time when stopgap measures, disguised and transformed by rhetoric, passed for original thinking. It was also a time when some writers and intellectuals attached their fortunes to radical movements that misunderstood or misgauged the course of events in America. Dreams were shattered, hence dreaming fell into disrepute. The supposed failure of one utopia, the Soviet Union, made belief in all utopias suspect. And despite the words of politicians and the disputations of intellectuals, the depression resolved itself in war.

To look back at the history of the 1930s as it was experienced by the *Partisan Review* and radical intellectuals in general is, therefore, to distort greatly the history of the period. Perhaps only one justification for doing so can survive historical perspective: the dependence in one way or another of our own decade and of postwar generations on the experience of the period. If there are striking parallels between today and that decade, parallels provided by a "new left," one of whose characteristics is the rejection of what remains of the old, and by its renewed belief in the compatibility of Bohemianism and radicalism which is reminiscent of Greenwich Village before World War I, then such a history is even more important, for it is incumbent upon subsequent generations to understand what is being rejected and what has been rediscovered.

Chapter 1

The New Paganism

Fundamentally, Socialism means, not merely a
political and economic revolution, nor even a
revolution in history, science, literature and art,
but both of these together. The conflict is
between two classes and the whole of the two
civilizations they represent.

William English Walling

But we had our bolshevists of the spirit before
ever America heard of the bolshevists of the
flesh.

"The Wanderers" from *Freeman,* 1920

Socialism to the radical American intellectual in 1900 often
meant the dream of society transformed, a dream pushed
toward realization by every event in the liberation of the human spirit and by every scientific advance; socialism meant
revolution in the broadest sense and the culmination of social
progress. The triumphs of modernity, the rule of reason and
science, and a renaissance of art and literature were its parts.
It absorbed in its broad path the art and thought of Wagner,
of Tolstoy, Gorki, Ibsen, of Nietzsche and Wilde. It represented
the fulfillment of the nineteenth century and the industrial and
scientific advances of that era, gathering in all that was new
and revolutionary in art and thought. Yet it was also a revolution against the century that had created it. To the socialist
intellectual in 1900 Walt Whitman, H. G. Wells, William
Morris, Oscar Wilde and many others were prophets of a new

8

order. There was no single literary style, no chosen school of radical writers, but there was a general faith in what the future could create out of the past. The vagueness of this vision reflected the diversity of the socialist movement itself, of the new Socialist party whose origins lay among anarchists, communitarians, and Christians. Change itself and the revolution of every aspect of human effort promised to add substance to the ideal society. To H. G. Wells, who influenced many early socialist writers, the advance of socialism included in the widest sense "all science, literature and invention." The reconstruction of society would usher in a new culture, a new literature and art, but there was no certainty at first about the nature of this culture except that it should be modern.[1]

The ill-defined intellectual socialism of the turn of the century had room for the schemes of a wide variety of social rebels. Just as it looked forward to a revolutionized American culture, it looked back upon a broad tradition of humanitarian literature that included many earlier artists who had invoked social justice. This tradition encompassed much of the American literary heritage—Emerson, Lowell, Whitman, and others; it looked also to England and the arts and crafts movement inspired by William Morris, to the poetry of Shelley and Markham, and to the writings of Strindberg, Ibsen, and Shaw. It included works that protested the exploitation of men and expressed the agelong search for a better world. But the intellectual socialism at the turn of the century also had within its ranks the forerunners of a cultural movement that emerged from American realism, radical journalism, and the writings of Upton Sinclair, Stephen Crane, Frank Norris, and Jack London. This embryonic movement was increasingly attracted to a distinctive sort of hero, the tramp-intellectual, exemplified in the life of Jack London and later celebrated by John Reed and Floyd Dell. In the first decade of the twentieth century both elements— traditional protest literature and revolutionary journalism—appeared in socialist publications. Only gradually did the writings of London, Sinclair, and others crowd out the revolutionary afterglow of the nineteenth century.

---

[1] H. G. Wells, *New Worlds for Old* (New York: Macmillan, 1908), p. 326.

The *Comrade,* founded in 1901 and edited by John Spargo, Algernon Lee, and others, typified the earlier, catholic tastes of American socialism. It printed the writings of diverse proponents of social change, from Whitman and Lanier to Strindberg and Heinrich Heine. Greeting their readers, the editors wrote: "*The Comrade* will endeavor to mirror Socialist thought as it finds expression in Art and Literature. Its function will be to develop the aesthetic impulse in the Socialist movement. . . ." Furthermore, the editors proclaimed, "We are in the early days of a great renaissance."[2] Although the magazine existed only four years, until 1905 when it was absorbed into the *International Socialist Review,* it unmistakably illustrates the transition from the earlier humanitarian tradition to the surefooted, positive attitude toward the creation of a socialist art and literature that eventually began to emerge in the *Review* and other radical publications.

Wilshire's Magazine, published by H. Gaylord Wilshire from 1901 to 1915, also mirrored in its earliest years the older spirit of American radicalism, expressed in mystical, utopian, and even religious terms, attached to Victorian humanitarianism, and symbolized by the "Man with the Hoe." Poetry and prose lamenting the plight of the proletariat was an important early feature of the magazine. The form of expression, the portrayal of workers, the language belonged to an older style and a different century. Like other intellectual socialist publications, the magazine drew slowly away from older forms of protest to newer expressions of socialist ideas on art and literature. The combination of the old and new resulted in the publication of the works of Keats, Shelley, Whitman, Howells, and Bellamy alongside those of newer writers such as Jack London and Upton Sinclair.

The gradual shift in taste that was characteristic of socialist intellectuals in some degree paralleled a change in the Socialist party itself, brought about by the increased activity in 1910 of the anarchist wing and the influence of their work on the party. Moreover, the party itself was growing in importance and seriousness during that period. Nowhere was this alteration more

---

[2] "Greetings," *Comrade,* I (October 1901), p. 12.

apparent than in the *International Socialist Review* founded in Chicago in 1900. One of the earliest cultural interests of the *Review* was the arts and crafts movement inspired by William Morris, a movement that, some socialists thought, might counteract the alienation that labor felt following the decline of skilled crafts. The discussion of Morris largely grew out of the Chicago Arts and Crafts Exhibition held in 1902 to which Jane Addams's Hull House contributed examples of handicraft and bookbinding. Commentators on the exhibition were clearly impressed by the efforts of Morris's American followers, as they were by his writings in general, but they were critical of the limited possibilities of the arts and crafts movement. They argued that Morris's ideas, profound as they were, would not be particularly significant in the struggle to change the structure of society. The influence of Morris receded during the first ten years of the century, but it is clear that the example he left and the ideas he advanced were once important to socialist intellectuals, just as the heritage left by utopian and cooperative elements still existed in the socialist movement. But it is just as clear that such influences were quickly being obscured.[3]

The last, most comprehensive statement of the older, eclectic attitude toward socialist art was Upton Sinclair's anthology, *The Cry for Justice.* Sinclair gathered together works by Blake, Cervantes, Emerson, Swift, Shaw, Gorki, Hugo, and others in addition to those of some new poets and writers such as Arturo Giovannitti and Jack London. What Sinclair called his "New Bible" was a collection of writings protesting man's exploitation through the ages, an anthology that was, as Jack London wrote, "The first gathering together of the body of the literature and art of the humanist thinkers of the world."[4] *The Cry for Justice* summarized a humanitarian tradition, but contained little to direct the creation of a new socialist culture. It symbolized the disorganization and diversity of socialist intellectuals that had existed since 1900.

---

[3] David Shannon, *The Socialist Party of America* (New York: Macmillan, 1955), pp. 55-80. *International Socialist Review*, 1902.

[4] Jack London, "Introduction," in Upton Sinclair, ed., *The Cry for Justice: An Anthology of the Literature of Social Protest* (Philadelphia: John C. Winston, 1915), p. 3.

While older writers such as Morris, Nietzsche, and Wells continued to be of some importance, several of the influences that were shaping the socialist movement itself affected attitudes toward culture. The increasing seriousness of the movement about 1910, the impact of the Industrial Workers of the World (I.W.W.), and the appearance of a new generation of socialist intellectuals coincided with the growing acceptance of new literary styles developed by Sinclair, Norris, and London. Cultural movements associated with American socialism in 1910 were undergoing rapid changes away from earlier forms of expression that looked back upon a humanitarian tradition to new forms that promised to develop into a cultural movement to supplement the political revolution.

One of the most important signs of change was the search for a revolutionary form of expression. "Perhaps the most important symptom of the progress of Socialism in America," wrote Upton Sinclair in 1911, "is the flood of Socialist books which are pouring from the presses nowadays, books written by native-born Americans and dealing with American questions from American points of view." This burst of socialist publication dovetailed with what some critics have designated as the end of the nineteenth-century literary world, the "Neo-Puritanic Era," as Gorham Munson called it, and the dominance of "Young America."[5]

This change in attitudes and styles among socialist intellectuals was reflected in the *International Socialist Review*. Poetry in the early issues of the magazine had been highly moralistic and expressed in elaborate and sentimental language. By 1910 the *Review* was publishing poetry that showed the strong influence of contemporary literary fashions, using simpler language, ordinary speech and slang, and was closer to the prose of Jack London and the poems written by members of the I.W.W. Hopes were sometimes high for the young poets and writers whose work appeared in the magazine. On one occasion John Spargo commented that James Oppenheim, later an editor

---

[5] Upton Sinclair, "Socialist Fiction," *Wilshire's Magazine*, XV (February 1911), p. 4. Gorham Munson, "The Limbo of American Literature," *Broom*, II (June 1922), p. 250.

of the *Seven Arts*, was one of the most important new socialist poets. One day, he concluded, Oppenheim would ."give us the first great American expression of the Social Revolution in Verse."[6] After 1910 little more was said of William Morris, arts and crafts movements, or cooperative schemes. Rather, events such as the Lawrence strike caught the imagination of the editors. The influence of the I.W.W. increased when Bill Haywood became an editor of the magazine in 1912 and the poems of anarchist Arturo Giovannitti began to appear. Significantly, the format of the magazine also changed about 1909 when it began to print the sort of cartoons, drawings, and poems that would characterize the *Masses*, founded shortly thereafter.

Early prophets of socialism and of a humanitarian commonwealth would be forgotten or ignored because of their presumed attachment to older forms of expression and seemingly archaic moral codes. The earliest socialists were sometimes pictured as puritanical in morals despite their political radicalism; men at war with themselves, in contrast to the new, liberated young socialist, a pagan radical born of the marriage of Bohemianism and socialism in Greenwich Village. A new generation of socialist intellectuals would lead a revolt, not only against a class, but against a century. Nonetheless, this revolt left unscathed a fundamental assumption of the previous era—the compatibility of most modern thought with progress and socialism. The revolt would also preserve and strengthen the image of the proletarian hero as a hobo, a tramp, a wanderer, a member of the I.W.W., a portrait that was captured in Hutchins Hapgood's *The Spirit of Labor* and personified in the life of John Reed.[7] Devotees of everything modern, the younger socialist intellectuals were nonetheless children of the nineteenth century.

The proletarian hero depicted as a tramp and hobo was celebrated in the songs of Joe Hill and the writings of the I.W.W., acknowledged by anarchists such as Emma Goldman, and, per-

---

[6] John Spargo, "Art and Literature," *International Socialist Review*, IX (April 1909), p. 817.
[7] Robert Rive La Monte, "The New Intellectuals," *New Review*, II (January 1914), pp. 45-46, and Floyd Dell, "Change in American Life and Fiction," *New Review*, III (May 1913), pp. 13-15.

haps most important, typified in the life of Jack London. London's career, part of it spent as a tramp, belongs in some sense to the tradition of Walt Whitman, the social outcast, the prophet, and the bard. In another sense, however, London's life reflects the widespread phenomenon of vagabondage, which was particularly important in the Western United States during the 1890s.

The emergence of the I.W.W. as an important labor organization brought to prominence the tramp and the migrant laborer who often joined the Wobblies. Moreover, the self-conscious celebration of vagabond life, always important in America, was given a revolutionary cast by the attention accorded to the Wobblies. A characteristic American social type was now depicted as a social revolutionary, but he could also be seen as the creator of a new sort of culture contained in songbooks and I.W.W. newspapers and as a prophet in his own life, a man on the fringe of society, yet capable of seeing clearly to its center.[8]

London became a kind of journalist for the social underworld, a type recreated later by John Reed, Arturo Giovannitti, and Michael Gold. London's career and his writing helped push the alliance of realism in literature and socialism—what Floyd Dell called the "journalistic" trend. Such journalism was radical, even revolutionary, because it implied that the journalist must not merely be the mirror of events, but a participant in their outcome. The works of Lincoln Steffens and John Reed exemplify this journalism pushed to revolutionary limits—the promotion of social change by fixing upon what were considered the radical implications of reality, the facts that cried out for change. Moreover, the immediacy of journalistic prose seemed best suited to describe the life of the underworld—the life of the migrant laborer, the urban immigrant, and the subjects drawn by London, Crane, and others.[9]

The conjunction of radical journalism and the socialist move-

---

[8] Jack London, "How I Became a Socialist," in Philip Foner, *Jack London: American Rebel* (New York: Citadel Press, 1947), pp. 4-5, 21. Nels Anderson, *The Hobo: Sociology of the Homeless Man* (Chicago: University of Chicago Press, 1923).

[9] Floyd Dell, in Lloyd R. Morris, *The Young Idea* (New York: Duffield, 1917), p. 148.

ment had begun by 1910. Intellectuals were becoming aware of the existence of an underground culture created by the I.W.W., and the image of an American revolutionary, a pro-letarian-intellectual, was sketched in rough form. The revolt against the nineteenth century, which obscured the earliest prophets of the new socialist order, had already set in. In 1914 one socialist critic wrote of the "Puritan-like narrowness" of the older generation of Marxist students. The renaissance in Green-wich Village, which gathered in existing currents of socialism, quickly revealed their meanings. Intellectuals who congregated in the new cultural center in lower Manhattan, although gen-erally denying the relevance of most of the previous century, acted on one of the most important premises of early socialism, the revolutionary potential of modern ideas. Instead of helping to preserve a humanitarian tradition, this stance increased the furious rejection of anything identified with the older genera-tion. What the Village intellectuals expressed, however, was not so much new as it was eloquent, coherent, and committed to action. Most important, this new movement was linked to the Bohemian life, which promised to create a society of experi-mental human relationships. The older ways, the dead prophets now seemed useless as intellectuals gathered together to revo-lutionize America.

The boisterous, self-confident beginnings of modern literary radicalism occurred in the few years before America's entrance into World War I: years of a sudden coming together of diverse ideas and personalities, and a time that future generations came to know as the classical period of the radical tradition. But the tradition meant much more than the growing prominence of socialist intellectuals; it was an intimate part of a larger literary revival. Two primary clusters of ideas appeared in the great flurry of changing philosophies, the "revolution" and the "renaissance" out of which most of the important literary fac-tions of the 1930s evolved. In this early period the two sides of literary radicalism had much in common; both were formu-lated in the optimistic, expansive atmosphere of Greenwich Village; both revolted against what they felt were the dominant ideas of the nineteenth century; and both found spiritual or political radicalism in the Bohemian life of the Village. As the revolution and the renaissance burst through the strictures placed upon intellectual life by the past, they found no immediate antagonism between modern ideas: socialism, anarchism, feminism, science, Freudianism all seemed to be linked together in a rebellion against tradition. It was assumed that literature—experimental writings of modern Europeans and the new self-discovery in American letters—was related to new attitudes in politics. The idea of change permeated a variety of expressions and activities. However, the association of literature and radical politics did not occur merely because of a vague attraction. It was precipitated by a general atmosphere in which ideas appeared to be interchangeable; it was developed by two important intellectual organs, the *Masses* and the *Seven Arts;* and it was given expression in the lives of John Reed, Max Eastman, Randolph Bourne, and others.[10]

Although World War I altered the mood of the Village and ultimately split it apart, it did not eliminate the association of literary radicalism with Bohemianism, nor did it destroy the supposed union of advanced art and radical politics. The sudden termination of the optimistic rebellion caused by the war acted in the long run to preserve the early spirit of the Village, for it shifted blame for the decline of the Village from the faults of the young intellectuals to the war. Whatever cracks there might have been in the assumption of compatibility between political, artistic, and social ideas were hidden when the whole structure was wrecked by the world conflict. Thus the period was preserved intact, optimistic, and successful for future generations.

The experience of the radical intellectuals in the 1930s not only in some ways parallels that of the generation that came to maturity immediately before World War I, but is also a development emerging from the events of those early years. Ideas about the nature of radicalism, conclusions drawn from an analysis of American culture, and definitions of the relation between the artist (particularly the writer) and society lingered on into the

---

[10] Meyer Schapiro, "Rebellion in Art," *America in Crisis*, Daniel Aaron, ed. (New York: Knopf, 1954), pp. 223 ff.

1930s. The apparently instinctive rejection of the middle class during the Depression years has much to do with the active intellectual revolution against the bourgeoisie before and after World War I. The radicals of the 1930s inherited a number of conceptions and misconceptions from their rebellious elders. Part of this legacy they rejected immediately, only to have to rediscover it later. Other parts they invested in the new intellectual enterprise of building a revolution and earned unexpected dividends.

The importance of the movement of young intellectuals who were gathered in Greenwich Village about 1910 does not depend on their actual role in the contemporary radical and socialist movements. They clearly existed at the outskirts of life in the Socialist party, which was the major radical organization. Nor did New York exert the commanding influence over such movements that it did after 1917.[11] Because of the later importance of New York and Greenwich Village in the Marxist cultural movement, the intellectual atmosphere and the personalities that survived from the prewar period in that city exerted a disproportionate influence on radicalism as a whole. Ideas associated with the enthusiastic experimentation in art and politics that characterized the beginnings of the Greenwich Village renaissance remained important as New York became the most influential center of American culture. The hero of the intellectuals in the 1930s significantly was not Eugene Debs but John Reed; what became the major cultural organ of the Communist party was founded as a revival of the old *Masses,* a magazine published by Bohemian-radicals in the Village. To write exclusively on New York intellectuals means that the radical scene before World War I must be consciously distorted. The justification for doing so is that the history of radical cultural movements itself swells the importance of the intelligentsia of New York.

Greenwich Village, to which Midwesterners and intellectuals from the East had fled in search of the Bohemian life, boasted

---

[11] James Weinstein, *The Decline of American Socialism, 1912-1924* (New York: Monthly Review Press, 1967). See also Hutchins Hapgood, *The Spirit of Labor* (New York: Duffield, 1907), for importance of Chicago.

a community that thrived on modern ideas and the experimental life. Before World War I and the thrust of the great traffic arteries through its boundaries, the Village was quiet, secluded, and charming. Moreover, the rents were cheap.[12] It was here, more than anyplace else, that the character of the American radical intellectual was determined. Although cultural revivals had swept the Midwest, Chicago in particular, the lure of New York quickly stripped provincial areas of their leading talents. In a secluded part of lower Manhattan an amazing diversity of men, women, and ideas were brought together. The geographic confinements of the Village seemed only to intensify the burst of energy that was released before World War I. Most important, it was here that the radicalism of Marx and the anarchism of the I.W.W. met and mixed with the new experiments in literature and art.

When the rents were low in Greenwich Village, recounts Floyd Dell, whose love affairs and literary adventures helped create the myths that surrounded Bohemia, the Village was inhabited by two sorts: the professional, middle-class people and the young Bohemians, economically unsure, who engaged their unestablished talents in literary and artistic odd jobs. By the beginning of the war in 1914, artists, intellectuals, Wobblies, socialists, and writers were mingling in the coffeehouses, restaurants, and apartments of lower Manhattan. What united them was their rebellion against tradition, respectability, and middle-class life. The rebellion boiled over into every aspect of contemporary life. "Everyone was cooking up some sort of revolution . . . ," related James Oppenheim, poet-editor of the *Seven Arts,* "socialism, sex, poetry, conversation, dawn-greeting—anything so long as it was taboo in the Middle West."[13] The aimlessness of this early enthusiasm for the new and frankly experimental was short-lived, for as youth searched for wider experience, the culture narrowed its vision in preparation for war. By the end of the war the critique of the young rebels,

---

[12] Caroline Ware, *Greenwich Village, 1920-1930* (Boston: Houghton Mifflin, 1935), p. 15.
[13] James Oppenheim, "The Story of the Seven Arts," *American Mercury,* XX (June 1930), p. 157.

and, particularly those of Randolph Bourne, flew straight to the heart of American civilization. The strenuous efforts of the Wilson Administration to silence political opponents deeply affected (possibly as much as any group in America besides the I.W.W.) the Village intellectuals who opposed the war and gave substance to their vague and exuberant prewar radicalism. There was ample evidence for a pessimistic appraisal of American society and for the conclusion that the United States was an impossibly provincial and hostile world for the artist.

Despite a wide variance of interests shown by the political and artistic sides of the cultural rebellion that began about 1911, the predominant figure of the Village ferment was the young writer. Through him attention was focused on America's cultural heritage, in a way that disparaged the earlier humanitarian writers. Van Wyck Brooks, whose voluminous critical writings did much to shape the attitudes of his generation, argued that there was actually no real literary tradition in America; on the contrary, literature was a history of false starts. The writer aged prematurely for he could not develop and refine his artistic talents. To Floyd Dell, traditional New England literature was largely irrelevant: "We can now discount almost to worthlessness—for our own purposes—the greater part of what New England took the trouble to say." The previous era meant little to the modern intellectual, and its literature explained almost nothing to the younger generation. "We had our own lives to live—and all these classical utterances of the nineteenth-century literature," Dell explained, "had no relation to our lives."[14]

Like many of their contemporaries, the young literary radicals blamed the social environment for America's intellectual and political dilemma. Repression interfered with the fulfillment of the individual and limited the social and psychological expression of the artist. This hypothesis was applied variously, from a narrow sexual interpretation to the broader sociological view ad-

---

[14] Floyd Dell to Bernard Shaw, draft of a letter, Davenport, Iowa, 1908, p. 2. Floyd Dell MSS, Newberry Library, Chicago, Illinois; hereafter cited as Dell MSS. Floyd Dell, *Intellectual Vagabondage* (New York: Doran, 1926), p. 106.

vanced by Randolph Bourne, who saw repression as a method used to gain economic and political power.[15]

To Bourne, who had attended Columbia University with the educated sons of immigrants, puritanism was a symbol of sterility, of clinging to old ideas about the nature of American society that were unreal and even oppressive. The puritan represented Anglo-Saxonism, New England exclusiveness, and a literature that had run its course. Bourne believed the new and important things that were happening in America bypassed this tradition, and he traced their origins to Continental Europe. Socialists also made the puritan a symbol of the socially repressive features of American society. Capitalism and religious puritanism, they felt, were complementary elements of middle-class rule. New forms of social and cultural enterprise, a "new paganism," was necessary as part of the revolution against capitalism. One puritanical attitude of American society was given enormous attention—conservatism toward sexual relations and women's rights. It was no accident that Socialists and Village intellectuals both championed the writings of Margaret Sanger and proclaimed the need to revolutionize marriage and sexual customs.

The vehemence of the Village rebellion was heaped on the caricature of the puritan, who was pictured as a cultural philistine and a moral hypocrite, armed with ideas from the *Saturday Evening Post,* the archenemy of Bohemia. This revulsion against puritanism was not limited to scorn for the vulgar contemporary version. To Van Wyck Brooks and others the puritan was the symbol of a social type historically associated with industrialism in America. Puritanism was the ethical system of the pioneers and the philosophy that drove American culture to acquisitiveness. H. L. Mencken's long essay, "Puritanism as a Literary Force," incorporated Bourne's arguments and acknowledged the historic origins of this presumably debilitating style of thought. The editor of the *Smart Set,* however, saved his sharpest remarks for the puritan in public affairs, the "professional sin-

---

[15] Theodore Dreiser, "Life, Art and America," *Seven Arts,* I (February 1917), p. 364. Randolph Bourne, "The Puritan's Will to Power," *The History of a Literary Radical* (New York: Russell, 1956), p. 157.

hound" and the "virtuoso of virtue." This awesome figure, bloated with political and financial power, had secured the passage through Congress of the Mann Act in 1910 and the Webb Act of 1913 (making the enforcement of "dry" areas easier), supported the Anti-Saloon League movement, and, worst of all, presided over the public morality with the power of censorship of the mails. The puritan was seen as a morally stunted and archaic figure, an intellectual subspecies who wielded a Stone Age ax against modern ideas and nonsentimental art. He was part of a cultural heritage considered at best dubious by a young generation of rebellious intellectuals who were excited at the thought of stretching life to the limits of experience and often indiscriminant in what they rejected.

Devotion to experience was an important part of the rebellion against the nineteenth century. Brooks felt that the American artist had neither realized experience nor understood life: he was repressed and his environment was denatured. Max Eastman, editor of the *Masses,* wrote of his friend John Reed, whose search for the chalice of proletarian revolution caught the imagination of many of the young Village radicals, that poetry was not just writing, but the "living of life." "We were carrying realism so far in those days that it walked right out of our books," Eastman remembered, "We wanted to live our poetry."[16] Realism did not mean the mere recording of unassimilated facts; it demanded the combination of a moral toughness and an ethical vision capable of coming to terms with the world as it existed and, if necessary, of changing it. It was this sort of toughness that enabled Lincoln Steffens, who exerted a wide influence over the young rebels—particularly John Reed— to conclude that corruption was the very essence of political activity. The vision made the difference, for it justified the younger generation in its contention that the world was fundamentally different from the nineteenth-century description of it.

The coexistence of a belief in the harshness of life and a firm faith in the relevance of literature to his view of society posed

---

16 Van Wyck Brooks, "The Splinter of Ice," *Seven Arts,* I (January 1917), p. 278. Max Eastman, *Heroes I Have Known* (New York: Simon and Schuster, 1942), p. 213.

an important question for the intellectual. What were the connections, if any, between the reality of 1912 America and artistic perception? With what catalyst could the artist bind unrefined experience to his new intellectual interests? Life,
particularly middle-class life, he felt, did not correspond to the
view advanced by his elders, and his own discoveries convinced
him that the history of American culture evidenced a deep split
between the realm of ideas and art and the world of business.[17]
The estrangement that many intellectuals felt from any cultural
heritage reinforced the assertion that tradition itself was at fault
because it had hidden reality from the artist under a slick
veneer of sentimentality. Thus the artist and society had both
suffered from repression. Discovery of what the intellectual saw
as a new reality placed him immediately at odds with the cultural tradition of his predecessors, and his first reaction was to
deny it as meaningful in any sense. On the other hand, reality
itself seemed radical, if one could only wipe away the blur
of archaic ideas; reality was revolutionary, and the journalist,
even the artist, could be its interpreter. Margaret Anderson, editor of the *Little Review*, wrote that her magazine was an organ
of art and revolution, because art and anarchism were "in the
world for the same kind of reason." Thus anarchism and revolution seemed to some intellectuals to be the political phase
of a cultural movement, ultimately as far-reaching and disastrous in its implications for traditional society as political upheaval.[18] But the intellectual was not as yet very comfortable
in the present, for he needed new ways of relating to his environment, and many of the ideas that had inspired older socialists continued to dominate his thoughts.

Science, particularly the revolutionary insights into modern
society developed by Sigmund Freud, was based on a view of
life that accepted facts that the young rebels felt their elders
had fastidiously avoided. Perhaps, science could even explain
the existence of a dreary reality and a culture that was singu-

---

[17] Van Wyck Brooks, *America's Coming-of-Age* (Garden City, N.Y.:
Doubleday, 1958), p. 4.
[18] Margaret Anderson, "Art and Anarchism," *Little Review*, III (March
1916), p. 3.

larly lacking in brilliance. The young intellectuals went to
school with the theories of Henri Bergson, Nietzsche, Wells,
Marx, and Freud, but they accepted only part of what the older
generation taught; Marx and Freud seemed to dominate their
new philosophy. Psychological explanations provided a valuable
clue to the behavior of the puritan and offered at least one explanation—sexual repression—for the mediocrity that seemed to
rule American letters. Walter Lippmann, who was a prominent
figure in radical Village circles, argued that the impetus begun
by Freudian researches offered "the greatest advance ever
made toward the understanding and control of human character."[19] The introduction into literary discussion of the Freudian
analysis of the subconscious created a justification to broaden
the critic's field of study, widening his awareness of the social
and subconscious backgrounds of art. Deductions from Freudian premises helped to explain the literary and cultural failures
that seemed to plague America by describing them as the result
of psychological disorders inherently a part of American culture.
Social repression was often seen as the primary impediment to
the development of culture.

It was because of their application of reason to the apparently
chaotic world of social relations that Darwin, Marx, Freud, and
other social scientists had created useful tools for understanding social reality and for offering ways to make it conform to
ethical standards. Science seemed to point to new sources of
continuity between reality and the vision of a new era. Walter
Lippmann argued that, "There is nothing accidental then in
the fact that democracy in politics is the twin brother of scientific thinking." It was Lippmann's belief that science could
uncover the nerve of human behavior and the sinews of social
and political life. It could search out the reality under folds of
archaic ideas. The result of his proddings was his conclusion
that an "invisible government" ruled politics, business, and
labor. Once this reality was acknowledged, with its origins in
the human psyche and with its political ramifications, the drift

---

[19] Bourne, "The Puritan's Will to Power," See also Van Wyck Brooks,
Days of the Phoenix (New York: Dutton, 1957), p. 21, and Walter Lippmann, *A Preface to Politics* (New York: Macmillan, 1913), p. 85.

in American society could be ended. "This is what mastery means," he argued, "the substitution of conscious intention for unconscious striving."[20]

To Max Eastman, editor of the *Masses* and a leader of the more political wing of the rebellion, it was Marxism, not Freudianism, that was the more important scientific theory. In advising young radicals to read Nietzsche in order to purge themselves of whatever softness they had, he insisted that even the tough-minded German had not been willing to follow science thoroughly to its conclusions. It was partly this feeling that science could bear the observer to the heart of a problem, and particularly a social problem, that made Marxism appealing to Eastman. Eastman stressed the scientific, experimental character of the political revolution. And Mike Gold, one young writer for the *Masses,* later an important figure in the literary left, related that "Eastman was a romantic figure in the Socialist-literary movement of the time. He was always talking about the duty of being scientific, 'a social engineer.' "[21]

With the past overthrown by a revolution in thought and the present urgently in need of thoroughgoing reform, the young intellectuals tried to visualize a future governed by their own dreams. This projection of a better world is a characteristic of the early years of the Village intellectual rebellion, although there was certainly disagreement about what the future should be and what means should be employed to realize it. Two principles, the idea of a cultural renaissance and the notion of a political revolution, expressed the desires of the younger generation and divided Bohemia into distinctive, but not antagonistic camps.

The large and active Socialist party provided a political arm to the rebellion of the young intellectuals. Before World War I, the Socialists were an important national party, with strength among Midwest workers and farmers, West Coast miners, as

---

[20] Walter Lippmann, *Drift and Mastery* (New York: Mitchell Kennedy, 1914), pp. 269, 275; and Lippmann, *Preface to Politics,* p. 19.

[21] Max Eastman, *Love and Revolution: My Journey Through an Epoch* (New York: Random House, 1964), p. 152, and Mike Gold, "*The Masses* Tradition," *Masses and Mainstream,* IV (August 1951), p. 48.

well as New York intellectuals. Morris Hillquit, the leading New York Socialist, relates that after 1905 intellectuals were attracted to the movement and it became "almost a fad." "Socialism," he continued, "became a favorite topic of discussion among New York's intelligentsia, and the intelligentsia were always strong on discussion."[22]

Within the Socialist party, particularly before 1912, the I.W.W., led by Bill Haywood, struggled for their policy of syndicalism against members who favored participation in elections or reforms rather than immediate revolution. Syndicalists and anarchists before World War I, relates James Cannon, an early leader of the Communist party, "were a recognized and respected part of the radical movement in those days." Max Eastman was even more enthusiastic: "The IWW was the only genuinely *proletarian* revolutionary organization that ever existed in America—one of the few that ever existed anywhere."[23]

The freewheeling syndicalism of Haywood and the Wobblies matched the spirit of the Bohemian rebellion. A kinship of style tied the Wobblies and the intellectuals, and it also united the Village writers and artists to an older tradition of American vagabondage that had itself become part of the I.W.W. Intellectuals striving for self-expression, for rapid change, and for a revolution against the ideas of their elders were attracted to the activist I.W.W. Floyd Dell expressed this affinity of the rebellion and the I.W.W. in his story, "Hallelujah, I'm a Bum."[24] The bum, often the symbol of the Wobbly, he wrote, discovered in Greenwich Village "a kind of tramp he had never known before—the artist kind. These painters, poets, story-writers, were

---

22 Morris Hillquit, *Loose Leaves From a Busy Life* (New York: Macmillan, 1934), pp. 55-56.
23 James Cannon, *The First Ten Years of American Communism* (New York: Lyle Stuart, 1962), p. 98, and Eastman, *Love and Revolution*, p. 126.
24 Floyd Dell, "Hallelujah, I'm a Bum," *Century Magazine*, CX (June 1925), p. 141. Dell recounts that he had originally planned this as a novel, but as he developed it he concluded that his comrades would not like the story since it had a passage in which the artist-heroine preached the doctrine of beauty and the futility of politics. Floyd Dell to Joseph Freeman, April 25, 1951, p. 25, Dell MSS. Albert Parry, *Garrets and Pretenders* (New York: Covici, Friede, 1933), pp. 272, 288.

old friends in a new guise. He and they understood one another perfectly." Not only did the Wobblies mingle with the intellectuals in the Village, but the anarchist Emma Goldman often met members of the *Masses* staff at the Liberal Club, which was located over Polly's Restaurant on Macdougal Street, and was an important center of Village radicalism.

That the I.W.W. was only one tendency in the socialist movement does not detract from its importance to Village intellectuals. For often, in their thinking about social revolution and the worker, the Wobbly or the Paterson striker was the prototype of the proletariat, and the I.W.W. the organization of the revolution. With the rise of New York as a cultural center and as the focal point of American Communism in the 1930s, this background loomed disproportionately large and tended to obscure the other equally important roots of American radicalism. Max Eastman, looking back on the period of the *Masses*, remarked on the implications of this intellectual-radical mixture: "I suppose that the most unique and important feature of the old *Masses* was that while maintaining an editorial policy essentially Marxian it drew into its pages the works of wide circles of the intelligentsia who had revolutionary feeling, *but no understanding of such a policy and very little conception what it was all about.*"[25]

The most famous meeting place in the Village for the interchange of ideas was the salon of Mabel Dodge. Mrs. Dodge, who occupied an elegant apartment on lower Fifth Avenue, opened her doors in 1913 and 1914 to "Socialists, Trade-Unionists, Anarchists, Suffragists, Poets, Relations, Lawyers, Murderers, 'Old Friends,' Psychoanalysts, I.W.W.'s, Single Taxers, Birth Controlists, Newspapermen, Artists, Modern Artists. . ."— all in the name of free speech. Often her evenings were planned in advance; for example, when Bill Haywood, Emma Goldman, Elizabeth Gurley Flynn, and Arturo Giovannitti argued the I.W.W. stand with Walter Lippmann and William English Walling. On another night artists listened to Haywood lecture

---

[25] Max Eastman to Ely Estorick, May 13, 1931, quoted in V. F. Calverton, *The Liberation of American Literature* (New York: Scribner's, 1932), p. 454. Italics mine.

on art, on the separation of the artist from society, and the need for a proletarian artist. One of the more important evenings was devoted to new discoveries in psychology, particularly those of Freud. Lincoln Steffens relates in his autobiography that this particular meeting was among the most serious and thoughtful.

Mabel Dodge in some ways exemplified the Village rebellion. Appraising her contribution to the Armory show of modern art held in 1913, she commented: "I felt as though the Exhibition were mine. I really did. It became, over night, my own little Revolution. *I* would upset America; I would, with fatal, ir-revocable disaster to the old order of things."[26] A revolution in the arts, made by a single person, destructive to the old order, and deeply personalized—these were the ambitions of the young rebel. He must be open to new ideas and intolerant of anything that blocked his self-expression. But Mabel Dodge was more than just a member of the younger generation. Her "evenings" were symbolic of the merging of revolutionary politics and modern ideas in the arts and sciences during the early days of the Village rebellion. Her interest in the I.W.W., the Paterson strike (she helped John Reed organize the Madison Square Garden pageant depicting the strike), and the Tannenbaum case (re-sulting from the arrest of a young radical who had led a group of bums into the Church of St. Alphonsus in 1915) is character-istic of the concern of middle-class Village intellectuals for political and social radicalism, a particular brand of radicalism that was immensely active, and youthful, a radicalism that re-called the comprehensiveness of the socialism of Wells and early radical magazines.

Just as Mabel Dodge could make her own revolution in art, so the Wobbly or the poet-anarchist John Reed felt that he could help bring down the old order with a single strike, or write a book that would shake the foundations of the world. The younger generation felt capable of changing society and of absorbing the ideas that the twentieth century was thrusting into their minds. The Bohemian could scarcely help being in-terested in political and social radicalism (though there were

26 Mabel Dodge Luhan, *Movers and Shakers*, Vol. III of *Intimate Memories* (New York: Harcourt, Brace, 1936), pp. 36, 83.

certainly some who were not), for so many new ideas glutted the atmosphere that there had not yet been time to compartmentalize them—this task would await the World War and the Russian Revolution. The particular attraction of the anarchist wing of the socialist movement to him was based in part on the fact that it shared with Bohemianism many of the same premises about life.

Although the rebellious younger generation was attracted to the Socialist party or the Wobblies, these political organizations were not his home. Rather it was through journalism and the arts, in the *Masses* and the *Seven Arts,* that the young intellectual made his mark upon the culture. In 1914 Floyd Dell wrote of the wonderful assortment of new ideas in the air, but of the need to distinguish among them: "The world needs criticism," he remarked, "I am inclined to think that the world needs criticism at the present time more than it needs feminism or socialism or any other . . . thing."[27]

The more political edge of the Village rebellion was upheld primarily by the *Masses*. It was through this journal and the group of intellectuals who wrote for it that the I.W.W. became established as the proletarian prototype: here, too, intellectuals attempted to join revolutionary politics to the broad interests of the rebellion. The magazine, edited during most of its run by Max Eastman and Floyd Dell, was founded in 1911 by Piet Vlag as the voice of the cooperative element in the socialist movement. By 1912, however, it was reorganized and its content changed under Eastman, a shift that reflected a trend among socialist intellectuals away from an interest in early forms of radicalism. The magazine described itself as "frank, arrogant, impertinent, searching for the true causes"; it was the loud, rough voice of the younger generation. Its pages contained the writings of John Reed, Floyd Dell, Amy Lowell, Sherwood Anderson, Amos Pinchot, John Spargo, and others, as well as the artwork of Robert Minor, George Bellows, Jo Davidson, and John Sloan. After Eastman became editor in 1912, the magazine became a center of the Bohemian rebellion against middle-class

---

[27] Floyd Dell to Arthur Davison Ficke, New York, March 23, 1914, p. 1. Dell MSS.

America. From serious discussion of feminism, strikes, and the
I.W.W. to the flippant portraiture of clergymen, immigration
officials, and big businessmen, the magazine was a free-for-all
proponent of revolution. Eastman pointed to the factor that
united this chaotic burst of writing when he commented: "Our
magazine provided for the first time in America, a meeting
ground for revolutionary labor and the radical intelligentsia."
Significantly, the foundation of the magazine occurred at a time
when Greenwich Village was developing a self-consciousness,
in other words, at a time when it was becoming a cultural center.
The *Masses* became a major spokesman of the rebellion and,
more particularly, its political side because it was published in
the Village by a group of its leading residents and because it
attempted to encompass the revolution in art, morality, and
politics. "There was no precedent in America," wrote Mike
Gold, "for its fascinating melange of wit, learning, bold new
crusading art and literature, sex enlightenment, reportage, socialism."

As first published in 1911, the *Masses* was allied to the center
and right of the Socialist party, attacking anarchism and up-
holding the Indianapolis convention of the Socialist party that
wrote violence out of the Socialist program. In 1912, however,
artist Art Young suggested that Max Eastman become editor of
the magazine and Eastman agreed. "I was reluctantly to become," he related, "the editor of a literary magazine, as a mere
means of arriving at a vehicle of political expression."[28]

By December 1912, under the editorship of Eastman, the
magazine reversed its previous stand on violence. It now opened
its pages to anarchism and syndicalism. The attraction of the
Masses to the I.W.W. was quickened by the spectacular strikes
that the union led. In some ways the Paterson strike was the
central event in the life of the magazine and, in fact, in the prewar Village rebellion. In June 1913 John Reed, now associated
with the *Masses,* went to Paterson, New Jersey, to report on the
silkworkers' strike. After his arrest there and release, he turned

---

[28] Max Eastman, *Enjoyment of Living* (New York: Harper, 1948), pp.
409, 416; and Gold, "*Masses* Tradition," p. 46. See also Max Eastman,
"New Masses for Old," *Modern Quarterly,* VIII (June 1934), p. 292.

his enormous energy to the organization of the pageant that re-enacted the events of the strike and used as actors the strikers from Paterson and their leaders, the I.W.W.'s Bill Haywood and Elizabeth Gurley Flynn.

Association of the *Masses* with the far left of the socialist movement occurred in two ways. Leaders of I.W.W. such as Haywood came to the Village where they met intellectuals around the magazine, and reporters such as Reed, Giovannitti, and Eastman traveled to strike areas to observe and sometimes join radical labor in action. Bill Haywood, who was expelled from the Socialist party in 1912 for advocating the use of violence to further socialist aims, became a hero of the Village intellectuals. East Coast intellectuals such as Eastman, Lippmann, Margaret Sanger, and Louis Boudin defended him against the sanctions of the party.[29]

The attempt to make the magazine "Socialistic, Anarchistic, Syndicalistic, Femministic, optimistic, and pessimistic," as poet-anarchist Arturo Giovannitti claimed it should be, was not without difficulty. Both Dell and Eastman, looking back on the pre-World War I period noted arguments within the *Masses* staff over intelligibility, propaganda, and artistic freedom. The split, commented Eastman, was between "art and propaganda, poetry and practical effort—between the very two interests whose satisfaction within the same covers had made the magazine unique."[30]

The *Masses* did succeed, however, in developing the political cartoon to a high level. Moreover, the sketches and drawings that it published were often able to project a radical view of society within the confines of advanced artistic technique. Preoccupation with urban settings and the forms and shapes of the modern city was typical of much of the artwork. But the *Masses*

[29] Daniel Bell, "Background and Development of Marxian Socialism in America," *Socialism in American Life*, Donald Drew Egbert and Stow Persons, eds. 2 vols. (Princeton, N.J.: Princeton University Press, 1952), I, p. 289.

[30] Floyd Dell, *Homecoming* (New York: Farrar & Rinehart, 1933), p. 251, and Eastman, *Enjoyment of Living*, p. 548. Eastman relates that in March 1916 the artists rebelled against the political posture of the magazine, against Eastman's contention that it should be class-conscious. Max Eastman, "Bunk About Bohemia," *Modern Quarterly*, VIII (May 1934), p. 207.

did not carry this urbanism to the extreme as that of its lesser known contemporary, the *Soil*. The latter magazine was much more a precursor of the celebration of mechanism and urbanism that was a part of the avant-garde movements of the next decade. Often the stories of John Reed or Floyd Dell or the poetry of Arturo Giovannitti presented ideas of the rebellion in fictionalized form. The magazine argued for the affinity of advanced art and literature and new political and social theories, but in general did little to illustrate it.

What related politics and art in the *Masses* was not the vision of a rejuvenated culture, but increasingly the belief in political revolution. The magazine acted to rivet the rebellion of youth to politics: within the context of radical politics, it expressed new ideas on sex, feminism, literature, and philosophy. Consequently the role of the intellectual was ambiguous, for he had to deal with a community wider than that of intellectuals and with forces broader than the cultural atmosphere, things that he did not always feel concerned him as an artist, but as a human being. Here a significant difference between the renaissance and the revolution is discernible. For Van Wyck Brooks and Randolph Bourne there was no question about the role of the intellectual; he was the leader of a rebellion who spoke to a community of like-minded youths. But what was the place of the intellectual, particularly the writer, in the revolution? Was he necessarily the leader? Could he use his gifts to serve politics?

Max Eastman was of primary importance in conveying the ideas of socialism and Marxism to the writers and critics who were drawn to the magazine and in trying to answer these questions.[31] The political commitment of the *Masses* was to the working class and the underprivileged. "This paper belongs to the proletariat," wrote Arturo Giovannitti, "It is the recording secretary of the Revolution in the making. As a recorder of great deeds and great faiths, it is the lineal descendant of the Book of Exodus and the Acts of Apostles."[32] One of the im-

[31] Egbert and Persons, *Socialism in American Life*, II, p. 189. The authors argue that Eastman helped to set the pattern for relating art and literature to politics and psychology.
[32] Arturo Giovannitti, "What I Think of the Masses," *Masses*, VIII (July 1916), p. 5.

mediate problems of the magazine was raised by this commitment, for like so many little magazines—particularly those of
the 1930s—it did not reach "the masses," but instead had a
relatively small readership, many of whom were middle-class
intellectuals. Other socialist publications such as the *Appeal to
Reason* and *Wilshire's Magazine* had a much larger circulation.
The political behavior of the *Masses* reflects the fact that it sat
at the edge of contemporary American radicalism, which was
centered in the Midwest in the Socialist party.

The *Masses* viewed events in the world through radical-
Bohemianism. The Mexican Revolution was of great importance
to the magazine, and John Reed, who traveled to Mexico, sent
in firsthand accounts on the progress of the revolution. Lincoln
Steffens was immensely influenced by this first great Latin
American social revolution and also went to view it for himself.
His comment on the reaction of New York intellectuals to this
upheaval is very suggestive: the Villagers supported Pancho
Villa because "he was at least a bandit," while Carranza, the
Mexican President, was middle-class.[33] Pancho Villa, in other
words, fit the image of the anarchist-Bohemian; he was a Mexi-
can version of the Wobbly.

Perhaps the most important Village figure to incorporate both
the political revolution and the social rebellion was poet-
journalist-politician John Reed. Reed's career was short and
brilliant. "He represented," his friend Eastman recalled, "the
Bohemian-anarchist ingredient in that extraordinary amalgam
of young rebelliousness, the *Masses* staff." Reed's contribution
to the tradition of Village radicalism by his writings and by the
example of his life is large. Immensely energetic, and a fine
journalist, he flew from one strike to the next, from the Mexican
Revolution to the Bolshevik Revolution. He represented the
epitome of the revolutionary journalist. Both his reputation as
a poet-adventurer and his writings in the *Masses* helped rein-
force the connections between Bohemia and the revolution.
Reed's sympathies lay with the I.W.W., the Mexican peasants,
and the Russian Bolsheviks, and his views of them often became

[33] Lincoln Steffens, *The Autobiography of Lincoln Steffens* (New York:
Harcourt, Brace, 1922), p. 715.

the views of the young rebellion. This combination of political radicalism and reportage projected itself through Reed's own perceptions. Where he saw the revolution, he also saw literature and art. Echoing the hobo tradition and the example of Jack London, he wrote of the Wobblies: "Wherever, in the West, there is an I.W.W. local, you will find an intellectual center—a place where men read philosophy, economics, the latest plays, novels; where art and poetry are discussed, and international politics."[34]

In Reed's life, then, there was no antipathy between art and politics; indeed, quite the reverse was true. He saw no divergence between the political anarchism of the Wobblies and the intellectual rebellion of which he was a part. Mabel Dodge, after their love affair was broken off, wrote that to say good-bye to Reed was to say good-bye to "the gay, bombastic, and lovable boy with the shining brow; to the Labor Movement, to Revolution, and to anarchy." He was surely, as Upton Sinclair called him, the playboy of the social revolution.[35]

A second group of intellectuals, less interested in immediate political applications of the rebellion in ideas, gathered around the *Seven Arts,* which became the prophet of a coming cultural renaissance. The magazine's opening editorial in 1916 stated: "It is our faith and the faith of many, that we are living in the first days of a renascent period, a time which means for America the coming of that national self-consciousness which is the beginning of greatness." This was an expression of a sentiment that was by no means unique. In the writings of Van Wyck Brooks, one of the editors of the *Seven Arts,* the idea had been incipient if not always expressed, that his cultural criticism was written to make way for a new period of great American art. Even H. L. Mencken in his later attack on puritanism ended with the expectation of a cultural renaissance. Walter Lippmann had felt, as early as 1913, that America was on the verge of a "splendid human civilization." Expressed by many young poets and artists of the twentieth century, especially those committed to artistic experiment, this cultural nationalism reflected optimism

---

[34] Eastman, *Heroes I Have Known,* p. 220, and John Reed, "The Social Revolution in Court," *Liberator,* I (September 1918), p. 24.
[35] Mabel Dodge, *Movers and Shakers,* p. 303.

about the potential of American culture. It was a basic ingredient in the belief in a cultural renaissance, a belief shared by such diverse figures as Mencken and Ezra Pound and discernible in a broad section of little magazines.[36]

The *Seven Arts*, published for little more than a year, is nevertheless one of the most distinguished of America's little magazines. Edited by James Oppenheim, Waldo Frank, and Van Wyck Brooks, it ran from late 1916 to December 1917. During this short period the magazine combined the moral rigor and vision of the young intellectuals with a strong emphasis on cultural rejuvenation. The result was the development of a sophisticated form of cultural criticism. Broader than literary criticism, cultural criticism focused on observation and measurement of the social environment from which the intellectual either gathered sustenance and flourished or drew the poisons that stunted his creativity. It did not attempt to inject politics into literature, but aimed at broadening the writer's awareness of all aspects of life, including the political. Van Wyck Brooks, commenting on the idea that united the *Seven Arts* group, stressed the devotion of American writers to a common cause —"an expression of artists for the community," as the opening editorial of the magazine put it. James Oppenheim recounted the sentiment that gripped the editors of the new magazine during its first days: "Well, Waldo [Frank], Paul [Rosenfeld], and I were wild enough to believe that the artists and critics could dominate America."[37] It is precisely this ambition and this feeling of allegiance to society that caused the magazine to smash itself headlong into the reality of World War I.

To Brooks, perhaps the major problem in America was the lack of a useful cultural heritage and the failure of the nation to produce true intellectuals. In writing of this idea he used, over and over, an image that filled the pages of the *Seven Arts:* the "young" intellectual who was as yet uncorrupted by Ameri-

---

[36] Lippmann, *Preface to Politics*, p. 317, and Ezra Pound, *Patria Mia* (London: Peter Owen, 1950), p. 26.
[37] William Troy, "The Story of Little Magazines," *Bookman*, LXX (January 1930), p. 480, and Oppenheim, "The Story of the Seven Arts," *American Mercury*, XX (June 1930), p. 157.

can culture, who could still assume his role as leader in the struggle for national fulfillment. The "middle-aged" or "old" intellectual was the symbol of the failure to live up to early promises.

The real leader of the *Seven Arts* group, related Oppenheim, was Randolph Bourne. Waldo Frank believed that it was Bourne who joined, through his work, "the political and cultural currents of advance." The merger of avant-garde attitudes and political thought by Bourne represents, in some sense, the culmination of one side of the rebellion of the younger generation. Bourne was eloquent in his plea for a revived culture, a new nationalism based on America's uniquely heterogeneous cultural heritage. "It bespeaks poverty of imagination," he wrote, "not to be thrilled at the incalculable potentialities of so novel a union of men." Bourne's plan for a new national culture was supported by a concept of internationalism. The literary radical must not merely be aware of alien culture, nor be an importer of intellectual fashions from Europe; he must be the leader of a community of young minds and a pioneer in the discovery of a united "Young World." Bourne effectively joined an awareness of politics to the idea of an impending cultural revival. The ranks of this army of the cultural rebellion would be filled with members of the younger generation.[38]

The necessity for a worldwide union of like minds was in part due to Bourne's feeling that all Americans were displaced: "Randolph was obsessed with a sense that we were all 'aliens,' " recounts Van Wyck Brooks. Writing to Brooks about his book, *Letters and Leadership,* Bourne emphasized the need for intellectual leadership which Brooks had discussed: "Of course I feel the necessity of this leadership more than anything in the world. . . . There is a certain superb youthful arrogance in your implication that it is we and our friends who are to be the masters."[39] Although Bourne and Brooks did not always discuss

---

[38] Waldo Frank, *Our America* (New York: Boni & Liveright, 1919), p. 199, and Randolph Bourne, "Trans-National America" and "History of a Literary Radical," *History of a Literary Radical,* pp. 41, 272.
[39] Brooks, *Days of the Phoenix,* p. 20, Randolph Bourne to Van Wyck Brooks, March 27, 1918, quoted in Lillian Schlissel, ed., *The World of Randolph Bourne* (New York: Dutton, 1965), p. 316; and Randolph

it in these terms, their theory of leadership was the basis of a program to create an American intelligentsia. Lewis Mumford, a later close friend of Brooks, wrote in the early 1920s that Randolph Bourne had been the center of a new intelligentsia, a group of writers and intellectuals devoted to the realization of the power of ideas. Like others of the rebellion, Bourne realized the importance of establishing a direct connection between his vision of culture and politics and a mode of expression.

The *Seven Arts* tried to fulfill Bourne's dream and its issues were filled with articles on "Young Italy," "Young India," and "Young Japan." What Bourne proposed, then, was a solution to the dilemma so ably posed by Brooks and others, which pitted the physical prosperity of the nation against the impoverishment of the culture. It was a plan to resuscitate the young, sensitive artist who was living in a close, intellectually stifling atmosphere and was doomed to premature middle age.

Bourne had a new vision of a culture based on a worldwide community of young intellectuals; his new community was to be structured by art and cultural criticism. The *Seven Arts,* in its farewell editorial, recounted its attempt to bring the potentialities of America to the surface and to create the basis for the new community: "From this standpoint, we looked upon art as a sharing of life, a communism of experience and vision, a spiritual root of nationalism and internationalism."[40]

Despite their obvious differences, the renaissance and the rebellion shared important assumptions. The younger generation had pronounced its judgment on the nineteenth century and rejected the presumably narrow middle-class cultural life that was its heritage. In a sense the younger generation was responsible for limiting the effects of this heritage because its view, its definition of the previous era, was narrow and sectarian. The revolutionary side of the rebellion found connections between art and literature and life in the modern age not, as the *Seven*

Bourne to Alyse Gregory, March, 1914?, Paris, p. 3, in Randolph Bourne MSS, Butler Library, Columbia University, New York.
[40] *Seven Arts,* II (October 1917), p. 2.

Arts group did, in cultural criticism, but in politics and in the lives of such figures as John Reed. Nevertheless, there are similarities between Bourne's prototype of the radical intellectual and Reed's Wobbly intellectual: both were seen as constants in an equation for social change. Despite the difference in approach, Bourne and Reed were part of the Village rebellion, and some of the same ideas and influences worked on both. The belief in revolution and the notion of a cultural renaissance shared common characteristics. Both projected into the future the vision of a rejuvenated society—a society of the young. Both considered the role of the critic or the intellectual important to the realization of this new world. Each saw the new society as nonbourgeois. But most important was the rejection of the past and the present for the sake of the future. The function of the critic and of the revolutionist was to destroy the old, stifling intellectual atmosphere and the oppressive class structure. There is a metaphoric unity, then, between the concepts of renaissance and revolution. But, more important, the younger generation felt at the time that there were real ties between social change and a new literary millennium.

Part of this compatibility was due to the style of the rebellion: its antipathy to an older generation, which sometimes saw a conspiracy between avant-garde art and political revolution; its emphasis on experimentation; and reliance on the intellectual as leader. But part of the similarity resulted from the concentration of the rebellion in Greenwich Village, thus making possible the interchange of ideas and people between the various sorts of reform. Bill Haywood and the Wobblies appealed to the *Masses* as well as other groups of intellectuals not merely because of a shared political vision, but because Haywood was also a familiar figure to Village inhabitants.

The desire to mingle revolutionary politics with experimental art existed as one part of the Village renaissance: the *Masses* and the *Seven Arts* were committed, each in a different way, to the achievement of this goal. Despite the implication that such an art might project a specific political commitment in avant-garde form, neither magazine drew this conclusion. Rather, the two publications expressed the idea of a combination of art and politics in terms of the renaissance or the revolution, but left only the vague outlines of a truly political art.

The effort to unite art and propaganda in the *Masses* was only partially successful. Unlike the *Seven Arts,* it did not examine the American cultural scene in broad essays. Its writers did not possess the critical interests of Brooks or Bourne. Its political bias was much stronger; its format, which was more journalistic, enabled it to scrutinize current political events, whereas the *Seven Arts* had to telescope such observations through the aloofness of the reasoned essay. What was organic to the *Seven Arts,* its merging of a radical vision of art and politics and its attempt to comment significantly on forces that related the two—or threatened to separate them—did not occupy the thinking of the *Masses* group, which called for a simultaneous rebellion in art, politics, and morality, but did not always demonstrate the relationships between these realms. It is true that the *Masses* advanced the cause of psychology, feminism, proletarian revolution, and modern literature, but it did so in a compartmentalized fashion. Part of the difference between the two publications is due to the fact that the *Seven Arts* was, in large measure, a critical journal, devoted to the clarification of the artistic atmosphere, and was more concerned with the unique problems that confronted the intellectual in modern society. Criticism in the *Masses* tended to be more specific, confined largely to book reviews. Eastman and his fellow editors did, of course, print the work of young poets and writers, but in their dash to keep abreast of political events they did not often find time to step back and assess the health of the culture.

America's entrance into World War I made the younger generation suddenly aware of its stake in the political and military adventures of the United States. The events of the war years drastically changed the tone and even the direction of the renaissance and the revolution. In her introduction to a collection of *Masses* poetry, Genevieve Taggard, herself a poet whose work had appeared in the magazine, wrote of the intellectuals before the war: "The age hadn't come to grips with anything much more serious than the problems of rancid meat. Even the

I.W.W. and the extreme left wing of the revolutionary movement shared the verbosity and romanticism of the time. Every-
body was playing."[41] But the period of play would soon end.
The World War and the Russian Revolution intruded into the
lives and minds of the younger generation. But if both events
swept away much of the gaiety of the young intellectuals, they
also clarified trends within the rebellion. The commitment not
only of the lives and industrial might of America to the war in
Europe, but the commitment of the culture itself in terms of
the goals that were projected and then tarnished at Versailles,
enervated reform movements at home and confused the Village
rebellion. What the younger generation had felt and expressed
about American society more or less vaguely before the war,
suddenly seemed to come true. And the reaction of Village intellectuals was often incredulous, as if they did not really believe some of their own predictions.

The war and the repressive measures taken by the Wilson
Administration against dissenters snuffed out the lives of the
two most important organs of the rebellion, the *Masses* and the
Seven Arts. The *Masses* found it impossible to distribute to local
news dealers and its August 1917 issue was barred from the
mails. In 1918 Eastman, Dell, Reed, and others were tried for
conspiracy against the government. Although the editors of the
magazine were acquitted, the magazine itself was dead; its
thinly disguised successor, the *Liberator*, was domesticated and
serious-minded in comparison. The *Seven Arts* folded after its
stand against the war, particularly in the essays of Bourne,
caused its financial backers to withdraw.[42]

Not only were the most eloquent expressions of the Village

---

[41] Genevieve Taggard, "Introduction," *May Days* (New York: Boni &
Liveright, 1925), p. 3. See also Lincoln Steffens's discussion of the implications of Versailles, Lincoln Steffens to Allen H. Suggett, June 28,
1919, Paris, in Granville Hicks and Ella Winter, eds., *The Letters of
Lincoln Steffens*, 2 vols. (New York: Harcourt, Brace, 1938), I, pp. 473-
474.

[42] "To the Friends of the *Seven Arts*," *Seven Arts*, II (October 1917).
Frederick Hoffman relates that an editorial dispute between Oppenheim
and others prevented the magazine's revival. Frederick J. Hoffman, Charles
Allen, and Carolyn F. Ulrich, *The Little Magazine* (Princeton, N.J.: Princeton University Press, 1947), p. 92.

quieted in this short period, but the boisterous voice of the I.W.W. no longer shouted the coming of revolution. Instead, the organization was persecuted for opposing the war and was soon lost in the shadow of the Russian Revolution. Moreover, the confusion caused by struggles within the Socialist party, the splits, and the formation of the Communist party (originally two parties)—all in the context of growing public hostility in the 1920s to the socialist movement—cut away at the structure of American radicalism.[43]

The agonizing question of whether to support the war, the urge to take a stand one way or the other, split the American intellectual community. But a more subtle division was caused by a change in mood. The affinity between the renaissance and the revolution was based on a belief in the imminence of social change and the ability of the younger generation to revolutionize society. But this feeling was no longer universal. Harold Stearns, who edited *Civilization in the United States,* a collection of essays appraising American culture, wrote in 1921 that rebellious youth was leaving the United States because it was conscious that it did not share the values of the society and because it felt that it could not change America. Paul Rosenfeld's comments on the death of Randolph Bourne mourned a cohesiveness that was lost to the young rebellion during the war: "He was a humanist; and the men left us are sociologists, political thinkers, professors, and critics."[44] The intellectual had disappeared and in his place stood the expert.

The war and the Russian Revolution inserted a quality of seriousness into the Bohemianism and radicalism of the New York intellectuals that had heretofore been missing. It forced choices on them that made it difficult to remain simultaneously sympathetic to revolutionary politics and to artistic self-expres-

---

[43] Irving Howe and Lewis Coser, *The American Communist Party* (New York: Praeger, 1962).
[44] Paul Rosenfeld, "Randolph Bourne," *Dial,* LXXV (December 1923), p. 560. See also Randolph Bourne, "Twilight of the Idols," *History of a Literary Radical,* and Harold Stearns, "What Can A Young Man Do?" *America and the Young Intellectual* (New York: Harcourt, Brace, 1922), pp. 159, 165. Also Brooks, "Introduction," *History of a Literary Radical,* pp. 10-13.

sion. Often there simply did not seem to be enough time to be a full-time artist and a practicing revolutionary. The community of young intellectuals would ultimately split apart, and, perhaps more important, the two figures still capable of holding the center, Bourne and Reed, would be dead by 1920.

The frustration of the renaissance was set in sharp relief by a brief flash of optimism released by the Russian Revolution. The political side of the rebellion edged toward Bolshevism and turned its sights in the direction of Moscow. John Reed captured the new mood in his account of the Russian Revolution, *Ten Days that Shook the World.* The enthusiasm for the work of Lenin and Trotsky fed back into the United States to nourish hope, at least temporarily, for the coming revolution in America.

As the political tendencies of the more aesthetic wing of the rebellion were muted, the revolutionary side became more isolated in its commitment to politics. The *Liberator* took on a new seriousness. Dell, Eastman, and particularly John Reed set out on the task of reporting and interpreting the Russian Revolution to American intellectuals. Reed's enthusiastic articles from Russia made the *Liberator* an almost unique source of favorable opinion about the Bolshevik Revolution. While magazines such as the *Saturday Evening Post* were violently critical, the *Nation* and *New Republic* opposed to the more violent aspects of the revolution, and many prominent socialists such as John Spargo and William English Walling antagonistic to the Russian movement, the *Liberator* printed Soviet documents, discussed new political and economic ideas, and commented on cultural events.[45] Writers such as Louise Bryant (John Reed's wife) took up the question, "Are Russian Women 'Nationalized?'" and the magazine even reproduced the mastheads from Soviet propaganda publications. The *Liberator* did not see the Russian Revolution as an isolated event. It reported for a short time on encouraging events in Hungary, France, Austria, and Germany. By the early 1920s the magazine had moved close to the new Communist party and began to publish articles by Charles E.

---

[45] Howe and Coser, *American Communist Party,* p. 26. Meno Lovenstein, *American Opinion of the Soviet Union* (Washington, D.C.: American Council on Public Affairs, 1941), pp. 31-33, 37.

Ruthenburg, Jay Lovestone, and William Z. Foster who were all to play important roles in the early Communist movement in the United States. In 1924 the magazine was merged with two other Communist publications, *Soviet Russia Pictorial* and *Labor Herald.*

The reaction of the younger generation to the Russian Revolution was conditioned, in part, by the work of the *Liberator* and its enthusiasm for the Bolsheviks. The feeling expressed by some intellectuals that their own destinies were wrapped up in the revolution indicates that the early stages of the Bolshevik Revolution fulfilled the dreams and the predictions of many of the prewar radicals. Reaction to the revolution was similar to reaction to the war: the shock at having been right was overwhelming. "What makes us rub our eyes at Russia," commented Max Eastman, "is the way all of our own theories are proving true. Nothing else could give us this crazy feeling of surprise!"[46]

The experience of revolution was considered instructive for the future of American society. Lincoln Steffens wrote from Petrograd in early 1917 that the first stages of the movement were "illuminating for the more orderly but equally profound struggle that we are having at home, and in Mexico and everywhere else. In other words we are seeing not Russia alone." The light from the revolution reflected upon American culture. In a remarkable article, "Lenin and Wilson," Max Eastman posed an imaginary confrontation between the two leaders, with Lenin, the physician-politician, probing for the secret motivations of Wilson's actions. What is most striking about this piece is Lenin's similarity to the prototype of the Village intellectual, armed with psychology and a tough-minded vision of a new community which enabled him to see through Wilson's rhetorical defenses.[47]

It seemed important to radicals to find American equivalents to Russian developments as a way of completing their own

---

[46] Max Eastman, "Revolutionary Progress," *Masses*, IX (August 1917), p. 1. See also Joseph Freeman, *An American Testament* (New York: Farrar & Rinehart, 1936), p. 139.
[47] Lincoln Steffens to Laura Steffens, May 6, 1917, Petrograd, *Letters*, I, p. 399, and Max Eastman, "Lenin and Wilson," *Liberator*, I (March 1919).

identification with the revolution. In one sense this was facili-
tated by a habit of mind acquired by the prewar rebellion—
that of seeing events (often isolated) as symptomatic of a whole
range of conclusions about the society. Thus the Paterson strike
had proven the strength of the worker and John Dewey's support for American participation in the war exhibited the limitations of Pragmatism. In the same way, Bill Haywood and the
I.W.W. had become symbolic of the proletariat; even those
who were antagonistic to radicalism felt that the I.W.W. represented—if it were not an actual part of—the Bolshevik world
movement. The comparison of events in America with those in
Russia became typical of the *Liberator.* But now one important
fact had changed. The revolution was of the present; it existed
in Europe and as such could no longer fulfill everyone's ideal.
Utopia had to cope with reality.

America's entrance into the war also cut a final link with the
traditions of the nineteenth century, particularly those identified
with England. Fighting in alliance with Great Britain had paradoxically inspired a struggle by American intellectuals against
the influence of English culture. The *Seven Arts,* consistent to
its call for a rejuvenated national culture, felt that America's
entrance into the conflict put the nation "at the beginning of our
manhood." It viewed the call for independence from England
as an assertion of national maturity. John Dewey, who supported
the war, wrote in the *Seven Arts* that the struggle "has shown
that we are no longer a colony of any European nation nor of
them all collectively. We are a new body and a new spirit in the
world." Randolph Bourne did not share Dewey's optimistic
analysis of the effects of the war: war to him was a sign of the
failure of American culture. Yet this view led him ultimately to
a similar, if more profound, conclusion about America's relation
to British civilization. The war demonstrated the failure of the
"melting-pot," which Bourne described as a nexus dominated
by Anglo-Saxonism, and not, as it should be, the center of a
new union of men. By failing to assimilate and use the diverse
resources of America's national experience, intellectuals had
fallen under the domination of British culture. Bourne saw the
task then as one of creating a new national civilization, a fur-

ther extension of the struggle taken up by the rebellion of young intellectuals.[48]

Bourne's friend, Van Wyck Brooks, writing after the war, claimed that America's dependency on England had vanished; it was now time to set precedents, not follow them. Harold Stearns summed up the conclusions of the intellectuals who had contributed to his volume, *Civilization in the United States,* by belittling the notion that the United States must be a cultural colony of Britain: "whatever else American civilization is, it is not Anglo-Saxon, and . . . we shall never achieve any genuine nationalistic self consciousness as long as we allow certain financial and social minorities to persuade us that we are still an English colony."[49]

The war warped and redirected the intellectual assumptions of the renaissance and the revolution. The spirit of the younger generation remained after 1917, but it was no longer dominated by the image of the young intellectual armed with revolution and artistic innovation and able to change society. The image was now the vagabond. As he had once drawn a sketch of the artist-bum to characterize the prewar period, Floyd Dell epitomized the 1920s with the figure of the intellectual vagabond.[50] The *Freeman* (of which Brooks was an editor) characterized this new type as a "wanderer," a sensitive intellectual who emerged from a society incapable of satisfying his moral and spiritual wants. He was an intellectual who viewed society from the inside. Joseph Freeman in his long intellectual autobiography gives a vivid account of his reaction to World War I, as he wandered from one idea to the next. Feeling the change in

---

[48] "American Independence and the War," *Seven Arts,* I (April 1917), pp. 2, 5; John Dewey, "In a Time of National Hesitation," *Seven Arts,* II (May 1917), p. 7; and Bourne, "War and the Intellectuals" and "Trans-National America," *History of a Literary Radical,* pp. 210, 260.

[49] Harold Stearns, "Preface," *Civilization in the United States* (Harcourt, Brace, 1922), p. vii. Brooks, *Days of the Phoenix,* p. 6. See also Joseph Freeman, "The Wilsonian Era in American Literature," *Modern Monthly,* IV (June-September 1927), pp. 130-136.

[50] Dell, *Intellectual Vagabondage,* and "Literature and the Machine Age," *Liberator,* VII (July 1924). Also "The Wanderers," *Freeman,* I (August 4, 1920), p. 510.

mood after the war, Harold Stearns asked in an essay, "What *Can a* Young Man Do?" His answer was that rebellious youth was leaving America, since it did not care about material success or well-being. Unable to change society, the young intellectual could do nothing but leave. Both Freeman and Stearns sailed for Europe, along with other Americans. The disillusioned league of youth—the temporarily frustrated renaissance—fed into the stream of expatriates, and the dream of a new national culture would in part be reconstructed on the shores of France.

The end of that decade that had launched the Village revival posed a question debated by two of the most important young intellectuals (now a bit older). The previous ten years had been filled with amazing events, some of which had touched the foundations of society. New ideas had been forced on Village intellectuals—solutions to war and poverty, and formulas for curing cultural depression. One essential problem that seemed pressing at the end of the decade revolved about the role of the intellectual in a movement to reconstruct society, a problem that did not really puzzle Bourne and Reed. To Max Eastman, the writer needed "guidance and careful watching by the practical and theoretical workers of the movement."[51] The intellectual could not be expected to lead a political movement, but should follow its general direction. Eastman's distrust of the intellectual was voiced over the efforts of European intellectuals, led by Henri Barbusse, to form Clarté, a separate movement of intellectuals for revolution. Eastman wrote to Romain Rolland that he had no faith in the statements of intellectuals who felt themselves to be "a class apart" or aloof from the proletariat. Van Wyck Brooks, answering Eastman in the *Freeman,* wrote that it was, in fact, the function of the intellectual to lead, to create a self-conscious culture that could contribute ultimately to a growing social awareness by the working class. Brooks was actually defending a position that he had expressed earlier. In 1918 he declared that "no true social revolution will ever be possible in America till a race of artists, profound and sincere,

---

[51] Max Eastman, "Inspiration or Leadership," *Liberator,* IV (August 1921), p. 8.

have brought us face to face with our own experience and set working in that experience the leaven of highest culture."[52] This was a restatement of Bourne's call for a league of youth and for the creation of an intelligentsia. But in the early 1920s its message had a hollow ring, because the hope for a renaissance as originally conceived was largely dead. Moreover, Eastman's argument shows how far in a political direction the rebellious tendency had gone from the prewar years.

Most important is the fact that this argument was a rehearsal for the literary wars of the 1930s: the two contending positions over the role of the intellectual in the revolutionary movement were here stated. Eastman's arguments foreshadowed the suspicion that the Communist party showed toward intellectuals in the 1930s, and Brook's rebuttals were much like those advanced by the *Partisan Review* and independent radicals. There were even broader implications to this dispute, for what was really at stake was the position of the intellectual in politics. The Communist and Socialist parties from the period before World War I through the Depression were often the most attractive political movements to an important segment of Village intellectuals. Thus the attitude of an intellectual toward the party was often indicative of his attitude toward politics in general. Was he, or not, to be considered a member of a special class? Could he lead the workers' movement as an intellectual, or must he follow the proletariat and its spokesman, the party? If he were a member of a separate class in society, what was the function of that class and what was its future? These were the questions at stake.

Unfortunately, Eastman and Brooks confused the issue by assuming that they were speaking of the same thing. Eastman was arguing that intellectuals in their relations to a specific political movement involved in a revolutionary struggle often strayed because of their independence of mind and position. Brooks was defining the function of an intelligentsia and defending the

---

[52] Eastman, *Love and Revolution*, p. 156. Van Wyck Brooks, "A Reviewer's Note-Book," *Freeman*, I (June 29, 1921), p. 382. See Daniel Aaron, *Writers on the Left* (New York: Harcourt, Brace, 1961), *passim*, for a full discussion of the positions in the debate. See also Van Wyck Brooks, *Letters and Leadership* (New York: Huebsch, 1918), p. 127.

role of the intellectual as the leader of a cultural revolution, a critical and literary movement that could bring clarity to the cultural atmosphere. The renaissance and the revolution were not, after all, exactly the same, whatever their similarities, nor was the writer as writer the same as the writer as politician. The same sort of confusion of issues persisted through the 1930s and clouded the arguments over the relationship of Marxism and politics to art and literature.

A rather deep schism between the political and more aesthetic wings of the Village existed after the end of World War I, but it was not quite as deep as might be expected. Both tendencies continued to look to European culture, the aesthetic side particularly to France and the political side to Russia. Although many young intellectuals left the United States, a significant number of radicals remained in Greenwich Village. The traditions begun in New York became the historical context for the radical-literary movement in the 1920s. Although transformed, the idea persisted that avant-garde art and radical politics were both part of the same revolution. The interchange of people and ideas was still possible, if not as easy as before. The continued importance of Greenwich Village and the growing centralization in New York of the Communist movement helped sustain and strengthen—even distort—the patterns of cultural radicalism drawn before the war. Radical departures in art, criticism, and politics had been intimately associated in the Village; transformed by history, this association would later be seen as organic—as a necessary connection between avant-garde art, criticism, and radical politics.

Chapter 2

Three Bohemias

What is art? Art is the tenement pouring out its
soul through us, its most sensitive and articulate sons and daughters.

Mike Gold, 1921

I am for them to the last drop, I am a patriot
for Russia; the Future is there: Russia will win
out and it will save the world. That is my
belief. But I don't want to live there.

Lincoln Steffens, 1926

The optimism of the prewar generation was overturned by
America's entrance into war: from the very first, the 1920s appeared to many young intellectuals to be a distinctively new
period, marked by sharp changes from the days when the rebellion encompassed an impending revolution in art and politics.
The amalgam of ideas that supported the burst of cultural and
political activity and the combination of individuals who advocated and practiced the revolution in art, politics, and even
life were scattered by the centrifugal forces of American culture.
The war itself became a dividing line between generations and
between attitudes. A feeling that the decade before 1920 had
been self-contained, separated from the nineteenth century and
choked off by the war, injected a sense of futility into the alliance between advanced art and political radicalism. To Lewis
Mumford, writing in 1925, the decline of faith in the ideas of
socialism and democracy spelled a decline in the importance of

the new intelligentsia which had begun to appear before the war. With Bourne dead and many intellectuals concerned more for their own prosperity than for the life of ideas, the intelligentsia was disappearing. After a short, enthusiastic plunge into support for the Bolshevik Revolution, the more political side of the rebellion was also discouraged: "Apathy had spread its opiate pall on the radical movement," wrote Art Young, "and many real earnest men and women who were with the *Masses* and of it were, temporarily at least, discouraged."[1] A general sense of disillusionment gave rise to the feeling that the prewar days were a time of optimism and intellectual experimentation, whereas the 1920s might be a period of discouragement and retreat. Because of a predilection to think of the 1920s as a period defined by the experience of the war, the history of the decade was in a sense written even before it was lived.

Greenwich Village Bohemianism before World War I had channeled European ideas in art, science, philosophy, and politics into the American intellectual environment. But in the 1920s, Greenwich Village was not the only Bohemia. Whatever its location, a Bohemia, because of its receptiveness to innovation, sometimes seems independent of its native sources; it is internationalist but not necessarily estranged from its surroundings. What unites Bohemians, and in fact makes a Bohemia possible, is the belief in the existence of a community of intellectuals, united in function and persuaded of the need to associate with one another. A Bohemia suggests freer, experimental social and sexual relationships, but it also implies much more. It is a highly evolved urban community, possessing none of the traditional cohesiveness provided by similarities of ethnic origin, nationality, religion, or family. It is hostile to the middle class at almost every point, particularly because it feels that the bourgeois definition of human relations is determined by economics.

The unity and similar commitments of Bohemian intellectuals indicate that this group might best be understood as a social class. Yet such a portrayal places a misleading emphasis on

---

[1] Lewis Mumford, "The American Intelligentsia," *World Tomorrow*, VIII (July 1925), p. 200, and Art Young, *On My Way* (New York: Horace Liveright, 1928), p. 298.

function and underestimates the dependencies that intellectuals
may have on other groups in society. Much of the source for
uneasiness that the intellectual may feel about his role in society
comes from the difficulty in demonstrating the assertion that
he is a member of a separate class, a member of an intelligentsia.
For it has never been precisely certain what characteristics define the intellectual, particularly in America, as opposed to a
member of the working class or the middle class. Moreover, the
lack of political and economic power felt by the intellectual often
gives rise to the belief that control over the direction of society,
however desirable, is impossible, or it creates a search for political allies in other sections of society; for example, in the working
class. The uniqueness of Bohemia to the intellectual lies in the
predication of its existence upon the notion of a community
and upon its ambiguous relations with other parts of society to
which it is inevitably related. The intellectual who feels isolated
from his society may look to Bohemia in much the same way as
the radical in a small, obscure political movement depends on
the revolution abroad.

One reason for a new mood in the 1920s among intellectuals
was the feeling that the old Bohemia had broken into pieces.
There was no literary capital in America the *Saturday Review
of Literature* lamented in 1924: "It is indeed one of the draw-
backs of American literary life that it has no general rallying
point."[2] The literary and political ideas of advance that had
been closely associated before the war were separated during
the 1920s into distinct factions, each linked to a particular group
of intellectuals. The literary expatriates who went to Europe
after the war felt little immediate political responsibility, but
rather sought an environment hospitable to their interest in
literature. Another offshoot of the early Village was the group of
intellectuals best exemplified by Van Wyck Brooks, who together with a small cluster of friends continued to rummage
through the American past in search of a viable culture heritage
and the causes for the premature death of genius in American
men of letters. A third element remained in Greenwich Village:

---

[2] "Solitude and the Writer," *Saturday Review of Literature,* I (August 23,
1924), p. 57.

these were the political radicals, interested in the new Communist party and publishing their political manifestos, their poetry, and their prose, first in the *Liberator* and then in the *New Masses*. During the decade the common ground between these three centers was gradually eroded. Each Bohemia lived and developed in its own direction during the 1920s, yet each still retained ties to the prewar Village rebellion. By the 1930s three distinct traditions existed, reaching back to the first attempt to unite radical politics and advanced art, traditions that would come together in the new renaissance promised by the Communist literary movement. But during the ten years after World War I the interchangeable parts of the prewar rebellion were shaped into ill-fitting theories of literature, politics, and psychology, a divergence that helps to explain the stresses that were ultimately placed on any new renaissance.

To some intellectuals in 1920 Brooks's description of the artist seemed more accurate than ever: the artist was starving on the barren intellectual soils of America and was shut out from any meaningful relation to tradition; or he was the restless vagabond that Floyd Dell depicted; or he was an expatriate in Paris. Hostility of the artist toward native social institutions and the sense that America had no cultural center indicated a less optimistic belief in the power of ideas and the strength of an intelligentsia.[3] The positive belief of the prewar Bohemia in the ability of the artist to change the world—just as he had once altered the course of his own life by tearing away from his roots in bourgeois society—seemed a false faith. The decay of the socialist movement put off the immediate prospects for political change, and the utopia that was being built according to Bolshevik blueprints in Russia looked "too much like work," as Floyd Dell said.[4] The tenuous combination between art and radical politics suggested by the *Masses* and the *Seven Arts* was one of the most vital elements of Bohemia lost in the wreckage

---

[3] R. P. Blackmur, "The American Literary Expatriate," *Foreign Influences in American Life,* David F. Bowers, ed. (New York: Peter Smith, 1952), p. 138.

[4] Floyd Dell, "A Psycho-Analytic Confession," *Liberator,* III (April 1920), p. 15.

of the war, and the failure of revolution and the artistic renaissance, both closely related to each other in the prewar years,
eliminated one way by which Bohemia appeared to mollify the
antagonism of the artist to society. Any attempt to reassert the
vital connection of the writer to his culture through the old sort
of Bohemia now seemed impossible.

Instead of a focal point for the interchange of international
culture, Bohemia itself became geographically decentralized. It
became less an ideal or a way of life than a location; it was
Paris, Moscow, or even Westport. In spite of common concerns
and an interest in one another's work, intellectuals associated
with three distinct Village tendencies grew apart during the
decade. Avant-garde art turned to explore new forms of literary
expression, displaying at first little interest in political movements; political radicalism under pressure of isolation and changing Soviet cultural programs defined the relationship of art and
politics in rigid terms. The tradition of Brooks and Bourne that
had seemed to promise the creation of a new American culture
now resided in Westport, Connecticut, where Brooks's criticism
increasingly emphasized nationalism in art and politics.

All of this apparent distinctiveness of the 1920s from the preceding decade is misleading, for disillusionment with American
society was always an undercurrent during the days of the rebellion and had already been eloquently and persuasively expressed
by Randolph Bourne and others before the end of the war.
Ambiguous as were Lincoln Steffens and Max Eastman toward
Wilson, not all radicals and certainly not all socialists dreamed
of a new world constructed upon the Fourteen Points. Nevertheless, a mood of disillusionment existed. The belief that had
pervaded the prewar Village that the intellectual could control
his own destiny and influence the direction of his society was
severely shaken by the war. Hope for a cultural renaissance
quickly faded before the wartime repression of dissent and the
postwar return to "normalcy." The dream of a social revolution
flickered on longer, but was snuffed out by the failure of revolution in Europe and the decay of radical politics in America.
Self-imposed exile to Europe was not necessarily caused by the
failure to sustain the excitement of the prewar Bohemia in New

York. Indeed, Greenwich Village continued during the 1920s to be a center of political and literary importance. But one crucial source that fed energy into the rebellion, the vigorous and large Socialist party whose spirit had infected both major political parties, seemed exhausted and confused. Instead of a literary renaissance, Greenwich Village had witnessed the death of the *Seven Arts* and the *Masses*. It was still possible for a sensitive young man to move from Iowa to the Village in search of self-expression. But it was scarcely more difficult and much more exciting to continue to France. Moreover, the internationalism of Bohemia made the transit across the Atlantic seem natural, and the assertion of middle-class control over public morality through prohibition made the trip all the more appealing.

Greenwich Village itself changed after the war. Its physical isolation gradually evaporated with the extension of subways and new roads through the area. Low rents, which were once a major attraction, increased about 40 per cent during the ten years between 1920 and 1930. Much of the prewar Village tradition nevertheless survived into the 1920s, even if in greatly modified form. The district was still a center of political radicalism, of sexual freedom, of Bohemian living and artistic creation, but it also became a highly successful tourist center. In the 1920s it was well-known for its restaurants and theatres, its free love and suicides, a notoriety promoted by the New York press. Older inhabitants such as Floyd Dell bemoaned this loss of innocence and the invasion of commercialism. But in spite of its profitable Bohemianism and high rents, it was the home of important literary figures such as Theodore Dreiser, Eugene O'Neill, Sherwood Anderson, and Edna St. Vincent Millay, figures who contributed to making the 1920s a distinguished era in American writing. Moreover, for many expatriates New York, if not the Village, was always a second home.[5]

The divergence between literary and cultural theories, the separate evolution of the three Bohemias during the decade, tends to obscure the assumptions that intellectuals often shared.

[5] Ware, *Greenwich Village*, pp. 15, 25; Parry, *Garrets and Pretenders*, p. 314; Allan Churchill, *The Improper Bohemians* (New York: Dutton, 1959), *passim*.

One of these was a feeling that the prewar experience was no longer relevant. This mood is perhaps best caught in Randolph Bourne's striking statement: "War is the health of the state." Literally, his aphorism is a comment on the need of the state to undertake war for the solution of political or economic problems; in other words, it was one explanation for America's entrance into World War I. What Bourne conveys in the very choice of his words, however, is a condemnation of the intellectual atmosphere preceding the war and his discouragement with Progressive intellectuals. The Progressive reform movement, which often stressed cleanliness, health, and social control, had relied primarily on the state, as opposed to the individual, to solve social problems. Here, however, was the complete inversion of the meaning of health: paradoxically, the state required violence, brutality, and corruption; the normal course of affairs was really the abnormal. War exposed the reality of social and cultural life.

A sense of cultural betrayal and of disillusionment that was felt by Floyd Dell's "vagabond," by many expatriates, and the "lost generation" of the 1920s provoked the search for a new realism and for a system of thought that could reveal the true nature of individual and social action. Socialists and Marxists had long maintained that capitalism periodically required a great bloodletting to refresh its economic organism, but this perception did not cause the generation of the 1920s to join the Communist movement. Marxism had proven right in its prognostications, but in Europe many Marxists had joined with their national governments to fight the war and betray their own principles of internationalism. There seemed to be a yawning division between political precepts and the ability of men to live up to them. Socialism was not so much wrong as it was irrelevant, and even the political radicals shared in rejecting the Bohemian socialism of the prewar days.[6]

Harold Stearns in his preface to *Civilization in the United States* pointed to this division as a basic fact of American society. "That in almost every branch of American life," he stated,

---

[6] John Aldridge, *After the Lost Generation* (New York: Noonday Press, 1951), p. 19. Freeman, *American Testament*, p. 233.

"there is a sharp dichotomy between preaching and practice; we let not our right hand know what our left hand doeth."[6] At the American Writers' Congress in 1937 Donald Ogden Stewart recalled the sentiments of one important group during the 1920s: "We of that long-lost younger generation began, as you remember, by being very disillusioned by the War, and disregarding any interest in things political as being of minor importance, we announced ourselves as determined to get down to the fundamentals of life and tell about them."[7] The search for an explanation for man's irrational behavior was not new. The young rebellion had also expressed a passion to understand the complexities of existence, and indeed many thought they were successful. Thus the search for reality began in the 1920s, not with a complete rejection of the previous decade, but with an extension of it. Many of Stewart's generation found that psychology best explained reality. And even for those who rejected them, the implications of the new psychology had to be answered.

The muting of the political content in the critique of society increased the importance of psychological and cultural criticism. The bourgeoisie, riding high upon the return to "normalcy," was still a symbol of a decadent American society. The hostility of the intellectual to middle-class society carried over from the previous decade, but was strengthened and changed. Occasionally it became a revulsion against modern industrial life. Waldo Frank proclaimed this notion in criticizing America: "Industrialism swept the American land and made it rich. Broke in on the American soul and made it poor."[8] But the rejection of middle-class America was rarely founded on an assertion of proletarian values or on the glorification of working-class life. The critique itself was initiated by a generation of middle-class intellectuals who were not interested in switching their own identity for that

[7] Stearns, "Introduction," *Civilization,* p. vi. Donald Ogden Stewart, "Address to the American Writers' Congress," June 4, 1937 (typescript), p. 2, League of American Writers MSS; hereafter cited as LAW MSS.
[8] Frederick Hoffman, "Philistine and Puritan in the 1920's," *American Quarterly,* I (Fall 1939), p. 253, and Frederick Hoffman, *The Twenties: American Writing in the Postwar Decade* (New York: Viking Press, 1955), p. 319. See also Frank, *Our America,* p. 45.

of the idealized worker. Instead, it was a deep and discouraging look at the soul of America.

The theories of Freud and other psychologists suggested fresh approaches to the understanding of society. But often psychology was turned upon the artist himself to explain his own maladjustment. Floyd Dell, sometimes called "Freud" Dell, remained favorable to the Russian Revolution; nevertheless, he increasingly devoted his attention to psychology.[9] Freudianism in its popularized version was applied to changing sex mores. It bolstered arguments for more liberalized sexual customs, and sex became an issue even to the more serious-minded Communist intellectuals. Thus when Dell asked in the *New Masses* "What is the correct revolutionary proletarian attitude toward sex?" in 1927, he started a discussion of the attitudes that the revolutionary movement might take toward marriage. Political radicals were obliged to debate the virtues of marriage and monogamy as well as the techniques of revolution.

The use of psychology to analyze middle-class life often resembled the way in which political, even Marxian, propositions were used to dissect society. Psychology could be made to explain the behavior of a whole class, a whole culture and not merely individual actions. Moreover, the characteristics ascribed to a class were seen to emerge from the structure of society itself. Middle-class culture was banal and puritanical because it mirrored the psychological repressions of its class. A few saw a strong tendency in psychological theory that led back to a Marxian analysis of society, that combined Marx and Freud to do battle for the freedom of the human mind. Thus the dream-world of surrealism to some intellectuals of the 1920s eventually joined Marx's call for revolution.

For those less impressed by the discoveries of psychology, the search for realism took a different direction. Malcolm Cowley in *Exile's Return* cited an important characteristic of his generation: a feeling of nonparticipation in the European war, a lack of experience.[10] The idea that life was something to be

---

[9] Floyd Dell to Fred Wieck, April 12, 1951, p. 3, Dell MSS.
[10] Malcolm Cowley points out that Hemingway, Dos Passos, Hart Crane, and Fitzgerald were not strongly influenced by Freud; Cowley to Fred

searched out, the sense that Americans lacked experience, the feeling of innocence were transformed into what Philip Rahv has called the "cult of experience," which expressed itself in a drive for individual freedom through sexual experimentation and through innovations in writing techniques. In his fight against the hostility of society the intellectual could at least appeal to experience, to a sense of having lived the sort of life that the middle class could never understand. The intellectuals of Floyd Dell's generation were "idealists and lovers of beauty and aspirants toward freedom; and it seemed to them that the whole world was in a gigantic conspiracy to thwart ideals and trample beauty under foot and make life merely a kind of life imprisonment."[11] One of the responses to this feeling of supression was the artist's desire to have a rich and full experience, to live this experience and write candidly about it.

Yet as much as the "lost generation," the "machine age" also characterized the 1920s. To some writers and artists Henry Ford was as representative of the times as T. S. Eliot or Gertrude Stein. To these intellectuals, the machine symbolized the possibilities of human advancement, of social reorganization, while it pointed to new subjects for art. The *Soil* magazine had captured this mood of the 1920s in its choice of a slogan: "It's not the man with the hoe, it's the man with the steam shovel." Everything modern in American life offered possible subjects for art; even the machine standing alone seemed to the editors a new form of sculpture. The potentialities of the machine age intrigued many American artists, some of whom lived in Paris such as Harold Loeb and Matthew Josephson. These two writers in particular tried to make their important little magazine *Broom* expressive of the new industrial culture.

Communist critics also celebrated the machine age and saw the Soviet Union as a place where the machine had triumphed

Hoffman, Gaylordsville, Connecticut, March 2, 1944, Malcolm Cowley Papers, Newberry Library, Chicago, Illinois, hereafter cited as Cowley MSS. Malcolm Cowley, *Exile's Return* (New York: W. W. Norton, 1934), p. 52.
11 Philip Rahv, "The Cult of Experience," *Partisan Review*, II (November-December 1940), p. 419, and Floyd Dell, quoted in Joseph Freeman, "Greenwich Village Types," *New Masses*, VIII (May 1933), p. 18.

in every aspect of life, in economics as well as art. Theories of futurism, constructivism, and proletarianism expressed a new civilization that celebrated the machine and the worker. But to some critics the machine age was more important for its impression on social relations. To Floyd Dell, for example, it meant the transformation of the family and marriage, and for him these were the most significant effects of the new era.

Not all intellectuals believed in a bright, mechanized future and warned of what might happen to society because of industrialism. Lewis Mumford, for example, criticized Communist intellectuals for their attachment to the machine and for worshipping the future. Instead he lamented the decline of skills that a worker needed for employment in a Ford factory. Joseph Wood Krutch, in *The Modern Temper,* analyzed the effects of mechanization on society and found them discouraging. The machine, he argued, had brought society neither the development it wished nor happiness nor wisdom, but rather the dogma of scientific optimism. It had brought despair and insignificance for man.[12]

In many cases this antagonism of the intellectual to the machine age symbolized a deeper uneasiness about himself and his social role. The desire for wider experience expressed dissatisfaction with the intellectual life in America which had been a subject of American art for many years. Even the optimism felt for the machine age in no way implied satisfaction with culture as it existed.

Speaking of the dislike for society that he shared with Theodore Dreiser, Sherwood Anderson, Sinclair Lewis, H. L. Mencken, and others, Isidor Schneider wrote of the 1920s: "I hated the society in which I lived, as a whole generation hated it. . . . Some of my writing of that period, as I read it now, has a tainted quality." What Schneider described in his own writing and in the work of others was a vigorous hostility to the prevailing

---

[12] Lewis Mumford, "That Monster—the Machine," *New Masses,* III (September 1927), p. 23. Joseph Wood Krutch, *The Modern Temper* (New York: Harcourt, Brace, 1929), pp. 75-81. See also Alfred Kazin, *On Native Grounds* (New York: Harcourt, Brace, 1942), pp. 205 ff., for a full discussion of realism during the 1920s.

cultural standards of the society. However the individual writer expressed this feeling, the antagonism involved the pervasive sense of a loss of his true, or what he believed to be his true, function in society.[13] It was, ironically, the notion of disrupted communication between a culture and its most articulate members and of the breakdown of positive exchange between interdependent elements of the community. Unable to relate to a society that did not share his estimation of his role, he had before the war partially overcome his sense of estrangement in Greenwich Village Bohemianism. But the Village tradition had changed. The literary intellectual felt obliged to find a new way of justifying his art and new theories for understanding his position in society, and each of the three Bohemias during the 1920s symbolized a new approach.

One of the most complex and well-known responses to the cultural environment in America after World War I was expatriation. The movement is diverse in its origins and its larger historical meanings, although it is linked to the intellectual atmosphere in America and to developments in Paris, the new Bohemia. For one thing, it seemed easier to be an artist in Europe. Kay Boyle, writing in answer to a symposium on "Why do Americans Live in Europe?" replied: "Americans I would permit to serve me, to conduct me rapidly and competently wherever I was going, but not for one moment to impose their achievements upon what is going on in my heart and in my soul." But hostility to America was by no means the only motive for going to Europe, for life seemed cheaper there and was often more exciting.[14]

Paradoxically, one of the most important results of exile was a new faith in America and a desire to rediscover it. Malcolm Cowley relates that his generation after crossing the Atlantic realized that American culture was not as inferior to European

---

[13] Isidor Schneider, *Daily Worker*, September 26, 1934. Schneider was an important Communist intellectual during the 1930s and 1940s. See also Solomon Fishman, *The Disinherited of Art* (Berkeley, Calif.: University of California Press, 1953).

[14] Warren I. Susman, "Pilgrimage to Paris" (unpublished Ph. D. dissertation, Department of History, University of Wisconsin, Madison, Wis., 1958), and "Why do Americans Live in Europe?" *Transition* (Fall 1928), p. 103.

civilization as they had once believed. In fact, the trip to Europe had strengthened and defined their essential national character. Joseph Freeman wrote of a similar experience. He became a sort of American patriot in Europe, even though he felt a strong sense of internationalism and alienation from American middle-class culture.[15] The ambiguity of the expatriate toward the culture of his country was often clarified by the European experience without, however, really altering his new literary interests or his hostility to the middle class. The rediscovery of America was not, for these intellectuals, merely the assertion of values long since discarded; it was the beginning of a belief in the present and future potentialities of American culture and a belief that these possibilities could be realized by ending middle-class dominance of culture. The trip to Europe also revealed how profoundly American culture had influenced Europe, how important advertising, jazz, and the skyscraper had become to the avant-garde artists of the Continent.

Malcolm Cowley's sensitive discussion of the exiles stresses the ambiguity of the writer toward America and his return, often to become a political radical. Cowley went to Europe in 1921 and became absorbed in the dada movement and in modern French literature, from which he translated into English such writers as Henri Barbusse, Maurice Barres, and Paul Valery. Growing up in America before the war and then traveling to France did much to divest Cowley's generation of strong ties of locality and tradition. What they found in Europe was not a vital, modern civilization; they often found a despair even deeper than that in America. T. S. Eliot, particularly in the *Waste Land*, which exposed the traditionless present, was a central concern to intellectuals of his generation because of the style and the severity of his judgment of contemporary society. Artists who sought to escape a world they had not made (or felt powerless to change) often searched for the essential qualities of life in primitivism or attacked the absurdity of civilization through dadaism. But just as often it was not escape, but the desire for experience that led Americans to Paris. When the

---

[15] Cowley, *Exile's Return*, pp. 101, 106; and Freeman, *American Testament*, pp. 183-185.

Depression began, Cowley relates, "Everyone seemed empty, without roots in yesterday or ambition for tomorrow." Yet pessimism was not the essential mood of expatriation, but merely one mood. When the exile returned he would bring with him his new tastes in art and literature, and he would seek a tradition of Americanism that best answered his needs as an artist. Often it was the Communist literary movement, optimistic and self-confident at the end of the decade, that seemed best to capture this vision of a revitalized America. It promised to destroy the middle class; it alone was willing to risk a revolution of social relations; most important, it promised a literary renaissance to complement social change, and an important role for the intellectual in this movement.

One of the most important effects of expatriation resulted from the wide contact of American writers with contemporary avant-garde European art. Expatriates varied widely in their interest and understanding of modern art movements; their artistic allegiances were diverse and sometimes contradictory. Some, however, were deeply involved in European avant-garde culture. Among the most experimental of exile publications was *Broom,* published in Europe during the early 1920s. Under the editorship of Harold Loeb and Matthew Josephson it collected the works of avant-garde American artists, as well as examples of European movements, dadaism and surrealism. Like *Soil* before it, *Broom* expressed the optimistic mode in its celebration of the machine and its interest in the revival of American literature. It was through Josephson, Cowley, and others that contact was established with the left wing of European cultural movements.[16]

One of these, dada, an organized insult to contemporary society, condemned and mocked traditional concepts of art: "Dada, recognizing only instinct, condemns explanation *a priori,*" wrote André Breton, "According to DADA, we must retain no control over ourselves. We must cease to consider these dogmas: morality and taste." Immediately after the end of World War I

---

[16] Harold Loeb, *The Way it Was* (New York: Criterion Books, 1959), pp. 90-100. Matthew Josephson, *Life Among the Surrealists* (New York: Holt, 1962), pp. 188-190.

dada had two forms, one more political in Germany, asserting not only the destruction of cultural and artistic dogma but a revolution of the state, and one in Paris, dedicated to artistic upheaval. The destructiveness of dada was expressed in the mock trials of literary figures, the interrupted plays, the manifestos, the poetry readings, and the exhibitions of the movement's advocates. Dada challenged the customs and values of modern society, but it also expressed itself in an art that stressed automatic and undisciplined writing or painting.

The restlessness of the dadaists gathered in Paris helped push one wing led by André Breton toward a new approach, surrealism. It was through surrealism that some of the implications of early German dada were realized, the commitment of modern art to the revolution. Surrealism, proclaimed by Breton and his followers before the mid-1920s, also wished to demolish society and culture, but it developed a political side. Intrigued by dreams, by unrefined thoughts, by automatism, the surrealists found Freud and psycholanalysis, even hypnotism, useful tools in liberating the repressed man. At the same time they claimed a whole new literary history, made up of the works of Dostoevski, Proust, Gide, Bergson, Baudelaire, and Rimbaud. But the surrealists went further than Freud in their attempt to liberate the individual spirit. Surrealism took up the cry of revolution as one part of its struggle to free life of the repressive aspects of society. In 1925 Breton, after reading Trotsky, announced that he had become a Communist. He wrote later: "Marx said, 'Transform the world'; Rimbaud said, 'Change life'; these two mottoes are for us one and the same."[17]

Thus, one wing of the advance artistic guard of Europe, first through dada and then surrealism, pointed toward a revolutionary combination of politics and art. Although the surrealism of Breton and the machine age culture of *Broom* offered at least the beginnings of a new relationship between radical art and

---

[17] Robert Motherwell, ed., *The Dada Painters and Poets: An Anthology* (New York: Wittenborn, Schultz, 1951), p. 203. Ferdinand Alquie, *The Philosophy of Surrealism*, trans. Bernard Waldrop (Ann Arbor, Mich.: University of Michigan Press, 1965), p. 56. Wallace Fowlie, *The Age of Surrealism* (Bloomington, Ind.: Indiana University Press, 1950), pp. 18, 110.

social change, this was not the primary interest of most expatriates; few Americans who went to Europe became absorbed in these movements. Rather it was Ernest Hemingway, Gertrude Stein and E. E. Cummings who became known as the prototypes of the American exile. Although few writers celebrated art for art's sake, an accusation made in the 1930s, few also committed their art to work for a fundamental change in society.

Symbolic of the impact of Continental literary influence was the *Dial*, a magazine published in New York, but devoted to the new art of Europe: a home bound voice of expatriatism. The magazine as it existed in the 1920s was in part an outgrowth of the *Seven Arts;* nevertheless its life was responsive to contemporary influences. Randolph Bourne, until his untimely death, was to be its political editor (subsequently the magazine did not concern itself with politics). Paul Rosenfeld was its music editor, and Waldo Frank and James Oppenheim were early contributors. Artists Boardman Robinson, George Bellows, and Art Young of the old *Masses* appeared in the magazine, but painters such as Picasso were much more important. The frequent appearance of Pound, Gorki, Cowley, Hart Crane, Ivor Winters, Paul Valery, and particularly T. S. Eliot (the *Dial* was the first to publish the *Waste Land* in the United States) and the interest shown in Joyce, Proust, Dostoevski, and Spengler made the journal a spokesman for international culture, especially for many experimental forms of modern prose and poetry. In addition to a profound belief in modernity there was the air of sophistication and naïveté born of the sense of discovery. The *Dial* was a partisan in a time of revolution in the arts.[18]

A difference between the *Seven Arts* and the *Dial* suggests the significance of the way in which modern European art was introduced to American audiences. A mainstay of the *Seven Arts* had been the critic; his purpose was to clarify intellectual trends in order to make artistic creation possible: he was a prophet

---

[18] Hoffman, *The Little Magazine,* pp. 197-198. *Vanity Fair* also did a great deal to introduce audiences to modern ideas in art and literature. See also Nicholas Joust, *Scofield Thayer and the Dial* (Carbondale, Ill.: Southern Illinois University Press, 1964), p. 23.

and a leader of the new cultural order. The *Dial* was more exclusively devoted to literary criticism. Gorham Munson, writing in the *Dial* of Van Wyck Brooks, called for a major effort toward aesthetic education in America. Brooks's sociological approach, he argued, made criticism subject to the changing patterns of history. The critic who explained a work of art in terms of locality and historical context was ultimately a provincial. The tendency to dismiss this "sociological criticism," which Munson's attack typified, wrongly associated the magazine and its writers with a theory of criticism that relied solely on aesthetics. The *Dial* did not go as far in severing the relations between art and its social context as did the New Criticism of the next decade, but the magazine did oppose the premises of the sociological and proletarian criticism that politically radical intellectuals developed.[19] Much of the avant-garde art of the 1920s was identified as reactionary by leftist literary critics (who often misunderstood or ignored it) because it developed without any clear connection to political radicalism and because the criticism used to explain it seemed to stem from a theory of art for art's sake. Writers such as Joyce, Eliot, and Proust were rejected in the early 1930s by literary leftists because these authors seemed to have no place in a culture moving toward socialism. The great variety of artistic experiment accomplished during the decade, and the radical implications of much of this art would have to await rediscovery until the late 1930s.

For Van Wyck Brooks and others who moved to Westport and other small Connecticut towns during the 1920s, the period was also a time for the rediscovery of America. But what Brooks sought was fundamentally different from the discoveries of the exiles or the political radicals. The move to the suburbs symbolized, just as the trip to France did, the splintering of an earlier unity between avant-garde art, criticism, and political radicalism. Other intellectuals who had been a part of the prewar Village were also scattered: Mabel Dodge, Waldo Frank,

---

[19] Gorham Munson, "Van Wyck Brooks," *Dial,* LXXVIII (January 1925), pp. 38-42; Hoffman, *Little Magazine,* p. 197; William Wasserstrom, *The Time of the Dial* (Syracuse, N.Y.: Syracuse University Press, 1963), p. 100.

and John Sloan, for example, went to the American Southwest. But in Brooks's suburban Bohemia resided one of the most important ideas of the old Village—the theory of letters and leadership by which Brooks and Bourne had sought to create an American intelligentsia. Now, however, Brooks's writings became more concerned with the discovery of a usable American past and consequently became isolated from trends in avant-garde art. Brooks still believed in the necessity of a great literary leader, but he also argued that "an age of reaction is an age that stirs the few into a consciousness of themselves." The exploration of his own consciousness led him to question any attempt at independence from American life, to reject expatriation: his concern with the cultural environment led him ultimately to grasp at nationality. Rather than find a new America, he rediscovered the old in the writings of the middle of the nineteenth century.[20]

Lewis Mumford, a young writer engaged in uncovering the origins of American architecture, replaced Bourne as Brooks's closest intellectual companion. Mumford had once believed that revolution could bring about a dramatic change in the quality of life: "I looked forward to an uprising on the part of the downtrodden, who would overthrow the master class and bring about a regime of equality and brotherhood." The community that he sought, however, did not appear after the war, and he became increasingly interested in reasserting the accomplishments of the American past, in a revival of regionalism, and in a rediscovery of the classic age of American literature. He argued that for the writer of the prewar decade American literature had begun with men such as Mark Twain, William Dean Howells, and Henry James. For himself, however, these writers were the "afterglow of a far more brilliant sunset, they are a darkening and a fading of the light which the great writers of the forties [1840s] had kindled in the sky." Not only did Mumford reassert the past in American literature, but he also called for a more diffuse culture, not to be centered in cities such as

---

[20] Van Wyck Brooks, *Emerson and Others* (New York: Dutton, 1927), p. 242-244, 250; and Van Wyck Brooks, *From the Shadow of the Mountain* (New York: Dutton, 1961), pp. 17 ff.

New York or Chicago, but to be tied to the diverse regions of the country.[21] Brooks's and Mumford's discovery of an American tradition of letters in Emerson, Hawthorne, and other early writers placed them at least in partial opposition to the avant-garde writers of the *Dial* and the authors of the new proletarian movement.

The most important organ that represented the views of the Westport Bohemia was the *Freeman*, a short-lived journal edited by Albert Nock with Brooks as literary editor. Located only a few doors from the *Dial* office, the *Freeman* was fundamentally different from its neighbor. In the pages of his regular column Brooks broadened his search in American history for a literary tradition and his call for assertion of intellectual leadership. Although he had a good number of friends who wrote for the *Dial*, he felt a sharp distinction between the two magazines, and between two sorts of criticism, one promoted by the "New York critics," who tended toward aestheticism, and those like Vachel Lindsey (with whom Brooks sympathized) who felt that art and literature were expressions of the people. The *Freeman* was not oblivious to European literature, but it had decidedly different tastes from the *Dial*. The *Dial* was attracted to innovation and experimentation in the arts, whereas the *Freeman* looked primarily to the tradition of European realism and naturalism. Having once expressed his faith in modern art before the war and in the league of youth promoted by the *Seven Arts*, Brooks became discouraged with developments in contemporary aesthetics. Moreover, the *Freeman* disparaged two of the greatest literary landmarks of the 1920s, James Joyce's *Ulysses* and T. S. Eliot's *Waste Land*. Brooks's political ties to the earlier period were also diluted. The *Freeman*'s vague leftism was of little interest to a generation that either avoided politics or looked to the Soviet Union.[22]

---

[21] Lewis Mumford, "What I Believe," *Forum*, LXXXIV (November 1930), p. 263; "The Emergence of a Past," *New Republic*, XL (November 25, 1925), p. 19; and "The Regional Note," *Freeman*, VIII (October 10, 1923), pp. 107-108.

[22] Brooks, *Days of the Phoenix*, p. 106, and Susan J. Turner, *A History of the Freeman* (New York: Columbia University Press, 1963), pp. 58-59, 129, 156.

A third offshoot of the Village rebellion, the political radicals, now joined by new Communist intellectuals, developed and refined new theories of culture, first in the *Liberator* and then principally in the *New Masses*. As in the previous decade, party politics were important to this group of literary radicals, but an important difference was that now the Communist party, not the socialists, inspired their activities. The group of literary radicals who remained in the Village after the war became the custodians of the prewar tradition. Moreover, the identification of Reed, Eastman, Dell, Robert Minor, Mike Gold, and Joseph Freeman with the Communists fed this tradition into the political-literary movement developed by the new Communist party.

In general during the 1920s radicalism suffered an eclipse. Aside from the debilitating effects of the war, the radical movement was weakened by the internecine war carried on within the Socialist party and between Socialists and Communists. In 1919 the Socialists were torn in two factions, with one forming the nucleus of two fledgling Communist parties (united in 1922) and the other retaining only a shell of its old identity and program. The division in the party developed ostensibly over a disputed analysis of American society in which a left wing, led by intellectuals such as John Reed and Louis Fraina, argued that the party must call for revolution and give up its demands for immediate reform. More significantly, however, this wing charged the party with opposition to the Bolshevik Revolution: that, in fact, the leaders were giving aid to its enemies. However untrue the charge, it raised the issue that from 1919 has been the major dividing line in the American radical movement —support or opposition to the Russian Revolution. One development that had an important impact on the future shape of American Communism was a large influx of foreign-born members into the Socialist party immediately before its crucial breakup, for it was largely from the newly recruited foreign-language federations, particularly the Slavic members, that the rank and file of the early Communist movement was gathered.[23]

During the 1920s the development of American Communism

---

[23] Hillquit, *Loose Leaves*, p. 290, and Shannon, *Socialist Party*, pp. 128, 132.

served to obscure the early history of American socialism and the roots of native radicalism, just as the Socialist party before it had lost its ties to the communitarian and nationalist movements. The new party identified with the old left wing of the Socialists led by Bill Haywood. Thus William Z. Foster, Secretary of the Communist party beginning in 1929, wrote in a history of his party that the main body of the Socialist party had been dominated by bourgeois elements: "Domination of the S.P. by these middle class intellectuals condemned the Party to a policy of opportunism." Foster claimed that the split in 1919 was based on the class origins of the members: the left wing was proletarian and the right wing bourgeois.[24] However, few of the socialist intellectuals who gathered in Mabel Dodge's elegant salon and supported Haywood, or wrote for the *Masses* or the *Liberator* were proletarians or of working-class origin. The Communist movement absorbed no pure working-class movement from the previous era, but the Bohemian-radical tradition of the prewar Village. This occurred for a number of reasons, but primarily because the *Liberator* was eventually turned over to the Communist party, because Reed was influential in the formation of the early Communist party, and because the Village intellectuals had identified with the romantic, freewheeling syndicalism of Haywood and the early Socialist left wing. The *Masses* and the *Liberator* accumulated the traditions that were passed on to the *New Masses*. They seemed to be the originators of a radical approach to culture just as the I.W.W. and the left-wing Socialists appeared to be the only legitimate bearers of American radicalism. The result of this process would be the retention of a major element of Bohemianism at the center of the Communist cultural movement. The new political party, populated largely by foreign-born members and outside the broader tradition of native radicalism of the Socialist party, was in an important sense estranged from American society at its very inception.

---

[24] William Z. Foster, *History of the American Communist Party* (New York: International Publishers, 1952), pp. 119, 124, 135, 148. See also William Z. Foster, *From Bryan to Stalin* (New York: International Publishers, 1937), p. 29.

The character of American Communism was established in the 1920s. At first the Communists were organized in much the same way as other radical movements, but by 1921 the Third International, dominated by the Soviet Union, began to exert control over its leadership and direction. Particularly after 1925 the party absorbed organizational characteristics of the Russian Bolshevik party, which made it responsive to changes in policy and leadership inside the Soviet Union. On the other hand, its close identification with the Russian party made it the recipient —the sole recipient—of the prestige that came from the Soviet Revolution.

A profound change in American radicalism, aside from its division over Bolshevism, was its isolation during the 1920s, due largely to the precipitous decline in activity and membership in radical parties. This is particularly true of the Socialist party, whose membership declined steadily from 1922 to 1929. Historian of the movement, David Shannon, estimated that in the later years of the decade the party was "all but dead." The American Communist party suffered a similar decline; from 16,000 members in 1925 it sank to 10,000 in 1928.[25]

The general decline of radicalism affected the attitude of intellectuals toward the movement. After the first enthusiasm over the Bolshevik Revolution, interest slackened. One could still read in 1921 of Isadora Duncan's enthusiastic letter to *Humanité* in Paris about her trip to Russia: "I am convinced that here in Russia is the greatest miracle that has happened to humanity for two thousand years." And one could read an advertisement in the *Liberator* in 1924 which told of a collective dairy and poultry farm being organized in Chicago with plans to move to Russia. But as the years progressed, the Soviet experiment appeared less an innovation in economic and human relations. "By 1922," Joseph Freeman recounts, "a reaction against the intense hopes generated by the Russian Revo-

---

[25] Theodore Draper, *American Communism and Soviet Russia: The Formative Period, Communism in American Life,* Clinton Rossiter, ed. (New York: Viking Press, 1960), pp. 20, 27-28, 153. See also Shannon, *Socialist Party,* pp. 163, 210, and Theodore Draper, *The Roots of American Communism, Communism in American Life,* Clinton Rossiter, ed. (New York: Viking Press, 1957), p. 184.

lution had set in among American liberals. The New Economic Policy inaugurated by Lenin seemed to them a betrayal of Communism." Floyd Dell points to a shift in the attitude of his generation: "After a brief enthusiasm, the intelligentsia has for the most part become indifferent to the new order in Russia— an indifference which masks a secret temperamental antipathy."[26] The New Economic Plan, instituted after the end of the Russian civil war, brought with it hard work and the necessity to realize certain practical and mundane goals of economic and political stability. Lincoln Steffens, who would deeply influence the next generation of intellectuals with the story of his growing faith in the Soviet Union, remarked in a letter in 1926: "I am for them to the last drop, I am a patriot for Russia; the Future is there; Russia will win out and it will save the world. But I don't want to live there. It is too much like serving in an army at war with no mercy for the weak and no time for the wounded."[27] And during the 1920s Steffens was also impressed by Mussolini's fascist experiment in Italy and, for that matter, by the successes of the American economy.

Theodore Dreiser relates that he was immediately struck by the Bolshevik Revolution and that it made him despair "of the miserable and degrading iniquity fostered by the capitalist system. . . ." The Soviet experiment was not particularly attractive or successful to him, but it presented an alternative that illuminated the faults of American society. John Dos Passos, comparing the post-World War II period with the beginnings of the 1920s, wrote of potentialities that seemed to be raised by both liberalism and Communism: "It was this sanguine feeling that the future was a blank page to write on, focusing first about the speeches of Woodrow Wilson and then about the figure of Lenin that made the end of the last war so different from the period we are now entering." For some intellectuals

---

[26] Irma Duncan and Allan Ross MacDougall, *Isadora Duncan's Russian Days and Her Last Days in France* (New York: Covici, Friede, 1929), p. 60. Joseph Freeman to Floyd Dell, July 2, 1951, p. 24, Dell MSS. Dell, *Intellectual Vagabondage*, p. 3.
[27] Lincoln Steffens to Matthew Schmidt, July 20, 1926, Carlsbad, *Letters,* II, p. 758.

the Russian Revolution at first meant little or nothing. Malcolm Cowley relates that he scarcely noted the triumph of the Bolsheviks when it occurred. Moreover, much of the art and literature produced under Lenin's New Economic Policy, he concluded, was a literature of disillusionment.[28]

There were those, however, who remained loyal to the Communists, who tried to transform the tradition of the Village and the heritage retained from early socialism into a movement that would combine literature and art with a call for revolution. But intellectuals who supported this goal did not always agree on the shape of the literature to come, nor on the premises that should guide its creation. There was little accord about the meaning of the Village tradition itself; more orthodox Communists stressed the political commitments of that early period; others emphasized the experimental social relationships, the new discoveries of psychology, and Bohemianism.

Two old Village residents, Floyd Dell and Max Eastman, who supported the Communists in the 1920s, argued for psychology and emphasized the compatibility of Marx and Freud. Both critics made an effort to bridge the gap between psychology and political radicalism, while they fought an intermittant war with those leftist critics who denied any validity to Freud. In a series of articles written in 1927 for the *New Masses*, the revival of the old journal of the rebellion, Max Eastman explored the possible theoretical antagonisms between Marxism and Freudianism. Taking Lenin as a model, he spoke of the professional revolutionist who was not a "midwife" of revolution but a scientist and an engineer. If one were truly scientific, he held, there would be no antagonism between Marx and Freud. On the contrary, there was a strong affinity between the two theories because both depended on the scientific method. Both thinkers were concerned with explaining behavior by means of unconscious motivations. "Marx's word ideology," Eastman con-

---

[28] Theodore Dreiser, "Where We Stand," *International Literature* (July 1934), p. 80; John Dos Passos, "Preface Twenty-Five Years Later," *First Encounter* (New York: Philosophical Library, 1945), p. 9; and Malcolm Cowley, "Where We Stand," *International Literature,* p. 82.

cluded, "is simply a name for the distortions of social and political thinking which are created by these [Freudian] suppressed motives."[29]

One of Floyd Dell's most interesting contributions to the *Liberator* was a "Psycho-Analytic Confession," written in 1920. As the revolution became a reality in Russia, Dell felt himself edging away from politics; as long as it was a long way off, "we could image it to be anything we liked." His doubts about revolution made him question his own motivations: "You work for the social revolution," he imagined his subconscious saying, "just as other people work to make a fortune." As before the war, Dell's interests were not limited to politics, and he began a series of discussions in 1923 in the *Liberator* on modern marriage and sex. Throughout the decade Dell emphasized psychology more and more until he all but abandoned radical politics.[30]

Another important advocate of modern psychology among literary leftists was V. F. Calverton. In his magazine, the *Modern Quarterly,* begun in 1923, he showed a constant interest in psychology and in the compatibility of Marx and Freud because of their attack on middle-class society. Calverton's writing on psychology continued through the decade; in 1928, for example, he published a book, *Bankruptcy of Marriage.* In an essay, "Sex and Social Struggle," in 1929, he argued that what society needed was a new science to be known as "psychosociology," which would reveal that problems of human relations were intimately related to the nature of the social struggle.[31]

Any radical who dismissed the theories of Freud thus had to confront three important literary radicals, Dell, Eastman, and Calverton, and had to fight the tradition of Bohemianism and the widespread vogue of psychology during the 1920s.

[29] Max Eastman, "Lenin Was an Engineer," *New Masses,* III (November 1927), p. 14.
[30] See Floyd Dell, *Love in the Machine Age* (New York: Farrar & Rinehart, 1930).
[31] V. F. Calverton, "Sex and Social Struggle," *Sex in Civilization,* V. F. Calverton and S. D. Schmalhausen, eds. (New York: Macaulay, 1929), p. 284.

Even as the *Liberator* gravitated closer to the new Communist party, it printed articles on modern attitudes to love and marriage. Perhaps one good explanation for the continued emphasis on psychology in radical circles and the discussion of sex during the 1920s is suggested by Dell's remark: "There is no doubt that one of the attractions of a radical political movement is the greater sexual freedom that it countenances or encourages."[32]

Aside from psychology, another influence of the early Village remained in the third Bohemia during the 1920s. This was the literary criticism evolved primarily by Dell and Eastman, often described as sociological criticism. As its name implies, this criticism emphasizes to various degrees the political, economic, and cultural background of a work of art. It claims, according to Joseph Freeman, an ancestry that can be traced back as far as the eighteenth century to the French and American revolutions.

Freeman, who became an editor of the *New Masses* and an important Communist intellectual during the 1930s, was a member of the younger generation of writers who were influenced by the criticism of Dell and Eastman. In 1922 Freeman and Dell discussed at length the relationship between literature and society and the need to inform the revolutionary movement of its literary heritage. The result was Dell's series appearing in the *Liberator* from 1923 to 1925, entitled "Literature and the Machine Age." Dell attempted to show in these articles the impact of sociological and cultural change on literature.[33] He called for a modern literature that could comprehend this new industrial society. On the other hand, he criticized the direction of much modern literature, particularly contemporary authors such as T. S. Eliot: "I would like to have our critics obliged to compare the sturdiness, the gusto and the simple

---

[32] Floyd Dell to Joseph Freeman, August 30, 1952, p. 9, Dell MSS.
[33] Joseph Freeman to Floyd Dell, July 2, 1951, pp. 15, 17-18, Dell MSS. Freeman claims that Dell influenced a whole generation of artists and writers who "grew up on the New Masses, the New Theatre, Partisan Review and other publications. . ." (p. 24). V. F. Calverton cites the importance of Dell's articles; Calverton, *Liberation of American Literature*, p. 456.

emotions of such a book as this [an industrial novel] with the
teary, beery pathos, the shivering disgust, the far-fetched ob-
scurities, and the sentimental and elegant attitudinizing of, for
instance, T. S. Eliot." Yet Dell's own novels were severely criticized by the literary left or merely ignored because they did not
live up to such standards. Dell called for a new literature of
industrialism, of radicalism, and of the machine age, but what
he meant was a literature that would explore changes in marriage
and love relationships, the two most important by-products, he
felt, of the new age.[34]

The influence of Eastman on left-wing criticism was also felt
through the *Liberator*. Like Dell, he avoided a prescribed
literary content and form, and he too expressed displeasure
over certain trends in contemporary art that he called the "cult
of unintelligibility," exemplified by Eliot, Joyce, Cummings,
Pound, and others. Perhaps the most important, however, was
his argument against the proposals of Clarté. According to
Freeman, this dispute immensely influenced young radical
writers.[35] The crucial part of Eastman's argument was that the
artist and writer were no more intellectual than the politician
of the Communist party and that the intellectual should take a
lead from the movement and not attempt to direct it himself.
It was not a great distance from this position to the idea that
the intellectual should also take the advice of the party in
literary matters.

Calverton's *Modern Quarterly* attempted to combine psychology and political radicalism during the 1920s in a criticism
that could encompass all depths of human experience. The
theme of completeness and the interrelation between aspects of
social life was stated in the first issue of the magazine by Scott
Nearing in his article, "Scientific Criticism: The Complete
Criticism." Calverton's magazine meant by "scientific" a sociological view of art, with content, form, arrangement of incident,

---

[34] Floyd Dell, "Charlie in the Steel-Mills," *Liberator*, VI (February 1923),
p. 28, and Calverton, *Liberation of American Literature*, p. 456.
[35] Max Eastman, "The Cult of Unintelligibility," *Harper's*, CLVIII (April
1929), p. 633, and Joseph Freeman to Floyd Dell, July 2, 1951, p. 22, Dell
MSS.

description, and analysis of character all determined by the environment. Calverton continued to develop his sociological criticism in essays on Sherwood Anderson, Dreiser, and other modern American writers. His ideal in literature was revealed by a manifesto published in 1927. He called for a new spirit of the age: "This attitude is that of a new realism, a tough-minded, skin-barred approach to life that is defiant of sentimentality and idealism." Although the magazine praised new Soviet art, Calverton equivocated about the future; it might be a "great catastrophe or a great renaissance." He called for a literary criticism that could take into account all aspects of life, but he was aware of the paradox that many literary modernists were radical in their technique and conservative in their ideology.[36]

The theory of proletarian literature, which gradually became the most important literary theory of Communist intellectuals, developed against the grain of the 1920s. Although it emerged from sociological criticism and had its roots in the Village rebellion, it was a more limited theory, more exclusive in what it held to be good literature, and more political in its content. In all of its various forms and expressions it was a literature that aesthetically recreated a revolution or demonstrated the necessity for catastrophic social change: it was a literature devoted to one class, the proletariat, and to one task, the destruction of capitalism. It transformed the Village heritage into a movement to create a new literature.

During the 1920s one of the principal efforts of the new proletarian critics was to exclude nonpolitical influences such as psychology from literary theory. The difference between literature for the masses and that for the intellectuals steeped in modern theories of art and psychology was often expressed in two contrasting metaphors: the effeminate intellectual concerned only with the workings of his own mind and committed to a theory of art for art's sake versus the tough, virile worker determined to remake the world. Speaking of a new workers'

---

[36] V. F. Calverton, "Sociological Criticism of Literature," *Modern Quarterly*, II (Summer 1924), p. 19, and V. F. Calverton, *Modern Quarterly*, IV (January-April 1927), p. 5. See also V. F. Calverton, "American Literary Radicalism," *Modern Quarterly*, III (September-December 1926), p. 260.

theatre in 1927, Mike Gold, the leading proletarian critic, wrote: "We don't want bored dilletantes, or the idle rich and patronizing. We want our audience to have a good time in the theatre and not to be bored with all the fake problems of the intelligentsia." A sense of moral righteousness often erupted in the writings of the critic who rejected the aestheticism and psychology current in the 1920s. "I do not want to know," commented M. H. Hedges in a *New Masses* review, "what are the sensations of the pale, thin young man as he enters the bed-room of his mistress, but what are the sensations of the robust young man as he sees his strength sapped by the furnace's mouth."[37]

The worker was pictured as a figure to whom psychology and the problems of the exile were irrelevant; he was uncomplicated, rational, and optimistic. As in the period before the war, when the proletarian was often pictured as a working-class Bohemian, some left-wing intellectuals tried to transform themselves into proletarians. "To us," Joseph Freeman relates, "Mike Gold appeared to be the outstanding 'proletarian' of the group. He affected dirty shirts, a big black, uncleaned Stetson with the brim of a sombrero; smoking stinking, twisted Italian three-cent cigars, and spat frequently and vigorously on the floor. . . ." Floyd Dell found the impersonation of the proletariat significant: "I used to mock at it occasionally in the *Liberator,* and my remarks deeply offended some of those who were indulging in that masquerade."[38]

Despite the rejection of the psychological interests that Dell and Eastman had passed on to the radical critics such as Mike Gold, the influence of the prewar picture of the working class was noticeable. The romanticism that had identified the proletariat with the I.W.W. survived, although it was overlaid with a new seriousness. Moreover, an important element was added, which was exemplified and to no small extent caused by

---

[37] Mike Gold, "White Hope of American Drama," *Daily Worker,* February 26, 1927, and M. H. Hedges, "War of Cultures," *New Masses,* I (May 1926), p. 20.
[38] Freeman, *American Testament,* p. 257, and Floyd Dell to Joseph Freeman, March 26, 1955, p. 1, Dell MSS.

the trial and execution of Sacco and Vanzetti. During its last stages the protest movement against the execution of Sacco and Vanzetti, two Italian immigrant anarchists convicted of murder under dubious circumstances, attracted the attention of an important segment of the American intellectual community, particularly writers.[39] Despite efforts of the two men to secure a reversal of their sentence, and over the protest of an increasing number of artists and writers, the execution was carried out in 1927. The shock of this apparent miscarriage of justice reverberated through literary circles. An estimated 144 poems were written about Sacco and Vanzetti; some of the best, by John Dos Passos, Edna St. Vincent Millay, Edwin Seaver, Alfred Kreymberg, and Babette Deutsch, were collected in a small volume of verse, *America Arraigned!*, printed in 1928. Other uses of the image of Sacco and Vanzetti occurred in six plays and eight novels, including works by John Dos Passos, James T. Farrell, Upton Sinclair, and Bernard De Voto. As immigrants, workers, and, in Vanzetti's case, intellectuals (the letters of Sacco and Vanzetti were published in 1930) these two men contributed to the literary identity of the proletariat. They reinforced an image of the working class as the raw material for a new social order.

In the Sacco-Vanzetti movement, which showed a long-term influence of the I.W.W., the image of the worker as a native-born American, highly individualistic, a man on the bum, a wanderer was merged with another view of the proletarian as an immigrant, a slum or ghetto dweller. James Cannon, one of the leaders of the Communist party before his expulsion for Trotskyist tendencies in 1928, wrote that the International Labor Defense, an organization begun by Bill Haywood while he was living in Moscow, was the center for the Sacco and Vanzetti defense. The I.L.D. was a "projection of Bill Haywood's influence," upon Cannon, Max Shachtman, and others who were important in the early Communist movement. But the image of the Wobbly-proletarian, the immigrant anarchist, was passed on in a more subtle way. The effects of the Sacco and Vanzetti

---

[39] Louis G. Joughin and Edmund M. Morgan, *The Legacy of Sacco and Vanzetti* (New York: Harcourt, Brace, 1948).

trial continued to operate in a "subterranean style" on the American intelligentsia, as Malcolm Cowley argues. And Sacco and Vanzetti were only the two most famous of the political prisoners in the 1920s and early 1930s. As a justification for condemning American society and as a focal point of identity with the masses, the trial and protest movement remained central to American writers and artists of the next decade. It was not labor unions or the working class, they claimed, that had worked to save these two immigrants; it was the intellectuals.[40]

Mike Gold was a major bridge between sociological and proletarian criticism, between the prewar Village and the Communist literary movement of the 1920s. Gold, who had been born Irving Granich on April 12, 1894, was the son of a Romanian immigrant. His early upbringing on New York's East Side, which he recreated in his novel *Jews Without Money,* was the source of both his radicalism and his optimism about political change. As a boy he held a number of odd jobs until he went to Boston in 1915. There he became a member of the I.W.W. until he returned to New York to work on the *Socialist Call,* a major socialist newspaper of the time. He joined the staff of the *Masses* shortly before it closed down and worked on its successor, the *Liberator.* Like John Reed and Lincoln Steffens, he was deeply impressed with Mexico, spending almost two years there during World War I. In more than one sense his career united the prewar Bohemia with the decade of the Depression: he was a Bohemian, as Floyd Dell delighted in reminding him, yet he denounced Bohemianism or any other way of life that did not identify with the proletariat. He combined a romanticism that was the heritage of the *Masses* and the *Liberator,* his own experiences in Mexico, and the memory of a childhood in the slums into a tough, almost puritanical belief in the righteousness of the workers' cause. In his own identification with the proletariat he pushed aside any independent role for the intellectual, arguing that literature itself

[40] Cannon, *First Ten Years of American Communism,* pp. 159-164, and Malcolm Cowley, "Echoes of a Crime," *New Republic,* CXXXIV (August 28, 1935), p. 79.

should stem from the masses. "What is art?" he asked, "Art is the tenement pouring out its soul through us, its most sensitive and articulate sons and daughters."[41]

Although the definition of proletarian literature was debated furiously by members of the literary left, its historical meaning is clear. Unlike other forms of criticism, it was concerned only in part with the evaluation of literature; it sought instead to create a literary-political movement. It looked forward to the moment of political upheaval and worked for this moment by combining propaganda and art in a manner that would, it hoped, arouse the proletariat and the intellectuals to revolutionary action. It attempted to depict the revolutionary urge that, proletarian critics claimed, was plainly revealed in social reality. It was thus a further development and politicalization of revolutionary journalism, of Wobbly literature, of realism, transformed and sustained by optimism. Furthermore, proletarian critics in America identified the revolution with the Soviet Union, thus providing a real utopia by which to assess the American reality. It was a literature that was adopted from Russian cultural experiments in order to recreate the Russian experience. It made the proletarian the hero, spoke about his life, practiced his speech, his manners, his social reactions, even as it tried to direct his politics. Above all, its character was determined by the fact that criticism came before the literary movement. Criticism was not called forth to justify an existing art, but to urge and argue for the creation of such an art.

Some basis for a literature created by the working class existed in America in the large Wobbly collection of poems, songs, cartoons, and speeches. This literature celebrated the proletarian life, the life of the bum, the striker, and the underdog. Although its production waned with the decline of the I.W.W., its heritage was passed on to Communist writers. In the 1920s, Wobbly publications, as well as Communist periodicals, were popular among hobos, and the tradition of early literary forms was kept alive in I.W.W. periodicals and such

---

[41] Stanley J. Kunitz and Howard Haycraft, *Twentieth Century Authors* (New York: H. H. Wilson, 1942), p. 547, and Michael Gold, "Toward Proletarian Art," *Liberator*, IV (February 1921), p. 21.

magazines as *Hobo News*. The picture of the Wobbly intellectual to which proletarian critics often returned was the same
that had intrigued Reed and Jack London.[42]

One of the first and clearest calls for proletarian art was
written by Gold in 1921. A recital of the worker's cultural potentialities, it was also an autobiographical celebration of the
proletarian life. Gold argued that previous American artists
were spiritually sick, pessimistic, and alienated. The artist must
turn to the proletariat to overcome the inadequacies of his soul.
The achievement of this was "the resurrection." Others had tried
but failed to achieve a new art form: "The *Little Review*,
preaching the duty of artistic insanity, and the *Seven Arts*,
exhorting all to some vague spirit of American virility, alike
failed, for they based their hopes on the Studies."[43] A new
literature could not come from the artists and intellectuals as
the renaissance had believed; it could come only from the
masses. The example to follow was the Soviet Union, which was
beginning to produce a working-class culture called Prolet-
Kult.

Gold's article combined three of the most significant traits of
proletarian art: the autobiographical, personal identification
with the working class, the prediction of an American renaissance (the cultural wing of a political revolution), and devotion to the example of the Soviet Union. On the last point Gold
was prophetic in identifying Prolet-Kult with the Soviet experiment, for it was by no means clear in 1921 that this artistic
theory would gain ascendancy in Russia, and as late as 1926
Leon Trotsky's brilliant *Literature and Revolution* rejected the
attempt to create a proletarian culture.

The writings of Gold, after a trip to Russia, did much to
popularize Soviet proletarian literature in American Communist circles. A mass recitation "Strike!", which was modeled after
similar Russian experiments, was one of Gold's first contribu-

---

[42] Joyce L. Kornbluh, *Rebel Voices: An I.W.W. Anthology* (Ann Arbor,
Mich.: University of Michigan Press, 1964); Alan Calmer, "The Wobbly
in American Literature," *Proletarian Literature in the United States*, Granville Hicks et al., eds. (New York: International Publishers, 1935), p. 341;
Anderson, *The Hobo*, pp. 185-250.
[43] Gold, "Toward Proletarian Art," *Liberator*, IV (February 1921), p. 24.

tions to the *New Masses*. He argued that the effectiveness of this art form derived from the genuineness of its working-class character: "It is proletarian because only revolutionary themes are intense and effective enough to be used; and because only proletarians can deliver a mass recitation; professional actors would seem silly in one."[44]

The influence of Soviet literary theories, translated by Gold and others, helped the development and acceptance of proletarian literary criticism, particularly after 1926. Before that time Soviet experimentation in literature, the theatre, and the film was relatively unknown except to readers of *Broom* and other avant-garde publications and to some readers of Communist journals. The direction of Soviet culture during the period of the New Economic Plan was not always clear. But by the time Soviet art and criticism were familiar in American radical circles, they had taken on the rigid and ultraleft characteristics typical of the late 1920s and the early 1930s. Thus they reinforced the rigidity of the proletarian art proposed by Gold and others.

Among the most important authors to write enthusiastically of the new Soviet art was Louis Lozowick, later art editor of the *New Masses*. Lozowick was a frequent contributor to radical journals, to such avant-garde publications as *Broom*, and to Jewish publications such as the *Menorah Journal*. He particularly stressed developments in painting and in the theatre that revealed the numerous schools struggling to express the revolution in art—constructivism, realism, proletarianism, and futurism. Moreover, Lozowick's constant theme was the modernity of Soviet movements; their acceptance of the machine age and their use of industrial materials and forms in art.

One aspect of New York culture that was especially responsive to Soviet experimentation was the Yiddish theatre. The foundation in 1925 of ARTEF (Arbeiter Teater Farband) established a Yiddish theatre devoted to the class struggle; it

---

[44] Joseph Freeman, "Past and Present," *Voices of October,* Joseph Freeman, Joshua Kunitz, and Louis Lozowick, eds. (New York: Vanguard Press, 1930), pp. 34-40; and Michael Gold, "Strike!", *New Masses,* I (July 1926), p. 19.

represented the realization of several years' efforts to begin such a group. Significantly, many of the arguments that surrounded proletarian literature in the 1930s were fought out as early as 1923 in *Freiheit,* the left-wing Yiddish daily, and *Thealit,* a magazine published by intellectuals seeking to organize a proletarian theatre. Many of the performers and producers who took part in this new theatre group had been trained at the Moscow Art Theatre. Furthermore, the writers and artists of the theatre were familiar with Soviet innovations in drama. Although the range of influence of the Yiddish theatre was limited, critics and writers such as Joseph Freeman and John Howard Lawson praised its efforts to create an art form that depicted the political revolution.[45]

Although a limited number of American intellectuals were familiar with Soviet literature, most radicals were probably more aware of the theories of literature and art than they were of actual examples. The most important disseminators of these theories and examples of Soviet art were the *New Masses,* the *Daily Worker* and its Saturday supplement, the *New Magazine,* and, to a lesser extent, the *Workers' Monthly* and the *Modern Quarterly.* The *New Masses* was organized by Joseph Freeman, Mike Gold, Hugo Gellert, and others in the spring of 1926 as a continuation of the old, defunct *Masses.* Contributing editors for the first issue included Sherwood Anderson, Van Wyck Brooks, Floyd Dell, Max Eastman, Waldo Frank, Lewis Mumford, Eugene O'Neill, Carl Sandburg, Louis Untermeyer, and others. At its inception the magazine attempted to be a broad grouping of intellectuals to include various political points of view.[46] During the late 1920s, however, it moved closer to the Communists, until eventually it became the chief literary organ of the party.

The early pages of the *New Masses* were filled with a discussion of the basis for a radical criticism of art and literature, but

---

[45] David S. Lifson, *The Yiddish Theatre in America* (New York: Thomas Yoseloff, 1965), pp. 432-481, and *Ten Years Artef* (New York: Posy-Shoulson, 1937), pp. 5, 6.
[46] See Freeman, *American Testament,* pp. 339 ff., for an account of the founding of the magazine.

it also reflected the 1920s through its discussion of sex and marriage. Gold, who contributed a significant amount of criticism to the magazine, took over the editorship in 1928. Looking back on his days with the journal, he recalled that he had tried to make it a magazine of proletarian art, "a kind of sublimated workers' correspondence." In accordance with the search for this new literature, the *New Masses* printed proletarian poems and stories that stressed the deadening life of the working class and presented an exhilarating vision of change.[47]

Another center of radical art and criticism that was tied directly to the Communist party was the *New Magazine,* the Saturday supplement to the *Daily Worker.* First edited by Robert Minor, once an artist for the *Masses* and a frequent contributor to anarchist publications, and later edited by Alex Bittleman, the publication presented a clear statement of the concept of art as propaganda. Minor wrote in 1926: "The essential characteristic of true art is exactly this: That it brings an incoherent mass of fact into a unified concept. Even the smallest good cartoon or verse does this!"[48] The *New Magazine,* in addition to extensive coverage of events in the Soviet Union and the American labor movement, printed stories by Gold and proletarian poems such as "The Scab," or "Lines to the Unorganized Unemployed." In its literary tastes the magazine was, in fact, as much a predecessor of the *New Masses* style of the 1930s as the early *New Masses* itself.

Despite Gold's influence, proletarian criticism was not accepted by the entire American literary left. John Dos Passos, who was something of a maverick leftist in the 1930s, argued in the second issue of the *New Masses* against a rigid radicalism and a Marxism that was imported. Gold's reply was to attack the pessimism of the younger writers. What he wanted was "a conscious exploration—with a compass" of the ranges of human

---

[47] Gold, "*Masses* Tradition," *Masses and Mainstream,* p. 54, and Norman MacLeod, "The Dynamic Theme is Revolution," *Little Magazine,* I (February-March 1934), p. 11.
[48] Robert Minor, "Art as a Class Weapon," *Daily Worker,* September 22, 1926.

experience. And that compass was to be the concept of proletarian art. The more independent *Modern Quarterly* was also
intrigued by developments in Soviet culture. A series of articles
printed in 1927 pointed to a new conception of the arts devised
in that revolutionary society: "In no other literature," remarked
editor V. F. Calverton, "is the clash of cultures revealed with
such vividness as in the contrast between the old and the new
Russia. . . . If this new literature is not yet a great literature; it
is at least a revolutionary literature." He added, "It is a literature that opens up the vistas of a new world."[49] Despite Calverton's praise, he was not entirely convinced that the proletarians
were the prophets of a great new literary movement.

One of the problems that grew out of the concept of proletarian literature, which many writers sensed almost instinctively,
was anticipated by Brooks and Eastman in their argument over
the role of the intellectual in the political movement. The career
of Robert Minor illustrates the dilemma of the artist and political activist. Minor concluded that there was an insoluble
problem in attempting to combine the life of the artist with
the life of the politician; so he renounced his artwork and
joined the Communist party. This conflict between art and
revolutionary politics was not due to the theoretical incom-
patibility of aesthetics and radical ideas, but to the attempt to
live two different lives simultaneously. It revealed how far-
reaching the implications of the proletarian movement might be.

A *New Masses* writers' symposium that hit obliquely at this
problem asked in 1927: "May society properly demand of the
artist, not merely good craftsmanship and good reporting, but
the transvaluation of values—and the creation of new social
values?" Of the critics and writers who responded, among them
Waldo Frank, Upton Sinclair, Genevieve Taggard, Edwin Seaver,
Edmund Wilson, and others, only Van Wyck Brooks felt that
society could, in general, demand the creation of new values
by the artist.[50] In other words, artists, although sympathetic to
the radical literary movement, expressed a reluctance to in-

---

[49] V. F. Calverton, "Revolution in Russian Literature," *Modern Quarterly,*
IV (June-September 1927), p. 101.
[50] "Are Artists People?" *New Masses,* II (January 1927), p. 7.

volve their own careers as writers in the search for revolutionary values. The attempt to combine the life of the politician with that of the artist was rarely successful. It was not often that the intellectual could follow the extreme solution proposed by Minor; instead, the attempt to achieve this union found expression in the semipolitical organizations of intellectuals such as the National Executive Committee of Proletarian Artists and Writers League (1926), the John Reed Clubs, and the League of American Writers.

Toward the end of the 1920s proletarian art and literature attracted the attention of an increasing number of radical intellectuals. Perhaps one of the basic reasons was that Communist critics such as Mike Gold tied proletarianism to the impressive achievements of Soviet culture. After the middle of the decade (especially in 1928) information about the Soviet Union was more widely available to American intellectuals. In addition to increasing interest from nonradicals, even Communists and their sympathizers tended more and more to focus on events in Russia. One important source for information about Soviet culture was the publication, beginning in 1926, of favorable travelers' accounts by Scott Nearing, Anna Louise Strong, and a number of others. In articles for the *New Masses* and the *Modern Quarterly*, for example, Nearing contrasted education in the Soviet Union and the United States. In 1926 the Vanguard Press began publication of a number of books that commented enthusiastically on Soviet life. The great influx of Soviet culture began, however, after 1928 with the translation into English of major works by Mayakovski and Ehrenburg. More important, from 1928 to 1930 forty Soviet films were shown in the United States. The result was a new phenomenon in America—the cult of the Russian film. *Potemkin* and other films offered striking examples of the merging of revolutionary themes with advanced artistic technique.[51]

By the end of the 1920s the political Bohemia that had re-

---

[51] Visitors' accounts include those of John Dewey, John Dos Passos, Henri Barbusse, and Dorothy Thompson; Philip Grierson, *Books on Soviet Russia, 1917-1942* (London: Methuen, 1943), p. 94; Lovenstein, *American Opinion of Soviet Russia*, p. 88; Freeman, *Voices of October*, p. v. Soviet authors

mained in New York fashioned a new theory to relate art and politics that was unlike anything proposed by its predecessors, the old *Masses* or the *Seven Arts*. It was a concept that went beyond the sociological criticism of Dell, Calverton, and others or the cultural criticism of Bourne and Brooks. By the end of the decade the influence of Eastman, Dell, and Calverton waned. Eastman was expelled from the Communist party for taking up the cause of Leon Trotsky, now in disfavor and in exile from Russia. Dell resigned from the *New Masses* in the late 1920s, and Calverton was read out of the movement in the early 1930s because of his association with Eastman. The proletarian movement succeeded in purifying its ranks.

Early in the 1920s Mike Gold had written an imaginary debate between himself and a more aesthetic-minded critic, which anticipated the attitude of Communist intellectuals some years later toward other literary groups of that decade. Gold's opponent defended the idea of a revolution of artistic form and attacked realism as a literary theory. Gold's defense is fascinating, for although he accepted the idea of a renaissance, he disparaged the other centers of literary criticism, the two other Bohemias, each striving in its own way for a cultural revival. The *Dial*, he felt, printed only foreigners, and second-rate ones at that; the magazine followed the vain lead of Henry James. A second center that Gold belittled was the *Freeman,* which he characterized as a group of writers in search of the Holy Grail of a great American culture. Finally, he castigated writers Dreiser and O'Neill whom he called pessimists, claiming that only Bolshevik art could be optimistic. Two themes of his article would dominate the thinking of proletarian critics of the 1930s: his attack on Greenwich Village as the source of bourgeois theories of art and his reiteration of the basic Americanism of proletarian art. Gold did not rely on foreign artists as the *Dial* did, he argued: "Yes, we may be crude, but at least, thank God, we are American."[52] With these words the proletarian movement,

---

were rarely available in English before 1928 or 1929, with the exception of some works by Mayakovski and some others; A. Ettlenger and J. M. Gladstone, *Russian Literature, 1900 to 1945* (London: Hutchinson, 1945).

in one sense, turned upon its own origins to attack its heritage of Bohemianism. Nonetheless, the influences of two previous decades of literary history remained at the heart of the proletarian movement in the 1930s.

At the beginning of the Great Depression, with the prestige of the new Soviet culture, the intellectuals around the *New Masses* and the *Daily Worker* offered other intellectual groups a cultural revolution to match the political revolution that seemed at least a possibility after 1929. It offered a map for the rediscovery of America which was carefully and intricately marked. It had nurtured and preserved an American tradition based on the *Masses,* the *Liberator,* and the Communist party. When the three Bohemias were eventually reunited during the 1930s, the Communist intellectuals were in a position to offer exiles a theory that predicted a rebirth of American culture and to proffer to critics such as Brooks, looking for a viable culture tradition, the vision of a revolutionary American past and future.

---

[52] Mike Gold, "Two Critics in a Bar-room," *Liberator,* IV (September 1921), p. 30.

Chapter 3

Revolution and Renaissance

It wasn't the depression that got me, it was the boom.

Malcolm Cowley, *Daily Worker*, 1932

In spite of these defects you feel in the Soviet Union that you are at the moral top of the world where the light really never goes out, just as you know in the Gulf of Finland, where the summer day never ends, that you are close to the geographic top.

Edmund Wilson, 1935

The radical movement of the 1930s owed its brief good fortune to the Depression which struck the United States after 1929. But before this economic catastrophe the outlines of the new cultural theory had already been completed; proletarian literature and art by the end of the 1920s had become an accepted blueprint for the cultural revolution. What the Depression made possible—the sudden influx of writers and artists into the Communist movement—was given direction and meaning by the theory of culture and the expectations for that theory proclaimed in the *New Masses* and other radical publications. A new union of art and politics was created by the renewed possibilities of a revolution and a renaissance. Yet the goal of the radical movement, the radical reconstruction of culture, which now seemed within reach, had been defined before the economic crisis and was related to issues of intellectual history in the 1920s and to the course of the Soviet revolution.

The *New Masses* in 1929 assumed leadership of an unwieldy movement it could not control and could scarcely direct and dependent on historical circumstances it did not always understand. The new radical movement drew to its ranks a wide variety of young writers whose beliefs and personalities often clashed with the new role they wished to play. Most important, the radical movement spawned a number of little magazines. The most significant among these was the *Partisan Review*, which remained deeply committed to revolutionary literature for a decade and reflected the complicated evolution of radical politics among American intellectuals.

From the earliest moments of the 1930s radical literature lived at three levels; represented by the *New Masses* proletarian critics and Communist party intellectuals, by more established writers and critics such as Edmund Wilson (who were influenced by the pervasive radicalism of the period, but remained more or less detached from any organizational ties to it), and by the unestablished writers who were among the first to become involved in the radical literary movement. As the 1930s progressed, these groups, by and large, continued to operate in distinct spheres, joining together once at the time of the Popular Front, but ultimately committed to different styles of literary life.

The importance attached to Marxism as a source of literary ideas is apparent in the little magazines of the left which devoted their enormous energies to the refinement of critical tools based on revolutionary socialism. Marxian criticism was the basis for a little magazine revival which attempted to live up to a new radical code, and which, in a sense, proved to be subversive to the established party organ, the *New Masses*. The origins of the *Partisan Review* lie in this movement and in the efforts of the editors to merge different levels of radical criticism and to avoid the secularism of some proletarians and the detachment of radicalized established writers. Although its editors shared the assumptions and expectancies of other young radicals, the *Partisan Review*, from the beginning, was aware of the obstacles to success of proletarian culture inherent in the shape and premises of the movement.

The rapid appearance of literary radicalism during the 1930s has been traced to the economic crisis. And it is true that the sudden plunge of the stock market in 1929 and the slow, steady decline of the economy for the next two years provided a focus, just as World War I had done, through which to assemble the images of a decade. Political, economic, and cultural events of the 1930s were viewed in terms of this momentous symbol of failure. But to relate the development of a set of ideas, particularly radical political and literary assumptions, to the downhill lunge of the economy and the feeble and sporadic reaction of society is, if unmodified, a mechanistic and false scheme. The relationship of major events such as wars and depressions to the intellectual positions of individuals is diverse and subtle, and the impact may depend on how precisely or imprecisely an event touches each person. To ask why intellectuals were attracted to radicalism in the 1930s is to raise a necessary question, but is in some sense also to doubt the wisdom of committing oneself to a movement that in retrospect seemed to offer little. There is no intrinsic force or logical necessity that drives the mind from the experience of a depression to radical politics. The attraction of the Communist literary and political movement was, of course, enhanced by the fact that it offered a revolutionary reorganization for a society that seemed pathetic in its response to crisis. But the literary radicalism offered to the intellectuals in the early 1930s by the Communist movement had little if any relation to the economic crisis: it was developed during the previous decade and ideologically obligated to a mixture of Marxism, the Bohemianism of Greenwich Village, Soviet Bolshevism, and a number of lesser influences. Moreover, it was defined, and continued to be, by its relations to Soviet culture, by its own self-conception, and by what sympathetic intellectuals felt it should be. Choosing a left-wing solution to the social and cultural crisis was a complex process involving the individual in an almost circular relationship to his new ideas. Literary radicalism was influenced and transformed by what writers wanted from it, just as many intellectuals changed their views for the promises of the radical movement itself. The pervasive feeling of betrayal by the Communist party at the end of the decade suggests that its sympathizers took these promises seriously. The Communist literary movement offered perhaps too much to the intellectual, rather than too little.

The Depression was an unforgettable trip through the capitalist inferno, but it was the vision of a new society, or at least a greatly altered one in terms of the peculiar problems and concerns of the American writers and artists, which attracted many intellectuals to Communism. Since the movement changed rapidly over a short period of time, the point at which a group of intellectuals became engaged in radical activities suggests some of their reasons for joining. When the party swung to the left in the last years of the 1920s and the early 1930s, it gathered in a group of young, often unknown writers and intellectuals. A move to the right in the mid-1930s drew into its ranks a large group with very different interests and flung into opposition many of its original supporters. This progression depends in part on the complex motivations of a cultural movement; it is not merely the story of Communist politics. Literary and intellectual issues were often as much at stake and antagonisms between very dissimilar intellectuals as important as the political questions hanging over the period. The breaks in the Bohemian community during the 1920s, based on differing attitudes toward the relation of art and politics, were temporarily rejoined by the Communist movement. But whatever its initial success in bringing together the divergent intellectual traditions of the 1920s, the party ultimately paid a great price, for it tied a literary movement to the vicissitudes of radical politics. Although quite serious in their stands on cultural matters, party intellectuals often had an even greater attachment to political questions. Often party critics stated the particular literary theory of the moment in political terms, thus making it impossible for writers to separate the issues of literature from the fortunes of the Communist political organization.

The first important group of intellectuals to enter the Communist literary movement were the young writers who joined the John Reed Clubs, founded in 1929 by party intellectuals in the memory of the flamboyant American literary Bolshevik. Their intense feeling that the 1930s would be a unique period and would have a completely different history from the previous decade did not prevent many of these early converts to literary radicalism from expressing a set of attitudes inherited from the 1920s. To them the proper relation of the artist to contemporary society was still obscure, if anything more uncertain, and the intellectual was increasingly aware of his hostility to the social environment. One typical expression of the writer's antagonism to his culture appeared in an article written jointly by William Phillips and Philip Rahv, editors of the *Partisan Review*, for *Poetry* magazine: "No honest and typical experience of our age," they stated, "can exclude a sense of the organized vulgarity and corruption of modern society." The isolation of the artist remained, and in this sense the 1930s were merely a projection of the previous decade. The mood of the 1930s was different, however, not because of the transformation of society, but because of its collapse and the writer's belief that political radicalism could help change his role in society. "The movement of history has again made possible," Rahv and Phillips continued, "the much desired integration of the poet's conceptions with the leading ideas of his time." Radicalism illuminated both the future and the past, but more important, it promised to end the complaint that the writer lived in a hostile world: in fact, it all but explained this problem away. "It wasn't the depression that got me," insisted Malcolm Cowley, "It was the boom. I saw all my friends writing the tripe demanded by the present order, stultified and corrupted and unable to make real use of their talents. After that I had to discover the reason for this state of affairs, which comes from the nature of a ruling class which lives by exploiting everyone else."[1] If American society seemed hostile to the intellectual, he could now claim the support of history in his struggle: it was possible, perhaps, that with a profound social transformation the intellectual would take his true place in society. In the meantime he could

---

[1] William Phillips and Philip Rahv, "Private Experience and Public Philosophy," "Social Poets Number," *Poetry*, XLVIII (May 1936), p. 104, and Malcolm Cowley, *Daily Worker*, October 14, 1932.

ally himself with the most progressive force, the potential source of revolution, the proletariat.

The breakdown of American capitalism and the great social injustices exposed by the Depression did not necessarily lead to pessimistic conclusions about the future. Of an older generation, Edmund Wilson nevertheless captured one mood induced by the crash: "Yet to the writers and artists of my generation who had grown up in the Big Business era and had always resented its barbarism . . . these years were not depressing but stimulating. One couldn't help being exhilarated at the sudden and unexpected collapse of that stupid gigantic fraud. It gave us a new sense of freedom and it gave us a new sense of power to find ourselves still carrying on while the bankers, for a change, were taking a beating." It is noteworthy that Wilson chose to write about the literary consequences of the crash with the idiom of a generation hostile to society. The possibility for intellectuals to feel estranged from their culture and yet closer to power over its destiny derived from their belief in the coming of a new social structure that would eliminate the problems of the old. "We were passionately eager to get away from our own class," wrote critic Granville Hicks, "and find a home with the proletariat."[2]

The young radical sought a cultural revival in which to play a central role. The radical literary movement promised him a renaissance and a political revolution—old and worthy goals—and a literary movement that would produce a new Jack London or a Walt Whitman. It promised a continuation of old traditions in America set to new purposes, and it asserted that the production of radical literature was work for a great future. The search for a new America during the 1930s

---

[2] Edmund Wilson, "The Literary Consequences of the Crash," *The Shores of Light* (New York: Farrar, Straus & Young, 1952), p. 498; Granville Hicks, "Communism and the American Intellectuals," *Whose Revolution?*, Irving DeWitt Talmadge, ed. (New York: Howell, Soskin, 1941), p. 87. Writing thirty years afterwards, William Phillips concluded precisely the opposite about the 1930s: the radical spirit and history were moving in different directions. To be a socialist in America was to be a utopian without power. William Phillips, "What Happened in the 1930's," *Commentary*, XXXIV (September 1962), p. 209.

ended in the vision of a society transformed by the proletariat
and the intellectuals. The way to overcome the isolation of the
artist was to end the isolation of American culture itself from
the progressive course of history. Once again a kind of Young
America was needed whose role would be to celebrate, to
propagandize, everything this time but to lead the new cultural movement. The result would be a new culture, a true
American renaissance led by the working class and the Communist party, and informed by intellectuals.[3]

The interests and concerns that the young radicals brought
to the burgeoning radical movement gave shape to the insub-
stantial leftist literature of the late 1920s. Intellectuals were
often attracted to the movement because of the vestiges of an
earlier Bohemianism, and their own knowledge and concern
for the literary world before 1929 helped to preserve the fading
images of the preceding decade. The diverse sorts of Bohemianism of the 1920s were poured into the mold of the
Communist literary movement, refashioned, covered over with
crisis-inspired earnestness, but they still retained some of the
outlines set in the previous decade. "The young mooncalf
[Floyd Dell's portrait of the young writer] plunged into this
new politico-cultural territory," wrote Alan Calmer who was an
early editor of *Partisan Review*, "But it did not resolve the
sharp conflict between his environment and himself. To be sure,
the John Reed Clubs did create something of an intellectual
center, a restricted milieu in which he could voice his esthetic
desires and judgments."[4]

In the early 1930s the Communist literary movement continued the purge of nonproletarian ideas that it had begun in
the previous decade and widened its struggle against competing theories of psychology, aestheticism, and Bohemianism. To

---

[3] Malcolm Cowley, "Twenty Years of American Literature," *After the
Genteel Tradition* (New York: W. W. Norton, 1936), p. 222, and Mike
Gold, "Discussion," *American Writers' Congress*, Henry Hart, ed. (New
York: International Publishers, 1935), p. 166.
[4] Newton Arvin, "The Passing of the Twenties," *New Freeman*, I (March
15, 1930), p. 19, and Alan Calmer, "Portrait of the Artist as a Proletarian,"
Saturday Review, XVI (July 31, 1937), p. 3.

establish themselves as the leaders of a cultural renaissance, the proletarian critics and writers attempted to lead the young intellectual from Bohemia to the steps of Utopia. The new radical would eventually be obliged to give up his allegiance to his previous literary tastes and interests if he had any, for in the early 1930s the Communist movement became increasingly intolerant of the preoccupations of the 1920s, and, paradoxically, of its own historical roots. Looking back on the 1930s, Mike Gold told the League of American Writers in 1941 that the Depression had stripped the literary world of its most cherished philosophies: Freudianism, Bohemianism, Humanism, Menckenism, Joyceism, and Midwest populism. Gold indicated in this bit of wishful historical analysis that the literary influences of the 1920s, particularly those associated with the expatriates, were swept away by the economic crisis. Wrong in his analysis, Gold nevertheless was certain of the direction in which the Communist literary movement had tried to lead the intellectuals, toward a rejection of the questions, and most of all, the answers, of the 1920s.[5]

Despite the fact that so many young radicals and even the older leaders Mike Gold and Joseph Freeman had been Bohemians, the *New Masses,* as the chief party intellectual organ, disparaged the idea that Bohemia had anything to offer the young intellectual. The radical movement could perform the function of an intellectual center with greater efficiency. The issue of Bohemianism set off a sharp debate between Joseph Freeman, Max Eastman, and others over the nature of Greenwich Village, and the meaning of the *Masses* heritage. Eastman, now bitterly opposed to the Communist movement because of his association with Trotsky, defended himself against charges that his had been a frivolous radicalism. On the contrary, he charged, it was he who had struggled against

---

[5] Michael Gold, "Untitled Address to the League of American Writers," June 6-8, 1941, p. 4, LAW MSS. E. A. Schachner, "Revolutionary Literature in the United States Today," *Windsor Quarterly,* II (Spring 1934), p. 28. Schachner argues that the *New Masses* tried to make Bohemians into Communists. Schachner was a member of the Communist party and secretary of the writers' group of the New York John Reed Club for two years.

the influence of Greenwich Village that had infected even John Reed and Robert Minor.[6] Both sides in the argument agreed that Bohemianism would debilitate revolutionary sentiments, but the Communist intellectuals tended to identify backsliders from their movement, all opponents of proletarian literature, with Bohemianism.

Greenwich Village, wrote Joseph Freeman, was actually a sort of halfway house furnished with partly formed ideas: "It combined a post-graduate school, a playground and a clinic for those who had broken with an old culture and had not yet found a new one. . . ." This picture of Bohemianism as a school or a hospital is an important one, for the radical intellectuals of the 1930s often condemned the atmosphere of the Village in the 1920s as degenerate and psychologically unsound: a significant change from the "moral health resort" as it was depicted before World War I. The seriousness of the economic crisis and the message of hope embedded in the slogans of proletarianism were often contrasted to the unreal preoccupations of the 1920s. The concept of Bohemianism (as a competitor of the radical movement) was denounced as bourgeois. More important perhaps, much of the literature of the decade was dismissed as escapist. Exile was denounced: Proust, Joyce, and others were considered dead-end, middle-class ideologists and not great literary experimentalists. In part because of this, the return of exile writers in the late 1920s and early 1930s was often accompanied by confessional writing or a renunciation of expatriation. Europe now seemed to many writers an escape, a place for shedding intellectual responsibilities, and America seemed once more to be the center of new opportunities. Exile, the avant-garde literature of the 1920s, and Bohemianism were often portrayed as aspects of the same social irresponsibility and intellectual abdication.[7] Reality, it was claimed, now marched with the armies of the proletariat. Thus the similar

---

[6] Eastman, "Bunk About Bohemia," *Modern Quarterly*, VIII (May 1934), pp. 200-201.
[7] Joseph Freeman, "Greenwich Village Types," *New Masses*, VIII (May 1933), p. 18, and Karl Radek, "James Joyce or Socialist Realism," *Problems of Soviet Literature*, G. H. Scott, ed. (Moscow: International Publishers, 1934), pp. 150 ff.

origins of the three Bohemias of the 1920s were obscured by the belief in a cultural revolution.

Aside from Bohemianism, the proletarian movement fought against another set of ideas, which it also branded as a rearguard action of middle-class culture—the humanist movement of the early 1930s. Led by critics Paul Elmer More and Irving Babbitt, this critical stance attacked pragmatists and philosophies of change and called for a gentle, measured Christianity. Humanism appealed to tradition as a guide for its literary judgments: "Any expression of a humanist society through the arts depends upon the acceptance of the artist of some sort of central authority," argued one of its exponents. But to Edmund Wilson, More's appeal to tradition and his rejection of science indicated that he was "really an old-fashioned Puritan who has lost the Puritan theology without having lost the Puritan dogmatism." To orthodox Communists, humanism was the epitome of a pathetic, outdated cultural philosophy, an elegant, old-age home for weary ideas. The most important attack on this philosophy was led by Michael Gold in the pages of the *New Republic*. Gold's scathing review of Thornton Wilder, in which he dismissed the author as a "poet of the genteel bourgeoisie," was a denunciation of the school of American critical and creative literature that ignored material progress and realism. "There is no question," remarked Edmund Wilson, "that the Gold-Wilder case marks definitely the eruption of the Marxist issues out of the literary circles of the radicals into the field of general criticism."[8]

The distance between the literary radicals and the humanists was great, for the subject matter, the style, and even the basic attitudes toward contemporary life were immensely different. In contrast to the humanists, Mike Gold's band of proletarian writers seemed well-suited to write of a world defined by depression and class struggle. Humanism in turn abhorred the

---

[8] Irving Babbitt, "An Essay at Definition," and Frank Mather, Jr., "The Plight of Our Arts," *Humanism and America*, Norman Foerster, ed. (New York: Farrar & Rinehart, 1930), pp. 39-42, 113. See also Edmund Wilson, "Notes on Babbitt and More," *New Republic*, LXII (March 19, 1930), p. 119, and Edmund Wilson, "The Literary Class War," *Shores of Light*, p. 589.

tough, hard-boiled prose of a Gold and the glorification of progress and historical change that was typical of radical writers of the early 1930s. The radicals who led the "Literary Class War," as Edmund Wilson called it, against the Wilders, Mores, and Babbitts denounced the attempt to bury what they considered the crucial issues of the day under a welter of ornate and didactic prose. Malcolm Cowley, for instance, in an editorial in the *New Republic,* argued that Irving Babbitt had rejected almost every writer since Rousseau. But one very important attitude was shared by members of both sides in this dispute— a hostility to a large part of contemporary literature. Both rejected the experimental art of the 1920s, both opposed a theory of art for art's sake (without proving that this theory had anything to do with the art of the "lost generation"), and both carefully weighed the didactic content of a work of art.

For much of the 1930s the central literary issue was the place to be given the culture of the 1920s and the importance of innovations in prose and poetry made during that decade. Radical intellectuals who attacked the humanists were united in their disgust at the appeal to a genteel tradition, but they were often divided in their attitudes toward the fundamentals of literature. Paradoxically, the appeal of proletarian literature and humanism to larger philosophic systems to which the writer must accommodate himself united these two very different approaches to literature on one of the central problems of the 1930s—the relationship of the artist and his work to the needs of society. Thus one of the literary issues that split the radical movement was only slightly removed from the implications of the humanist debate. It became a burning question to critics, after their first enthusiasm for proletarian literature, to decide which tradition was most relevant to literature and what place the literature of the twentieth century should occupy in the coming cultural renaissance.

The publication in 1931 of *Axel's Castle,* Edmund Wilson's study of the symbolists, was a less dramatic but more subtle and influential attempt to reappraise some of the literary presuppositions of the 1920s and illustrated perhaps better than the humanist controversy how important radical political ideas would be to the 1930s. Moreover, Wilson's position helped to give respectability to new approaches to literature, such as proletarian criticism, even though he did not condone them. Wilson, in his book, contended that Yeats, Joyce, Eliot, Stein, Proust, and Valery belonged to the symbolist movement: ". . . that second swing of the pendulum away from a mechanistic view of nature and from a social conception of man. . . ." Very conscious that he was writing at the end of a period, Wilson suggested that the critical premises of these writers and their works could no longer serve as guides for young poets, nor would their renunciation of experience, their escape into the chambers of the imagination or the haunts of primitivism satisfy the new literary world. Wilson's pronouncement upon Marcel Proust has a memorable finality to it: "Proust is perhaps the last great historian of the loves, the society, the intelligence, the diplomacy, the literature and the art of the Heartbreak House of capitalist culture. . . ." T. S. Eliot's criticism, he remarked, imposed on the reader a "conception of poetry as some sort of pure and rare aesthetic essence with no relation to any of the practical human uses for which for some reason never explained, only the technique of prose is appropriate."[9] Edmund Wilson's study was important to the younger critics of the 1930s because of his ability to relate the rhythm of literary movements to a long-range cycle of cultural and economic history without betraying the sort of mechanistic intellectual scaffolding that often showed through in other attacks on the 1920s. He did not reject the accomplishments of the symbolists, but allowed his radical orientation to indicate the reasons for the end of the movement and the direction that a new literature might take. He provided persuasive arguments for the radical's call for a new literary movement without specifically calling for proletarian literature.

Also related to the issues of the 1920s was the uneasy and

---

[9] Edmund Wilson, *Axel's Castle: A Study in Imaginative Literature of 1870-1930* (New York: Scribner's, 1931), pp. 19, 119, 190. Both Phillips and Rahv relate that they were influenced by Wilson: William Phillips, "The Wholeness of Literature," *American Mercury*, LXXV (November 1952), p. 107, and interview with Philip Rahv, April 26, 1965, New York.

often incomplete radicalization of the young intellectual. Often it took form in a denunciation of the interests of that period. Speaking of his own intellectual progress, Philip Rahv wrote: "As so many other middle class intellectuals, though I studied Freud, Nietzsche, Proust, Joyce, Rambaud, etc., I really knew and saw nothing. We lived on the carrion of Eliot, writing poems that were an unspeakably sad reflection of the end-of-the-world mood, affected, semi-conscious and petulant." To William Phillips, joining the radical literary movement amounted to a painful readjustment of values and a need to see the literature of the 1920s in a new perspective.[10]

The problems of the intellectual in a working-class movement went beyond the initial difficulties in adjusting himself to new ideas, for the important Communist critics suspected the dependability of writers and artists. "It is true that the intellectual brings into the movement many of his bourgeois hangovers and ideologies which are dangerous," wrote Mike Gold, "but they can be controlled." Moreover, Gold identified this suspicion with an older American distrust that had been expressed by the I.W.W. Only in characters such as John Reed did the problem of class seem resolved. Because Reed immersed his life and art in revolutionary journalism, he became a symbol for the Communists of the potential role of intellectuals. Some radical critics advised an extreme solution to the identity problems of the intellectual: the artist or writer must become a proletarian so that his adherence to the working class would be complete.[11]

To become a literary radical and a proletarian artist in the early 1930s, an intellectual was forced to deny, in part at least, traditional ideas of the role of the writer or critic. Thus the idea of an awakening, a shattering of the dreamlike world of the 1920s, became a countertheme to the symbol of the great crash in characterizing the Depression decade. The young radicals expressed a new urgency; they could be the forerunners of

---

[10] Philip Rahv, "For Whom do you Write?" *New Quarterly*, I (Summer 1934), p. 12. Interview with William Phillips, April 30, 1965, New York.
[11] Michael Gold, "Notes of the Month," *New Masses*, VI (August 1930), p. 5, and Granville Hicks, "The Crisis in American Criticism," *New Masses*, VIII (February 1933), p. 5.

a renaissance, especially if the issues raised by the new theories of proletarian literature and the question of art versus propaganda could be decided. "Writers felt that they were at the dawn of a golden age," related Rahv and Phillips in 1937 looking back on the early years of proletarian literature, "and that these questions must be settled quickly lest they retard the expected burst of creative glory."[12] The renaissance of American culture depended on the intellectual, particularly the critic, to point the way to a revolutionary basis for art, a new criticism and a new audience, but the intellectual would have to follow the general lead of the party, which was the vanguard of social transformation.

The radicalism of intellectuals in the early 1930s was still more complex than a reaction to the economic wreckage that cluttered society and a faith that they could participate in the rebuilding of American culture. The Soviet Union added a further dimension as the example of the ideal economic and cultural system and as the testing ground for radical theories. Edmund Wilson perhaps best captured what it meant for the intellectual to identify with the Bolshevik Revolution when he wrote after a trip to Russia in 1935 that in the Soviet Union one felt at the "moral top of the world where the light never really goes out." Radical literary criticism, as proletarian art, would ultimately stand or fall not only by the virtue of its accomplishments in America, but also by the success of the Soviet Union in political and cultural affairs. Communists identified with the Bolshevik Revolution because they wanted to make its prestige their own and because the roots of indigenous radicalism were by the 1930s forgotten or distorted. One of the most important of the earliest radicals, Floyd Dell, by now exiled from radical literary circles, relates precisely the opposite intellectual orientation during the 1930s. "Some six years ago," he wrote in 1939 of the Hitler-Stalin pact, "as if in a nightmare, I foresaw some such possibility as this, and it made novel-writing too difficult—it damn near gave me a nervous break-down:

---

12 William Phillips and Philip Rahv, "Literature in a Political Decade," *New Letters in America,* Horace Gregory, ed. (New York: W. W. Norton, 1937), p. 170.

and I've been detaching myself from that situation ever since. . . ."[13] Even for those who opposed literary Communism, the Soviet Union was a central problem of intellectual life.

The connections between political revolution and a cultural revolution were indisputable in the Soviet Union. It appeared that cultural change, as Marx implied, was responsive to economic change. Granville Hicks, a major leftist intellectual of the 1930s, wrote that he considered this connection very important to him and his friends: "We knew that the Soviet Union was no utopia, but what we saw of Russian literature and art convinced us that something interesting and important was going on, and we wished the revolution well." In his desire to Americanize the Soviet experiment, Mike Gold asserted that an important link existed even in the literature produced by the new American writers and the heroes of the Russian Revolution. "The style of Lenin," he commented, "is curiously the style of Ernest Hemingway and other young writers today."[14]

The investment of hopes with the Soviet Union and the belief that it was on its way toward overcoming the antagonism of the artist to society by creating a new society—and new artists —was a development that had profound effects on the character of the radical literary movement in the United States. A dependence on ideas originating abroad in no way intimidated intellectuals, many of whom were convinced of America's cultural inferiority. Moreover, many radical literary figures became convinced Communists or sympathizers, not because of their own experience as part of an exploited class, but as a result of the intellectual process of reading about the new society in Russia; this made them dependent on the cultural attitudes of the Communist party, which mediated between the intellectuals and the Soviet Union. Thus the history of the Communist movement and its organizational relationships to Russia during the

---

[13] Edmund Wilson, *Travels in Two Democracies* (New York: Harcourt, Brace, 1936), p. 321. Floyd Dell to Elizabeth Lancaster, 1939, p. 2. Dell MSS.
[14] Granville Hicks, *Where We Came Out* (New York: Viking Press, 1954), p. 25, and Michael Gold, "Three Schools of U.S. Writing," *New Masses,* IV (September 1928), p. 13.

early 1930s are part of the background of literary radicalism and part of the context from which the *Partisan Review* emerged. Bolshevik Russia provided an example of the new society to the future editors of the magazine and to many of their intellectual companions who were convinced of the need for a radical transformation of society and a new culture.

The internal political struggles in the Soviet Union by which Stalin eventually eliminated most of his powerful enemies and asserted control over the international Communist movement were fought out in terms of issues that inevitably involved the American Communists. The success of the Russian leader in translating what was often a struggle for power onto the plane of ideological dispute and in forcing the Soviet leadership to divide according to right or left positions in domestic, foreign, and Comintern policy meant that Soviet attitudes toward culture were often linked to general Soviet assessments of the world political situation. Sensitive to changes in Russian policy, American Communism was not always immediately responsive to changes in the American climate of opinion. But in a general sense the attitudes of the Communist party literati toward the function of culture were constant. Literature was always viewed in relation to politics and never particularly prized for itself. Within this framework, however, there was room for profound change in literary and critical attitudes, changes that reflected the pronouncements of the Soviet Union on cultural matters and were simultaneously in line with the general movement of American letters.

Stalin's swerve leftward beginning in 1928 was an effort to outflank Nikolai Bukharin, a former ally against Trotsky, and to overcome domestic economic difficulties by collectivization in agriculture and by rapid industrialization. Translated into Comintern policy, the new left turn emphasized the revolutionary potential of the international working class and the necessity of struggling against Social Democrats (as the Socialist party in the United States). In practical terms it meant the replacement of Jay Lovestone, who had been identified with Bukharin, by William Z. Foster as head of the American Communist party.[15] This change of policy extended even into Soviet attitudes toward cultural matters. The period from 1928 to about 1932 was one of extreme leftism, during which the Soviet Union fought to industrialize itself and the Communists distrusted any party other than themselves, any class other than the proletariat, and any social role other than that of a worker.

The closeness of the American Communist literati to the international movement is indicated by their anxiousness to accommodate to changes in Soviet policy. At the second Congress of Revolutionary Writers at Kharkov, U.S.S.R., held in 1930 and attended by several important American radicals, including Mike Gold and Joshua Kunitz, the new Soviet policy was asserted in the demand for more genuinely proletarian literature in the United States and elsewhere and for a struggle against unstable fellow travelers (Social Fascists). Practically, this meant the exclusion of such men as Upton Sinclair from participation in the Communist-sponsored John Reed Clubs. Criticism of the quality of the *New Masses* as an intellectual organ was raised at the conference, and the American delegates incorporated some of these criticism in their own resolution concerning the future tasks of American proletarian and revolutionary literature.[16]

Another suggestion of the Kharkov conference was that the proletarian movement be wary of the petty bourgeois past of its new recruits and that it be careful to re-educate and remold the thinking of its allies.[17] Whatever indigenous distrust of intellectuals already existed in the American movement was thus reinforced by similar attitudes coming from the Soviet Union. And during the early 1930s the *New Masses* and the Communist intellectuals continued the process of purging their ideological ranks of elements deemed untrustworthy because of their lit-

---

[15] Draper, *American Communism and Soviet Russia,* pp. 302-305.
[16] Walter B. Rideout, *The Radical Novel in the United States, 1900-1954* (Cambridge, Mass.: Harvard University Press, 1956), p. 141, and "Resolution of the American Delegates on Proletarian and Revolutionary Literature," *Literature of the World Revolution* (Moscow: International Publishers, 1931), p. 122.
[17] "Resolution on Political and Creative Questions of International Proletarian and Revolutionary Literature," *Literature of the World Revolution,* p. 89.

erary interests or their reluctance to follow the lead of the party. One implication of the Russian advice, one deduction from the premises of proletarian literature could eliminate this problem of intellectuals. Perhaps true proletarian literature, a small minority of critics concluded, could be created only by workers.

The precariousness of the proletarian movement was not ultimately founded on this reluctance to deal with intellectuals as intellectuals. Rather, as an official and comprehensive theory, it absorbed a great many related issues and was further complicated by the heated discussion of radical literature among its proponents, during the first half of the 1930s. Since it was promoted by an American movement that reflected changes in Soviet policy, its ultimate success—unless it were to touch off an immediate burst of fine literature—depended on the course of Soviet policy.

In addition to the feelings of the young intellectual for his culture and for the promise of Communism, there were other reasons, which, being more practical, seemed to justify his interest in the radical literary movement. During the first years of the Depression ordinary channels of publication seemed constricted. Unknown writers and artists found it more difficult to enter into established literary and artistic circles. Because of their radical views, they were often intellectually isolated, and the problem of finding a sympathetic audience was a serious one, as it had always been. But now this dilemma seemed explainable in terms of the cultural decadence of America. Maxwell Bodenheim commented on the plight of the writer in 1934: "No proletarian worker on the face of the earth is more shamelessly and deceitfully exploited than is a poet in any capitalistic country." The lack of an audience for serious prose and poetry was a sign to other writers of the failure of the culture. Isidor Schneider wrote of the 1920s that authors thought that they "were assembling an audience of the rebellious and adventurous minded," but had discovered that such an audience was very small.[18] The Communists offered a theory to explain the predica-

---

[18] Maxwell Bodenheim, "The Revolutionary Poet," *Little Magazine,* I (February-March 1934), p. 1, and Isidor Schneider, "For Whom do you Write?" *New Quarterly,* I (Summer 1934), p. 10.

ment of the writer and a movement to change it. Only a radical interpretation of art, wrote Mike Gold, gave the writer a world philosophy, and only the proletarian movement promised a new audience (the working class) and the literary organ of a cultural renaissance, the *New Masses*.

A number of little magazines that were committed to radicalism, to printing the poems and stories of young writers and to finding a new audience sprang up around the self-designated leader of the literary revolution, the *New Masses*. As the semi-official spokesman of Communist letters the *New Masses* was drawn in contradictory directions. It was naturally responsive to changes in the political and cultural attitudes of the American Communist party. It reflected political maneuvers of the party upon occasion, while it ignored or played down the theoretical aspects of literary criticism. Moreover, it did not always take the lead in printing new prose and poetry as might be expected. Thus a major problem of the magazine was its closeness to the Communist political organization, which involved its pages in party affairs. Furthermore, it was unable to decide on the nature of its audience; was it for intellectuals or for workers? The magazine attempted to be too broad in its function; thus it succeeded often in being merely superficial.

Communist intellectuals were convinced in the early 1930s that proletarian literature was meaningful and important as a literary theory. But at the fringes of the *New Masses* group there existed a rapidly growing movement of young radical intellectuals who believed even more seriously (or more exclusively) in the literary renaissance, the idea of a new culture and the necessity not to cut themselves off, as they felt the expatriates had, from their roots in provincial or working-class America. This group saw in proletarian literature a new combination of advanced art and radical politics. But unhappily the inflexibility of bourgeois culture and the difficulty that an author experienced in establishing himself or finding an intelligent and understanding audience were problems for leftist literature too. The *New Masses*, whatever its pretensions to being a worker's correspondence, printed, by and large, the work of well-known writers, or at least intellectuals who were established in Left circles. For the young radical who desired to contribute to the literary revolution, or who wished to help lead it, the question remained: how could he take his place in history—even if only in literary history? The little magazine movement was a response to this question. It offered a chance for publication and an opportunity to tap the vast, untouched audience of the future, the proletariat. Dissatisfaction with the quality of the *New Masses* came from official party sources in the 1930s and also from new recruits to the movement. Because of the promises of Communism, and because young radicals took them seriously, the failure of the *New Masses* to establish itself as an outstanding leader in a literary renaissance was a serious problem. The foundation of a number of little magazines in the early 1930s, among them the *Partisan Review*, occurred partly to compensate for the deficiencies of the *New Masses*.[19]

The center of the little magazine renaissance was the John Reed Club organization, founded in 1929, with branches in New York, Chicago, Boston, and other major American cities. These organizations of writers and artists provided a meeting ground for radical art and political activity. They fulfilled the function that Earl Browder, secretary of the Communist party, proposed: "One of the means whereby the Party hopes to assist in linking up literature with life, lies in participating with you [writers] in organizing this field; organizing the writers, organizing a growing audience, and furnishing the connecting links between these two basic factors in cultural life."[20] Although some established writers and artists (particularly in New York) worked with the clubs, a unique characteristic of the organization was that most of the artists and writers who belonged were unknown. The clubs attempted to become the articulate spokesmen for the leftward movement of young and inexperienced intellectuals. The New York club, which was large enough to be divided into sections, participated in a variety of

---

[19] *New Masses*, VIII (September 1932), p. 21, and Wallace Phelps [William Phillips], "Three Generations," *Partisan Review*, I (September-October 1934), p. 52.
[20] Earl Browder, "Communism and Literature," *Communism in the United States* (New York: International Publishers, 1935), p. 314.

political and cultural activities. Among the most noteworthy of the opportunities that it offered to young writers and artists were the John Reed Club Writers' School, which listed Joshua Kunitz, Kenneth Burke, Horace Gregory, and Edward Dahlberg as lecturers, and a John Reed School of Art, which advertised as instructors Robert Minor, Hugo Gellert, William Groper, Raphael Soyer, and others. The Reed Clubs were the foundation on which the proletarian movement was to be built.

It is not surprising that the theory of proletarian literature absorbed the John Reed Clubs and their publications more than it did the *New Masses*. Many young writers and artists, who were unable to find their way into print, established magazines through their local Reed Clubs devoted to a new literature. Because their writings were crude or revolutionary (politically), many of these writers had not, as yet, secured access to larger publications—even to the *New Masses*.[21] By 1934 the clubs could boast a number of radical publications including *Left Front, Left Review, Leftward*, the *Cauldron, Blast, Dynamo*, the *Anvil, Partisan Review*, the *Partisan*, and the *Hammer*. These belligerently titled little magazines published the proletarian poetry and prose of the young literary radicals; they struck the opening notes in the expected literary renaissance.

The history of two little magazines that antedate the Reed Club publications played a role in the early history of the *Partisan Review* and helped to set the tone for other radical journals. One of these, the *Rebel Poet*, was among the most authentically proletarian of the radical little magazines. It was also the first publication to which Philip Rahv, one of the two important founding editors of the *Partisan Review*, contributed editorial work (he also wrote a translation of a poem and a manifesto for young writers). The magazine, edited by Missouri novelist Jack Conroy, began publication in January 1931. Part of a literary underground even in its relations with the Communist movement, the *Rebel Poet* belonged to an international organization

---

[21] Charles Allen, "The Advance Guard," *Sewanee Review*, LI (July-September 1943), p. 426. Allen discusses a number of major writers who first published in obscure, often radical little magazines.

of Rebel Poets, which was headed by Ralph Cheyney of the I.W.W. and was thus linked to the literary heritage of the Wobblies. Conroy also edited *Unrest*, an annual volume of international revolutionary poetry. *Unrest* was self-confident and combative; the introduction to its 1931 volume proclaimed the dawn of proletarian culture in language which became typical of the radical movement: "We know the future belongs to us. What we say now will appear commonplace and indisputable to our ancestors, and the fulminations of most of our critics will seem grotesque and absurd." Rebel Poet groups, functioning somewhat like the John Reed Clubs, were started in New York and other cities to further the efforts of proletarian poetry. Conroy's magazine, however, was short-lived because of financial difficulties and complications with postal authorities.[22]

The *Anvil*, also edited by Conroy, superseded the *Rebel Poet*. Founded in May 1933, it preceded the John Reed Club magazines, which became common the next year. In 1935 an attempt was made to form an Anvil League of Writers and a group of Friends of the Anvil to contribute to the magazine and help in its financing. Even though the magazine had a rather large circulation for a publication of its type, it was moved to New York, where it was submerged in the John Reed Club, and in 1936 it was combined with the *Partisan Review*, also a Reed Club publication at the time. Conroy's attempt to make his own proletarian movement was short-lived, but important.

The foundation in 1934 of the *Partisan Review* took place in part as an expansion of the institutional framework of the Communist literary movement, but also as a reaction to the failure of the *New Masses* to perform its anticipated cultural function. The magazine's character was immediately influenced by the theories of criticism developed in the earliest writings of Philip Rahv and William Phillips. It was affected by their particular

---

[22] Jack Conroy and Ralph Cheyney, *Unrest* (New York: Henry Harrison, 1931), p. 8, and Jack Conroy to the author, January 5, 1965. See also Jeff Rall, "1933 and 'The Disinherited,'" *Industrial Worker*, May 22, 1963. Rall relates that "The *Rebel Poet* was hastened to its early demise by the curious fact that it was printed in, of all places, a cow shed. This led to its suppression by the postal authorities on the grounds that it was too unsanitary to be sent through the mails."

concern for the implications of proletarian literature, to which both were deeply committed, and by their criticisms of the existing Communist movement. Within the movement, despite the rigidity of its attitude toward intellectual deviance from accepted policy, there was a rather wide difference of opinion in literary matters and room for men like Phillips and Rahv. Adherence to the idea of proletarian literature, perhaps the most rigid literary theory ever held by the left, was not the exclusive test of allegiance to the radical movement. Ultimately, the interests of party intellectuals such as Gold, Minor, and even Freeman were political, not literary. Authors who remained favorable to Communism and defended the Soviet Union (which did not seem a particularly compromising intellectual position in the early 1930s) were judged more by their politics than by their peculiar literary style. Because the party used political criterion, the early Communist literary movement remained surprisingly flexible; in fact, this was a source of criticism of the *New Masses*. Some little magazines complained that the establishment radicals did not really promote revolutionary literature and that they equivocated on the purity of the new movement.

Two such young men who wished to help shape the proletarian movement were William Phillips and Philip Rahv. William Phillips, like many of the new radical generation, was born into an immigrant family. Although his father had been a socialist, his own interests were at first not political, but philosophical and literary. At City College, where he received a B.A., he absorbed the new literature of the 1920s, of Eliot, Joyce, Cummings, and the expatriates. Later, at New York University, he received an M.A. and taught there through 1932. Significantly, his first writing was creative, a play, and his first criticism was sent to the *Horn and Hound*, a periodical that stressed literary innovation. To members of his generation the end of the 1920s and the bleak inaugural of the 1930s seemed simultaneously to shut off the possibilities for life in society and to make change appear more certain and near. But it was not merely the offering of change by the Communists nor the creation of an example and a model in the Soviet Union that attracted young men like Phillips; it was also the vision of a new culture and the high place to be given the intellectual and the writer in the revolutionary movement.[23]

Early in the 1930s Phillips became active in the New York John Reed Club, where he was made secretary of the writer's group and was listed as a speaker for the organization. His earliest work for the radical press included two book reviews for the *Communist* in 1933 and a critical essay for the *Dynamo* in 1934. Perhaps because he was still intrigued with the literature of the 1920s, he seemed preoccupied from the beginning with the attitude of the proletarian movement toward the art of that decade. He accepted the judgment that radical literature and radical politics were related, but was troubled by the distance between revolutionary politics and the important avant-garde writers of the 1920s and before, who in their own way had been artistic radicals. He did not accept unquestioningly the movement's harsh judgment that these writers represented bourgeois decay. To him an essential problem was to explain in a poet such as T. S. Eliot the simultaneous existence of a radical approach to literary technique and of reactionary political stands. After reading Croce, Eliot, Edmund Wilson, and other modern literary critics, he began a book, which he never completed, that attempted to formulate a Marxist literary criticism to explain such paradoxes.[24] Thus, whatever temporary faith he might have had in an American revolution, it was cultural radicalism that was his abiding interest.

Phillip's earliest writings demonstrate his serious involvement in the idea of a new literary movement. In defense of the cultural potential of the proletariat he argued, for example, that critics like Ortega y Gasset belonged to the modern school of literary criticism that had assimilated into its vocabulary and structure of thought a defense of capitalism common to both fascist and social democratic theory. This early review shows clearly the influence of the rigid leftism curent in the early 1930s, a characteristic that evaporated rather quickly from his

---

[23] William Phillips used the pen name Wallace Phelps until 1935. Interview with William Phillips. Biographical material supplied by William Phillips.
[24] *Ibid.*

writings. Nevertheless, Phillips remained well within the general assumptions of the Communist movement in his later articles in the *Symposium* and the *Dynamo*, even though he raised two interrelated questions that could have been interpreted as a challenge to the fundamentals of proletarian art. The first related to the place of aesthetics in the new literary movement and the role of traditional critical standards. Should these, as the movement seemed to suggest, be cast aside? He argued on the contrary that some standards in criticism were permanent. He was reluctant to discard all the old assumptions about criticism despite the radical changes that history seemed to suggest and the cultural revolution demanded. In his article for *Dynamo*, "Sensibility and Modern Poetry," he argued that the problem of the carry-over from bourgeois art, that is, the accomplishments and traditions of literary history, was the major problem for Marxian critics. On this issue he wished to compromise. He concluded, however, with a plea for the author to immerse himself in the vision of the proletariat: "When a poet's sensibility is rooted in the proletariat and adjusted to traditional poetry, he has the equipment to produce good proletarian poetry."[25]

The attempt to retain high aesthetic standards and to preserve the literary achievements of the past (particularly of the 1920s) marked Phillips's early literary criticism as much as his commitment to the new literature based on a revolutionary moral scheme and a new audience, the proletariat. His ambiguity toward such literary figures as T. S. Eliot and his attempt to work out a theoretical approach that would allow him to appreciate, yet go beyond, the accomplishments of Eliot led him to conclude that if a new literature were to be born, it would have to be the product of a true proletarian culture, one that would be as fertile in literary potential as had been bourgeois culture. Proletarian literature, in other words, must become truly avant-garde.

---

[25] Wallace Phelps [William Phillips], "*Class*-ical Culture," *Communist*, XII (January 1933), pp. 93-94; William Phillips, "Categories for Criticism," *Symposium*, IV (January 1933), p. 41; and Wallace Phelps [William Phillips], "Sensibility and Modern Poetry," *Dynamo*, I (Summer 1934), p. 25.

Philip Rahv, the other important founder of the *Partisan Review*, was a member of a Russian Jewish family that, like many others, came to the United States after the Russian Revolution. Born in Kupin in the Ukraine, Rahv was fourteen when his parents settled in Providence, Rhode Island, where he went to high school. From there he went to the West Coast, working in advertising until he returned to New York in 1932. Although he was fascinated by politics during the 1930s, his first and strongest interest was literature, so much so that before his early twenties he scarcely bothered to read daily newspapers.[26] When he arrived in New York, like Phillips and others he responded to the movement promoted by the John Reed Clubs, an opportunity perfectly suited to the young, unestablished writer, anxious to participate in the literary and cultural revolution that seemed possible in those early years of the Depression.

In addition to his activities in the Reed Clubs, Rahv also wrote for a number of left publications, some of them predecessors of the John Reed Club magazines. More politically inclined than Phillips, he was closer to the Communist party and by 1932 was secretary of the monthly magazine, the *Prolit Folio*, published by the Revolutionary Writers Federation affiliated with the International Union of Revolutionary Writers. He also joined the Rebel Poets group in New York, even though his interests were quite different from those of Jack Conroy, editor of the magazine. In the Rebel Poets group Rahv fought for more critical writing and more theory and against a conciliatory policy toward liberal or socialist fellow travelers. Conroy, on the other hand, had little interest in literary criticism and wished to keep the magazine a publication open to a wider group of young poets. There was so much bickering and factionalism, related Conroy, that he dissolved the group in New York, and the magazine folded shortly thereafter.[27] In the fall of 1932 in the *Rebel Poet* Rahv spelled out his program for the proletarian literary movement. He felt the literary tide had turned against

[26] Philip Rahv to the author, March 22, 1966.

[27] *Prolit Folio*, I (October 1932), and interview with Jack Conroy, February 27, 1965, Chicago; also Jack Conroy to author, January 5, 1966.

bourgeois art; anyone could see that the bourgeois critics were fighting a rearguard action. The time had come for the young writers who worked in the offices, factories, and farms to choose the side of the class-conscious proletariat. However, to do this, American intellectuals needed a Marxian education. Older forms of literature that had attempted to rise above the issues of a class society—the works of Lawrence, Joyce, Huxley, Mencken, and Faulkner—all pointed in a direction that was "irrelevant to the historical process of development which society is now undergoing." It was the task of the young intellectual, particularly the critic, to restore the function of literature to its proper place: "The ideological revolution must precede the political revolution—the sincere writer is herewith offered a magnificent opportunity to vitalize his creative talent within the seething vat of world important problems." Literature was the "nerve center" of culture; hence it could not remain neutral in the face of the corruption of capitalist society.

One of the major difficulties experienced by the new proletarian movement was the failure of its literary ideology to keep pace with its political ideology. The work of left-wing critics had softened the public attitude toward the new literature, but it was still imperative to merge a revolutionary, literary ideology with an integrated Marxist view of the world. The difficulty, as Rahv would later acknowledge, was in developing a theory that could link art and propaganda. His antipathy to compromise with prevailing schools of literary criticism reflected how much he had absorbed proletarian theory: "We must sever all ideological ties with this lunatic civilization known as capitalism," he wrote.[28] Although Rahv's first critical writing is notable mainly for its sweeping and overenthusiastic generalities, it nevertheless contains a hint of certain later characteristics. Most important, however, is his idea that Marxism could be the basis for a literary theory and that this revolutionary philosophy was as important for literature as for politics.

Yet Rahv was not prepared, any more than was Phillips, even

---

[28] Philip Rahv, "Open Letter to Young Writers," *Rebel Poet* (September 1932), pp. 3-4. Rahv wrote a number of letters to Jack Conroy in 1932, discussing these issues; Jack Conroy MSS.

while seriously contemplating the literary revolution, to bury the culture of the past. In a fascinating article for the *New Masses* in August 1932 he proposed the adaptation of the concept of catharsis and of Aristotle's theory of the completed action to proletarian literature. The new working-class literature could recapture the dramatic energy expressed in the Greek concept of the release of the emotions, he argued; for the proletarian, however, the release would not come through emotion, but in class-conscious action. It was exactly at this point, he insisted, that American writers fell flat; they lacked any dramatic resolution to their work. Significantly, he revealed at this time a dislike for naturalism in literature, which he never abandoned. Writers such as William Faulkner, he concluded, left the reader with nothing but "stylized photography." Theirs was not the literary road to revolution.

Rahv was rather pessimistic about the ultimate comprehensiveness of the proletarian movement. Most writers, he felt, would eventually end up in the bourgeois camp rather than with the workers. Unlike proletarians, writers had embraced the revolution not because of the misery and chaos of capitalism, but because of the example of the Soviet Union and the intellectual strength of Marxism. This acute observation shows that from the beginning, Rahv was aware of the central phenomenon of American literary radicalism of the 1930s: its dependence, in one way or another, on the Bolshevik Revolution. The test of the radical intellectual was his attitude toward the Soviet Union.[29]

Like Phillips, Rahv was impressed by the poetry of T. S. Eliot and deeply concerned with the ideological implications of his work. Eliot was not unintelligible or obscure, as he had seemed to Eastman; he was wrong. "In him," Rahv wrote, "one experiences the whole gamut of post-war disenchantment, the entire complex of spiritual and intellectual problems that torture and stultify the creative course of modern thought." He concluded that Eliot's experience was not relevant to the proletarian renaissance, although his early work was admirable and he was

---

[29] Philip Rahv, "The Literary Class War," *New Masses*, VIII (August 1932), pp. 7-10.

fundamentally modern in his approach to literature. Paradoxically, Eliot seemed keenly aware of the problems of modern
society, yet out of step with history. If the writer became aware
of the political implications of literature and of the political demands of culture, if he realized the role of class struggle in
society, and if he could join the proletarian movement, he might
avoid Eliot's dilemma; then he could "take his place within the
scheme of history."[30]

When Rahv and Phillips entered the Communist literary
movement, they did so at a moment when it promised to transform society and revolutionize culture; their writings indicate
the attractiveness of a literary revival. The revolutionary movement promised to end the dilemma of the American writer.
The malaise felt by the artist in the 1920s that was caused by
his profound dislike for the cultural environment of America,
his frequent ambiguity toward the value of everything but his
own work, looked insignificant on the face of the literary
renaissance that would be one part of a thorough social and
political upheaval. As before World War I, the critic promised to
be the central figure of the renaissance, for unless he could
clarify the current literary mind, creativity might be stunted and
lost. But unlike that other period, the relationship of art to politics was fundamentally different, for literature and politics were
now fused—not in the cultural criticism of Bourne and Brooks,
nor in the alliance between radicalism in art and politics of the
Masses, nor even in the directions indicated by dada and surrealism, but in the formula of proletarian art that combined art
and politics and left little room for what had already been produced by the avant-garde. Rather, the movement promised a
new sort of avant-garde. Much of what troubled the writers of
the 1920s was dismissed as a fake problem, and many of the
extracurricular interests of the intellectuals were viewed as obstacles to a true understanding of literature. If the Communist
movement offered a home for the exile and a vision of a new
America, it did so in terms that some of the older, established

---

[30] Philip Rahv, "T. S. Eliot—An Essay," *Fantasy,* II (Winter 1932), p. 17,
and Rahv, "For Whom do you Write?" *New Quarterly I* (Summer 1934),
p. 12.

intellectuals could not accept. But many of the younger writers accepted the movement on its own terms, as the vanguard of a new era of letters.

Rahv and Phillips were very much a part of this younger generation of writers caught up by the promises of the proletarian movement. Nevertheless their attitudes, even at the beginning, demonstrate an equivocation about some of the premises of proletarian literature. Whatever their enthusiasm for the Communist movement, the problems of the 1920s, especially the ambiguous relation of the artist to society, had not been solved entirely to their satisfaction. Nor could T. S. Eliot or the avant-garde, for that matter, simply be dismissed. The important question of the artist's relation to American literary and critical traditions, even to the traditions of European literature, had not yet been answered by the proletarian movement. And their certainty that America lacked a Marxist tradition meant that radicalism, like avant-garde art, would be identified with European thought. Thus Rahv and Phillips tended to search for the solutions to problems of American culture in Europe.

The earliest characteristics of the *Partisan Review* were formed by the interaction of the institutional manifestations of the radical literary movement such as the John Reed Clubs and the *New Masses*, by the ways in which Rahv and Phillips related to such institutions, and by their special views of the function of criticism. Rahv had expressed early doubts about the *New Masses* and the sectarian nature of the left, but this did not reveal any disillusionment with radicalism: it pointed to a special conception of art and criticism that he shared with William Phillips and which would be the principal mark of the *Partisan Review*. It was into the midst of a rising intellectual movement, at the beginning of a great literary renaissance, or so many thought, that the *Partisan Review* was founded.

Chapter 4

The First Partisan Review

Marxism fights the vulgarization of literature
by its "leftist" hangers-on; it will not and cannot support the desire of a group of primitives
to hypostasize their lack of talent and to repudiate the cultural heritage.

Philip Rahv, *The Little Magazine,* 1934

When the *Partisan Review* appeared in late 1934, it was substantially similar to other John Reed Club publications that had
suddenly come into existence during that year. The *Partisan*
was unique, however, in that it immediately became involved
at the center of the Communist literary movement: it originated in New York where most radical intellectuals had congregated and it was published by the most important branch
of the John Reed Club. After April 1935, when the Reed Clubs
were abandoned by the Communists for their new League of
American Writers, the *Partisan* became an independent socialist
publication, still a part of the radical movement but without
organizational ties. From this point on its relations with the
Communist party deteriorated until the end of 1936 when the
magazine discontinued publication.

The two crowded years of the first *Partisan Review* can be divided into three noteworthy periods: the Reed Club days, the
period from April 1935 to the end of the year when the magazine was combined with Jack Conroy's *Anvil,* and the remaining
ten months before the magazine folded in October 1936. In
some respects each period is marked by a particular mood. The

118

first was a time when the proletarian renaissance seemed close at hand, and therefore the need to settle questions of revolutionary criticism was the most pressing. The second, although short, exhibited indecision about the direction of the magazine. The last was important because the editors grew harsh in their assessment of the proletarian literary movement. The gradual disaffection of Rahv and Phillips with the Communists is a complicated process that relates to their changing literary tastes, their evaluation of the progress of proletarian literature; to the difficulties of publishing the *Partisan,* and to striking events in the Soviet Union such as the Moscow Trials.

From its first issue in February-March 1934 it was apparent that the new publication would be different from its more sectarian comrade, the *New Masses.* Although the latter was now published weekly, it nevertheless apparently did not have enough time or space for extensive discussions of literature and criticism.[1] Because of growing political demands upon the time of its intellectuals, the Communist literary movement was willing to allow the creation of a new magazine of culture that in some sense would be a competitor of the *New Masses.* The new publication promised to print the best writings of the New York John Reed Clubs. From the position of the Communist party, the foundation of the *Partisan Review* was basically another step in the proliferation of its influence in literature and a complement to the work being done principally in the *New Masses.*

Joseph Freeman, an editor of the *New Masses,* agreed with the complaint offered by Rahv and Phillips that the *New Masses* was too political; he agreed, in fact, to help them organize a new publication devoted exclusively to literature and criticism. The encouragement of the Communist party stopped short of any direct financial contributions to the new magazine, but it aided efforts to secure necessary funds by endorsing the new publication. Mike Gold, who was perhaps the best-known Communist writer and critic at that time, presided over a fundraising lecture for the *Partisan* delivered by John Strachey at

---

[1] Browder, *Communism in the United States,* p. 314.

the auditorium of the downtown building of the City College of New York.[2] The speech, "Literature and Dialectical Materialism," netted enough profits to publish the magazine for two months. Beyond this, Rahv and Phillips relate, they did not consider the problem of finances.

From Phillips and Rahv's point of view, the establishment of the magazine was not only an extension of the cultural activities of the Reed Clubs, but also a chance to clarify the foggy thinking that enveloped the Communist version of proletarian literature. It would now be possible to concentrate on the theoretical implications of the new critical system in one magazine. Radical literature had developed beyond the first rough proletarian poems that appeared in the *Rebel Poet* and other magazines, but to the young editors of the *Partisan Review* the movement still lacked maturity. Anxious to systematize the scattered critical insights of the literary left, the new magazine in effect challenged the *New Masses* for leadership of the proletarian renaissance. It hoped to provide the broad cultural criticism and the specific analysis of individual literary works that the *New Masses*, when it adopted a more political format, was forced to abandon. From the beginning the *Partisan* was an intellectual center for a radical critique of the left literary movement.

The opening editorial expressed the political assumptions of the new magazine and assessed the progress of radical literature. "Partisan Review," it announced, "appears at a time when American literature is undergoing profound changes." After listing the causes for these changes—all of which were linked to international political and economic events—the editorial

---

[2] Daniel Aaron, *Writers on the Left: Episodes in American Literary Communism, Communism in American Life*, Clinton Rossiter, ed. (New York: Harcourt, Brace, 1961), p. 298. Freeman elsewhere has described the foundation differently. He says that he, Gold, and Hicks were early editors (in addition to Phillips and Rahv), but that the three editors stepped out of the magazine to do other things, leaving Phillips and Rahv in control. Joseph Freeman to Floyd Dell, April 13, 1952, New York, p. 8, Dell MSS. See also Testimony of Leonard Mins, U.S. Congress, House, Special Committee on Un-American Activities, Hearings, *Investigation of Un-American Propaganda Activities in the United States*, 78th Congress, 1st Sess., 1943, Vol. 7, p. 3425.

pledged the magazine to publish creative and critical literature from the viewpoint of the revolutionary working class. It would avoid the liberalism of the middle class and the narrow-mindedness that had at times invaded the radical movement itself.[3] The first issue listed an editorial board that included a number of dignitaries from the radical literary movement: Freeman, Edward Dahlberg, Joshua Kunitz, Edwin Rolfe, and others. Granville Hicks, Grace Lumpkin, James T. Farrell, and Joseph Freeman, all well-known in radical circles, contributed criticism, stories, and poetry. The magazine, it appeared, would be graced by the best work of Communist intellectuals and sympathizers.

To Rahv and Phillips, who from almost the beginning guided the direction of the new magazine, proletarian literature was a visible edge of the future, a projection of the time when political revolution would dramatically sweep away archaic capitalist institutions and bourgeois culture. Proletarian literature as they understood and wrote about it was both a literature for and about the working class, which grew out of an emerging revolution, and literature that would answer the problems of the modern intellectuals. They were aware, as were most writers of the day that intellectuals during the 1920s had often thought of their relationship to society in terms of estrangement or had at least expressed hostility toward middle-class life. Thus proletarian art appeared to overcome the problem of the artist who existed without a homeland, for it promised a new country and a new sort of artist. Thus, behind the young editors' belief in the necessity of creating proletarian literature lay the legacy of unanswered problems left over from the previous decade. When the proletarian movement was shunted aside in 1935 and 1936 by the Communists, who then desired respectability and not revolution, the problems of reconciling radical ideology with artistic experimentation, of ending intellectual alienation, once more seemed immediate, but very different. When radical literature of the early 1930s faded, it did so for two reasons: because it was weakened by the Communists' pre-

---

[3] Joseph Freeman claims to be the author of this first editorial. Aaron, *Writers on the Left*, p. 298. However, William Phillips argues that he was not.

occupation elsewhere and because it did not solve the problems that many of its enthusiastic supporters felt it would.

Proletarian literature and the promised cultural renaissance meant more to the *Partisan Review* than to the *New Masses*. As the radical literary movement faltered in 1936 and then shifted directions, the *Partisan* turned to discover what had gone wrong and what had transformed the bright promise of a new literature into a dull performance. This search led from a re-examination of proletarian literature to the premises of Marxist criticism, back into the literary and critical accomplishments of the two decades before the 1930s. When the *Partisan* was revived in 1937, it initiated a process of rediscovery and reanalysis of the culture of the twentieth century, a process that highlighted in the magazine flashes of modernity upon a background of eclecticism.

Two book reviews in the first issue of the *Partisan* by Rahv and Phillips set the tone of literary criticism that would prevail in the magazine. However mild, they represented the first shots fired in the literary controversy that was waged and ultimately won against the accepted practice of proletarian art and criticism. Both articles used arguments that indicated a disagreement between their own authors and more orthodox leftists. Both editors felt that it was wrong to make literature the vehicle for ideas that were politically expedient at the moment. Rather, literature should reflect what was permanent and new in proletarian culture. It should not merely promote the class struggle. Second, they argued that literary history must be preserved, even if it was largely the history of middle-class authors writing for middle-class audiences. Briefly stated in the first issue of the *Partisan,* as yet ill-formed, these ideas were developed and broadened until they eventually became the rationale for rejecting the whole movement two years later.

In his analysis of Hemingway's *Winner Take Nothing,* Philip Rahv criticized current left letters for exhibiting an idealization and sentimentality that intimidated the reader. To overcome this tendency, he advised, it would be well to learn from the artistic traditions of bourgeois art, at least those that had little relation to ideology or the defense of capitalism. The danger of contamination by middle-class art was actually rather small, and the writer could learn much from its positive accomplishments. Careful not to make this a broad defense of all traditional art, Rahv nevertheless denounced as left sectarianism any theory that completely rejected bourgeois art.

Phillips's review of Henry Hazlitt's *Anatomy of Liberalism* was a fairly standard example of contemporary leftist criticism. But he emphasized the importance of the critic as a guide in creating proletarian culture and of objective standards in literary criticism. He briefly mentioned an argument that he had used once before: proletarian literature must arise from the experience of a proletarian culture, as an expression of a growing class consciousness. It was therefore important for the writer to immerse himself in this culture to attain a revolutionary perspective.[4] Phillips's expectation that proletarian art would emerge from the expression of a working-class civilization was based on an analogy with the view that great European art had been created in the process of developing a bourgeois culture. This notion that literature was an organic part of a larger culture provided a convincing argument for proletarian literature, as long as the possibility existed that a working-class society would eventually replace capitalism. Moreover, it provided persuasive reasons for rejecting the artificial and sectarian proletarian art that was then characteristic of the Communist movement. Both Rahv and Phillips in these first reviews hinted at what would be the three most important stumbling blocks of the proletarian movement: the relation between proletarian and bourgeois art, the question of reconciling form with content, and the conflict between art and propaganda.

Despite their early hesitations, the editors were firmly in the Communist cultural movement. The literary millennium did not seem far away to Rahv in the second issue of the magazine in May 1934. The new working-class novels and the literary maga-

---

[4] Wallace Phelps [William Phillips], "The Anatomy of Liberalism," *Partisan Review*, I (February-March 1934), p. 49. Rahv criticized this article in *International Literature* for not dealing with Hazlitt's addendum which attacked Marxism. "Marxist Criticism and Henry Hazlitt," *International Literature*, No. 2 (1934), pp. 112-116.

zine renaissance indicated to him the depth and direction of the
new movement. Proletarian literature could not be distracted:
"No hue and cry of propaganda, no lugubrious headshaking of
wiseacres, and no amount of sneering on the part of those who
persist in training their palsied hieroglyphics on the fly-paper
of bourgeois class impotence, can arrest its progress." The style
of Mike Gold with its strident optimism about the ability of the
Communists to withstand attacks by the bourgeoisie echoed in
Rahv's writing. But Rahv made an additional remark which
carried him beyond Gold. He praised two new novels by Ar-
nold Armstrong and William Rollins because they had avoided
the "communist self-consciousness that results in formula"; they
had not made the mistake of rejecting the literary heritage.[5]
His simultaneous faith in proletarianism and the need to preserve the literary tradition—two views commonly thought to be
mutually exclusive—was possible because of his belief in the
cultural renaissance and the success of the new literary movement. Whatever uncertainties might exist about the literature
so far produced, uncertainties aired even in the first issues of the
Partisan were unimportant when placed beside the expectancies
of the movement. When the great proletarian writers appeared,
the place of the literary tradition would be decided.

Two other factors made the editors' early criticism of left
literature relatively unimportant. One was their incomplete understanding of what the literary tradition meant: from its context the word "tradition" in the early pages of the magazine
implied little more than respect for past standards of literary
performance. Second, the editors attempted to circumvent and
even explain away the problems of the movement, to systematize its contradictions through the application of the Marxist
dialectic. Out of the mixture of opposing literary traditions a
new and more advanced combination would be created. The
accomplishments in avant-garde art of the first decades of the
century, although rejected by proletarian writers, were nonetheless part of their consciousness. Thus bourgeois literary
movements, whatever their ideological entanglements, were

---

[5] Philip Rahv, "The Novelist as Partisan," *Partisan Review*, I (April-May
1934), pp. 50, 52.

seen by Rahv and Phillips as predecessors, as the foundation of proletarian literature. The critic could reject the ideology of past generations as a second step in the dialectic process, yet feel that the influence of their writings was a part of the contemporary critical atmosphere. What this Marxian theory camouflaged was an ambiguity about the past, a feeling that the critic could not accept tradition completely nor, on the other hand, reject it.

This ambiguity appeared prominently, as it often did, in connection with T. S. Eliot. Reviewing Eliot's *After Strange Gods* in the second issue, Phillips denounced the reactionary political and religious stands of the poet. Eliot had gone so far toward conservatism that critics expected (and perhaps even hoped) that he would make some conclusive statement of allegiance to fascism. The poet had not committed himself yet, but the mixture of feudal and Catholic themes in his latest book left no doubt about the direction of his thought. "Only the blind would hesitate to call Eliot a fascist," Phillips concluded.[6] In one sense Phillips seemed to wish that Eliot would state his reactionary politics openly, not only because this was the direction in which he seemed headed, but because it would clarify the whole issue. If he was a real fascist, Eliot could be read out of contemporary literature. It could then be stated with certainty that his literary and cultural assertions led to an intellectual dead end. But Phillips's attack on Eliot settled little, not even for himself. It merely indicated the importance that he attached to squaring Eliot's reactionary politics with his acknowledged radical approach to modern literature.

In the discussion of such problems the *Partisan* occasionally published the works of leading European Marxist critics which dealt with the difficulties created by proletarian literature. An article by George Lukacs, "Propaganda or Partisanship," discussed the conflict of art versus propaganda. To eliminate this conflict, argued the Hungarian Marxist, the artist should record objective reality. The writer should hold a mirror up to his subject and therein capture the images of the class struggle, for

---

[6] Wallace Phelps [William Phillips], "Eliot Takes His Stand," *Partisan Review*, I (April-May 1934), p. 52.

reality itself demonstrated the Marxist call for revolution. This sophisticated justification for proletarian art was really a dismissal of the problem of art versus propaganda as the magazine saw it rather than a successful answer. Four months later in the *Little Magazine* Rahv dismissed Lukacs's proposals. The critic's use of the word "propaganda" to denote recreation of objective reality was irrelevant to Americans, Rahv argued, because writers here did not understand the term in this way. The attempt to make the word "propaganda" a legitimate tool of criticism, he continued, was misguided. On the contrary, it should be reserved as a derogatory category for the vulgarization of literature by the "leftists"—that group of "primitives" who sought "to hypostasize their lack of talent and to repudiate the cultural heritage."[7]

An editorial in the third issue of the *Partisan*, written jointly by Rahv and Phillips, is the first substantial evidence that the two young editors had assumed control over the intellectual direction of the magazine. The editorial also represented a refinement of their views on radical literature; it strongly attacked those left sectarian writers who, they felt, substituted revolutionary orthodoxy for creative ability. Proletarian literature had great promise, they contended; the writer could attain a degree of rapport with his audience and with a class which would give him a sense of confidence and responsibility unknown in previous decades. Denial of this power of the new literature to bring together the writer and his audience left only the discouraging alternative of accepting the conclusions of the previous decade, when the writer was pictured as a social outcast and his literature was considered inconsequential. Proletarian literature, on the other hand, suggested a movement so profound in its implications that it could end the estrangement of the writer from his society. It was the only useful answer to estrangement.

Shifting the direction of their argument, Rahv and Phillips went on to state that the literary problems that baffled the radical movement had not yet been faced squarely by writers

---

[7] Philip Rahv, "Valedictory on the Propaganda Issue," *Little Magazine*, I (September-October 1934), p. 2.

and critics. Within the movement there existed a wide variety of backgrounds, training, and perceptions—divisions that could no longer be ignored. There was, for example, a large group of writers whose knowledge of the proletariat was based on a "tourist's visit" to areas where working-class struggle had flared. Ignorance of their subject matter condemned some writers to producing crude, polemical tracts rather than literature because they assumed that one could translate economics directly into novels and poems. "Leftism," as they called it (a term taken over from Lenin who had used it to belittle the extreme and unrealistic proposals of other radicals), was a great obstacle in the path of the Communist literary movement. In denouncing this characteristic Rahv and Phillips did not hesitate to mention names—H. H. Lewis, George Marlen, and others—but these were minor writers in the radical galaxy. They did avoid an assault on a more important source of leftism in the critical writings of leaders such as Mike Gold. However wide of the mark, their repudiation of leftism was in part an attack on the *New Masses* and on the older established proletarian critics.

In a final section Rahv and Phillips turned to the literary works of fellow travelers. They argued that the right wing of the new literary movement must be given leadership in order to overcome the backwardness of their political views. But these comments on the right wing were of slight importance and added little more than balance to the argument. The basic problem of the proletarian movement as the editors of the *Partisan* saw it was the isolation of radical political ideology from the rest of human experience and history. Rahv and Phillips insisted that writers must create characters who knew the class struggle as an actual part of their lives and culture. If leftism were eliminated, the creation of a genuine proletarian culture would become possible. The writer should also be sensitive to the culture of the past, for modern literature was part of the context of revolutionary art. These two young critics of the proletarian movement demanded in effect that literature cease to pretend that it was propaganda: literature reflected politics only when it depicted social forces as a part of a general perception of reality. Only in this sense was literature a part of the radical movement: a work of art could never be judged merely by its agitational effectiveness.[8]

If it had not known it before, the *New Masses* shortly realized that the *Partisan Review*, despite its disavowal of any such designs, was now an active competitor for leadership of the radical literary movement. Rahv and Phillips were candid about the quality of the *Partisan*. It too was guilty of leftism and low literary standards, but the editors pledged themselves to a continual search for critical principles that might guide the movement. By its very nature the magazine exercised judgments for the left movement in selecting manuscripts and in theoretical criticism. Still, the magazine wished to remain a part of the literary revival of which the *New Masses* was the "central organ." Political questions, the editors concluded, should be left to the pages of the *New Masses*.

The dominance of Rahv and Phillips over the editorial function of the magazine did not produce a uniformity of tone, quality, or critical position for the early *Partisan*. Short stories and poems varied in quality from the conversion formula, typical of leftism, according to which a worker realized his exploitation and joined a strike as the first step to revolution, to the more sensitive poetry and prose of James T. Farrell, John Dos Passos, and later, Ignazio Silone and Archibald MacLeish. Much of the creative work in this period came from writers who were, in one way or another, established. Contributors Joseph Freeman, Grace Lumpkin, Edwin Seaver, Meridel Le Sueur, Genevieve Taggard, Kenneth Fearing, Horace Gregory, and John Dos Passos had all appeared in the *New Masses* during the first years of its publication. Midwesterners like Richard Wright, Nelson Algren, and Farrell had published first in other magazines. Nevertheless, the early *Partisan Review* did promote some of the better new proletarian writers. In 1936 the *New Masses* praised the magazine for supporting the work of young radicals, many of whom had not yet appeared in the

---

[8] Philip Rahv and Wallace Phelps [William Phillips], "Problems and Perspectives in Revolutionary Literature," *Partisan Review*, I (June-July 1934), pp. 5, 9.

New Masses itself. But there remained a fundamental contradiction between the criticism and the creative work of the
magazine. While calling for a literary renaissance, the *Partisan
Review* printed the prose and poetry, with a few exceptions,
of a large group of minor authors. The tension resulting from
the demand for high standards of creative excellence, from the
fact that the editors were writing criticism for what amounted
to a secondary literary movement, could not ultimately be resolved without sacrificing either literary standards or the movement itself.

In the fourth issue Rahv and Phillips in separate articles extended their critique of leftism and their attempt to settle the
outstanding issues of radical criticism. Repeating an earlier
argument, Rahv insisted that proletarian literature alone could
capture the central meaning of contemporary life; it alone could
express the movement of history and the heroism of the masses
in a tragic, yet affirmative statement. However, he was more
concerned to explore the relationship of this new tragic mode
to the despair and negation preached by bourgeois art. An important distinction, he argued, first ought to be made between
the commercial and the intellectual art of previous decades.
Intellectual art should not be dismissed by the revolutionary
critic (as Rahv felt it had been), for it was an important
predecessor of the proletarian movement. The advanced art of
James Joyce, for example, both retarded and accelerated the
radicalization of the intellectuals. Because of its rejection of
middle-class life it served to stimulate some to social awareness,
others to social inactivity. Unfortunately, many of the previous avant-garde writers had failed to develop their critique of
bourgeois society beyond negativism, and at this point a new
conception of art was necessary. Proletarian literature, Rahv
concluded, had grasped the fundamental truth about capitalist
life and enabled the writer to choose the revolutionary affirma-
tion of a new society and thus go beyond the art of the past.[9]

A notable new element was Rahv's concern for the role of the
intellectual. To him, the important writing of the previous

---

[9] Philip Rahv, "How the Waste Land Became a Flower Garden," *Partisan
Review*, I (September-October 1934), pp. 37-42.

decades retained an integrity and value for contemporary writers because it had been produced by intellectuals and was not the sort of commercialized art that was used to propagandize the virtues of capitalism. The ramifications of this point were, of course, still only implicit, but the article reveals Rahv's belief in proletarian art as a literary mode of utmost importance to the intellectuals who created it. It was not just a sophisticated translation or dramatization of partisan politics.

William Phillips, in the same issue, also turned to literary movements that had preceded proletarian writing. In an interesting application of the Marxian dialectic, he wrote of the two previous decades as literary generations. The genealogy of revolutionary writing could be traced to the dialectic interaction between the generation of Dreiser, Anderson, Lewis, and Sandburg (the regional American writers) and the generation of the exiles. "The lost generation negated many of the values of the preceding one," he wrote, "although both operated in the same framework of capitalist culture. In rejecting this culture the proletarian generation effects a higher synthesis of both earlier periods." The interaction of American provincialism and expatriate cosmopolitanism created the potentiality for a new literature. Revolutionary writers and critics who understood and attempted to assimilate the past were "clearing the road ahead for a great proletarian art," unlike the primitive leftists who repudiated the bourgeois heritage, or the rightists who failed to understand how art could be bent to revolutionary purposes.[10] To Phillips, a literary theory derived from Marxism was an intellectual tool to be used to understand and preserve the best literature of the past while creating the basis for a great new culture. The Depression had made this culture all but inevitable: it had eliminated occupational outlets for young writers and critics in publishing houses; hence the younger generation would by necessity abandon the bourgeoisie.

The effects of *Partisan Review*'s attack on leftism and its roundabout jabs at leading proletarian theoreticians were almost immediately acknowledged in radical literary circles. Granville

[10] Wallace Phelps [William Phillips], "Three Generations," *Partisan Review*, I (September-October 1934), pp. 54, 55.

Hicks, who became literary editor of the *New Masses* in 1935, publicly questioned the need to continue the upstart publication. Did the magazine operate in a way compatible with the "effective utilization of our forces?" he asked. The appearance of reviews that were duplicated elsewhere and of proletarian literature that could be published in other magazines did not seem to him to justify the existence of a separate publication. Starting such little magazines, he continued, was a sign of "bohemian individualism" and was not really compatible with "the intellectual discipline of revolutionaries."[11] Hicks's remarks signified recognition of the competitive nature of the *Partisan Review* and other little magazines by establishment leftists. The threat implied by his suggestion that the left movement begin a discussion of magazine reorganization was not carried out, but it raised the possibility of the eventual censure of the *Partisan* editors.

Perhaps one of the reasons that the magazine received only a mild reprimand from orthodox radicals was the growing popularity of its critical position among John Reed Club writers. At the National Convention of the Reed Clubs, held in Chicago during September 1934, both Rahv and Phillips addressed the gathering. More important, however, several speakers before the writers' commission meeting denounced leftism and the sloganized tracts that had previously been hailed as literature. From this evidence the *Partisan* concluded that it had been "exerting a wide influence among young writers."[12] After only ten months of existence the *Partisan* had emerged as one of the most important proletarian magazines aside from the *New Masses* and by all indications had won over a segment of the left intellectuals, particularly the younger writers, to its position on proletarian literature. Despite this initial victory for their point of view, the editors had as yet only faintly sketched the guidelines for a proletarian art; their contributions in a positive sense had been limited.

---

[11] Granville Hicks, "Our Magazines and Their Functions," *New Masses*, XIII (December 18, 1934), p. 23.
[12] "The National John Reed Club Convention," *Partisan Review*, I (November-December 1934), p. 60.

The attempt to gain leadership of such a literary movement and provide a workable theory of radical literature seemed to demand close examination of the conditions that had made proletarian literature seem necessary. Yet the persistence of low-quality writing in left journals was an impelling reason to continue to focus criticism on current standards of radical literature. This, ultimately, reinforced the desire of the editors to explore and borrow from other literary movements. At first this was expressed in several attempts to draw up a comprehensive new theory of revolutionary art that would bolster the magazine in its argument against sloganized literature.

William Phillips's essay in February 1935 explored the problem of aesthetic standards from a new direction—from the separation between form and content that inevitably resulted when proletarian critics pronounced judgment on literature according to its revolutionary qualities. Phillips hinged his argument on Marxian theory: it was the radical approach, he felt, that should bring together, not separate, form and content. The article, however, raised more questions than it answered. It was apparent to Phillips that form and content, or the structure and ideology of a work, were aspects of one unified vision. This vision or "sensibility," as he called it, was a three-dimensional projection of the writer's view and his intellectual environment. Content and form were interrelated—content did determine form—but there was "no prophetic principle which enables us to foresee the form which a content must take." Proletarian literature could therefore provide no simple formula to relate content and style. On the contrary, revolutionary writers were confronted with the necessity of forging a new sensibility, but in doing so they should realize the persistence and relevance of the sensibilities of traditional literature. The writer should be concerned with aesthetics. He must re-evaluate the literary heritage, set standards in revolutionary literature, and revise his attitudes toward traditional culture. These were the issues that should be settled by radicals. Even T. S. Eliot, he continued, as a practitioner of traditional literature had a vision of modern life that he had transformed into an important idiom "for the dislocation of bourgeois perspectives amidst a tightening commercial way of life," a vision that could be relevant to the new school of proletarian writers.[13]

Phillips's article repeated many of his previous conclusions, and he continued to stress the importance of traditional literature. The success of the new literary movement, however, now seemed somewhat more remote. Furthermore, the example of the new Soviet culture did not seem relevant or inspiring to him, as it did to other leftist critics. Neither Phillips nor Rahv relied on events in Soviet literature to bolster their literary arguments, nor did they seek to hide the failings of the American movement beneath praise for Soviet accomplishments, as some more orthodox proletarian writers did. True, the Soviet Union was very important to the *Partisan,* but, significantly, Phillips and Rahv in their own writings appeared less concerned with Soviet literary events than with the more relevant problems of a cultural revolution in the United States.

André Malraux's praise for Russian culture in the same February issue made precisely the point that Rahv and Phillips had skirted—that the renaissance had arrived in the Soviet Union. Malraux's article is fascinating, for it hinges on the idea of the alienation of the modern artist, a psychological state that had impressed the editors of the magazine as a major, unsolved problem of bourgeois culture. Malraux argued that the problem of estrangement had been solved by the conscious allegiance of the Soviet writer to his society. The result was a totalitarian society in the sense of the writer's active acceptance of his own civilization. The artist's self-importance and introspection had diminished but this was because the objective reality of the new society was so real and overwhelming.[14]

Despite the importance of the issues involved, the *Partisan's* criticisms of proletarian literature came at a time when the Communist literary movement was beginning to edge away from sponsorship of revolutionary culture. Beginning with the Popular Front, proclaimed in 1935, the Communists made a significant

---

[13] Wallace Phelps [William Phillips], "Form and Content," *Partisan Review,* II (January-February 1935), p. 36.

[14] André Malraux, "Literature in Two Worlds," *Partisan Review,* II (January-February 1935), p. 14.

reversal in tactics which, translated into cultural affairs, sought to unite writers according to their political commitment to reform in the United States and support for the Soviet Union's basic foreign policy. The new emphasis on antifascism and expression of eagerness to make alliances with more sympathetic members of the middle class made a good deal of sense in a world that did not starkly divide between bourgeois and proletarian, between reactionary capitalism and socialism. The John Reed Clubs were one of the first casualties of this policy change; they were replaced in 1935 by the League of American Writers, which was designed to provide the framework to accommodate the new, more flexible approach to literature and sympathetic intellectuals. The American Writers' Congress, at which the League was created, met three months before the formal announcement of the Popular Front, but the conference nevertheless marked a transition to the new policy.

At the Chicago convention of the John Reed Clubs in the fall of 1934, Alexander Trachtenberg, an important official of the Communist party, had suggested the organization of a National Writers' Congress which would meet in 1935. The implication was that the party was about to shift its attitude toward intellectuals. When the Congress assembled in New York in April, there were hints of a significant new direction for the Communist-sponsored literary movement. Between the Chicago meeting and the Congress most of the John Reed Clubs were dissolved, a decision made even before the convention of the Reed Clubs. In effect, this shattered the proletarian movement, for it undercut the original strength of the radical literary movement among the young unestablished writers who had populated the clubs. The destruction of the John Reed Clubs eliminated the organization that had sustained the radical literary movement and the radical little magazines. Most of the small left-wing publications that had grown out of the Reed Club movement, cut off from financial and moral support of the Communist party, suspended publication in late 1934 and in 1935. The "Call" for the Congress, reprinted in the February 1935 issue of the *Partisan Review*, was signed largely by established leftist writers, but not by Rahv and Phillips. Moreover, the announcement reflected an altered set of priorities for the radical literary movement: the defense of the Soviet Union and opposition to fascism were most important, while the struggle to create a revolutionary literature was given only slight attention. The belief in a literary renaissance was still present; the "Call" proclaimed that a "new Renaissance is upon the world," but this did not refer to the creation of a proletarian literature.[15]

From the first the *Partisan Review* had a special relationship to the new League of American Writers. One indication of this was the special pre-Congress issue of the magazine, combined with the *Dynamo* (another small left literary publication) for the purpose of "presenting a united creative front on the eve of the first Congress of American Writers." The editors expressed hope that the Congress would promote clarity "in the movement of American intellectuals to the left." The new organization of writers and artists, they hoped, would make possible "a more profound and more extensive revolutionary literature."[16] For the *Partisan Review* the possibility of creating proletarian literature was still real, even though the Writers' Congress and the new League of American Writers symbolized abandonment of proletarianism by the Communists. And although the policy of the party changed gradually, the commitment of the *Partisan* to a radical, new literature remained much the same. At first the effects of the new Communist policy were negligible on relations between the magazine and the Communist left, for there was still room in radical letters for a publication dedi-

---

[15] William Phillips, "What Happened in the 30's," *Commentary*, XXXIV (September 1962), p. 205. A letter from Walter Snow to Jack Balch (also sent to the *Partisan* editors) relates some of the details of the dissolution of the clubs. The Communist party, according to Snow, had closed down the New York Reed Club without informing most of the members. Only party members were told. One of the reasons for this was the friction between artists and writers. The party also wished to eliminate those writers who produced nothing. Snow concluded that only about 50 per cent of the local Reed Club writers would receive invitations to the Congress. Walt Snow to Jack Balch, February 6, 1935, p. 1, Conroy MSS.

[16] "Forward to the Great Alliance," *Partisan Review*, II (April-May 1935), p. 3.

cated to class-conscious writing. Moreover, from the Congress in 1935 until late in 1936 the League of American Writers considered making the *Partisan* its official organ.

The *Partisan* devoted a special issue to the Writers' Congress, in which it discussed the most pressing critical problems that, the editors felt, faced the revolutionary cultural movement. There were articles by Edwin Rolfe on proletarian poetry, Edwin Seaver on the proletarian novel, and Phillips and Rahv on criticism, followed by discussions of their merits. Seaver's article on the novel attempted to settle the problem of defining this art form. The identity of a proletarian novel, he concluded, depended not on the class origin of the writer, but on the revolutionary purpose of his work. The writer must not merely understand the world; he must seek to change it. The discussion of Seaver's article, particularly by James T. Farrell, is important, for it supported the general position of the magazine against leftism. Farrell argued, as he would even more extensively in *A Note on Literary Criticism* (1936), that the function of the critic was being destroyed by those Marxists who believed in the facile theory that economics directly determined culture. There was too little attempt to understand what an author was trying to do and too much emphasis on "revolutionary scholasticism."[17]

Itself rather scholastic in style, Phillips and Rahv's article on criticism went even further than Farrell's description of the radical literary movement. The function of criticism, they contended, was to guide and temper literature; it could not be a weapon in the class struggle. Criticism touched the masses only in an indirect way. A critic should never base his judgment of a work on its propaganda content: criticism was a weapon of literature, not of politics. And art and literature were no less remote from immediate contact with the class struggle. Literature influenced those most susceptible to it, the intellectuals, and acted as an instrument for reorienting social values, not as an agitational device.

---

[17] Edwin Seaver, "What is a Proletarian Novel," *Partisan Review*, II (April-May 1935), p. 8. James T. Farrell, "Discussion," *Partisan Review*, II (April-May 1935), pp. 13-15.

This attempt to disengage literature from the immediacy of political strife led Rahv and Phillips to a very important conclusion, which further justified a careful consideration of the value of bourgeois literature. A specific work of art, they wrote, could not be understood by its political impact or by the general ideology to which it might be linked, but only in reference to its specific content and to its form. A novel of Proust's, for example, might reveal elements of bourgeois ideology, but it contained other stylistic and intellectual elements that were of more interest to the critic. "Revolutionary literature," they argued, "is not the literature of a sect, like surrealism or objectivism; it is the product of an emerging civilization, and will contain the wealth and diversity which any cultural range offers."[18] Its validity rested on the proven reality that class struggle was the central experience of society. Revolutionary literature to Rahv and Phillips was part of a revolutionary culture, not an appendage to a political movement. As a rich and complicated culture it could absorb the contradictions that existed in the literary heritage.

Comment on this essay by Newton Arvin and Granville Hicks indicates some of the effects of the *Partisan*'s critique. Arvin agreed basically with the argument of the article. Even more important was Hicks's acknowledgment that many leftist critics had failed to employ aesthetics in their judgments. Hicks's concession is noteworthy because of his stature in orthodox radical circles. The literary editor of the *New Masses* did not agree, however, that Rahv and Phillips were right on every count, and resented what he felt was their scornful attitude. He concluded that if one could grant that there was a lack of aesthetic knowledge, one might also ask what sort of criticism should be applied to fellow revolutionaries. "There is a distressing amount of the most uncomradely sniping and back-biting," he charged in reference to the intensity of Rahv and Phillips's literary polemics.[19]

---

[18] Philip Rahv and Wallace Phelps [William Phillips], "Criticism," *Partisan Review*, II (April-May 1935), pp. 17, 25.
[19] Granville Hicks, "Discussion," *Partisan Review*, II (April-May 1935), p. 29.

All of this discussion would be irrelevant after the turn toward respectability initiated by the Communists in 1935. The American Writers' Congress, held at Mecca Temple in New York City during the latter part of April, created the League of American Writers, the most important leftist intellectual organization during the remainder of the 1930s. The John Reed Clubs, which had demanded that the writer engage his craft in the proletarian movement and that he recreate the class struggle in his art, were dead. They were replaced by a broader organization of writers which sought the commitment of the artist to a set of political principles and which recruited him as a middle-class intellectual and not a converted proletarian. The principal object of the new organizations was to create a cultural group united against fascism and favorable to the Soviet Union.[20]

The old principles of the proletarian struggle against capitalist culture did not disappear immediately, nor did the new League suddenly adopt all of the characteristics of the cultural Popular Front. The first Writers' Congress occurred three months before the official Soviet announcement of the Popular Front, and it was still dominated by a discussion of proletarian literature. Philip Rahv relates that when Kenneth Burke asked that the word "people" displace the word "worker" in a resolution, he was shouted down. Nor did the Congress dissociate the fight against fascism from the broader struggle against capitalism.

Instead, the political and cultural ramifications of the Popular Front appeared gradually. For the writers who had participated in the John Reed Clubs, the theory of proletarian art was still important, even if the movement as a whole was moving away from this conception. A continuity of membership inevitably meant that there would be some ideological carry-over. Malcolm Cowley, looking back on those years in 1937, pointed out in an address before the League of American Writers that the revolutionary literary movement actually experienced several changes during the 1930s. He felt that from 1932 to 1934 proletarian literature was the most important radical literary theory. From

---

[20] The application for League membership emphasized the political nature of the organization which, it said, was to "enlist writers in all parts of the United States in a national cultural organization for peace and democracy and against fascism and reaction . . . ." LAW MSS.

1934 to 1936, he maintained, the discussion of art and politics had broadened to an argument over the validity of Marxist criticism.[21] In a more general sense, however, Joseph Freeman was correct when he wrote somewhat later that the Congress joined together two tendencies in American letters, one liberal and the other radical. The Congress, in other words, broadened the definition of the radical movement in an effort to find new allies in the American community. Its new stance brought together radical intellectuals and liberal writers. Especially important among these new recruits were the writers who followed Van Wyck Brooks in his search for an American literary tradition and in his attempt to revive a nationalist cultural heritage.

The actual meeting of the Writers' Congress was important to the *Partisan Review* in a number of ways. Granville Hicks, in a speech on the dialectics of the development of Marxist criticism, repeated the admission that he had made recently in the pages of the magazine. The critique of the revolutionary literary movement offered by Rahv and Phillips, he conceded, was essentially accurate. He did differ, however, in his view of Marxian aesthetics, for he felt that there was little hope of developing a permanent set of critical categories, as Rahv and Phillips seemed to demand. But their definition of the problems that beset proletarian literature seemed correct. Too little attention had been paid to the technical problems of the writer and to the complex relationship between experience and creation. It was clear from this speech that the editors of the *Partisan* had made headway in their effort to revolutionize radical theory, but in the long run it meant little, for it occurred at the very moment when the Communists were planning to abandon proletarian literature.[22]

The end of the Reed Clubs and the beginning of the League cut the *Partisan* loose from any specific organizational ties to the left. For a number of little magazines this independence

---

[21] Philip Rahv, "Two Years of Progress—From Waldo Frank to Donald Ogden Stewart," *Partisan Review*, IV (February 1938), pp. 23-24. Malcolm Cowley, "Seven Years of Crisis," address delivered June 4, 1937, p. 10, Vol. II of *Proceedings of the American Writers Congress*, LAW MSS.
[22] Granville Hicks, "Dialectics of the Development of Marxist Criticism," *American Writers' Congress*, pp. 96-98.

ultimately proved fatal, for without the creative and financial contributions of Reed Club members most revolutionary periodicals folded. Subject to the same sort of pressure, the *Partisan* gravitated toward association with the League of American Writers, but never affiliated with it. At the Writers' Congress Hicks had proposed that the new organization publish a magazine that would not be exclusively Marxist to enable a larger number of writers to contribute. It seems clear that the *Partisan* was considered for this role. Moreover, Rahv and Phillips were both active in League functions during 1935 and 1936. A third important result of the Reed Club dissolution was that it enabled the national chairman of that organization, Alan Calmer, who worked with Alexander Trachtenberg in the Communist publishing apparatus, to join the editorial board of the magazine. As an editor he contributed a series of important articles attacking the persistence of leftism in the radical literary movement.[23]

Three months after the Writers' Congress Georgi Dimitroff in a report to the Seventh Comintern meeting in Moscow proposed the tactic of the Popular Front; after this, the implications of the League's founding became clearer. Although the *New Masses* denied that the new tactic meant that the Communist movement had even temporarily given up its revolutionary aspirations, the policy was quite clearly a defensive one. The change from an almost exclusive interest in the revolutionary potential of the working class during the period of leftism (1928-1933) to a more pragmatic theory that emphasized the desirability of alliances with progressive elements of the middle class was in part a reaction to the growing strength of fascism in Europe. The change from united front tactics to the Popular Front diluted the revolutionary commitments of the party and changed its approach to writers.[24]

---

[23] Rahv was asked to join the Finance Committee of the League in 1935; "Minutes of the League of American Writers," May 16, 1935, New York, LAW MSS.

[24] The Communists previously had a policy of the united front, whereby they tried to secure participation of non-Communists in their own strikes and political activities. However, the Popular Front meant a dilution of the aims of the Communists for the sake of obtaining participation by other groups—often on the others' terms. For discussion of the united front, see Earl Browder, "Struggle for a United Front," *Communist,* XVIII (October 1934), pp. 931-967.

As before, changes in Soviet policy were reflected in the attitudes of the American Communist party and affected its relations with the literary world. The *New Masses* drifted toward a policy of encouraging antifascist writers and paid increasing attention to the pronouncements of liberals. The Popular Front was an attempt of the Communist political movement to secure middle-class allies, and it did not matter that these allies might not believe in Communism or even in socialism. The only condition for membership in the Popular Front was antifascism. In an article for the *Communist*, Dimitroff wrote that the most progressive elements of society should be preserved to aid this cause.[25]

This change struck at a major premise of proletarian art—that the writer must identify and merge himself with the working class to create great art and that he must go beyond and even reject the literary accomplishments of the bourgeoisie. In a sense, the move to the Popular Front meant the substitution of the party for the proletariat. The effort to secure allegiance to the revolutionary working class evaporated in the attempt to identify intellectuals with the party and its program. Proletarian literature, which had sought to create a revolutionary new culture as the counterpart to political upheaval, withered as its sponsors turned to more established writers who could be counted on to participate in the party's new cultural organizations. Gradually during 1936 and 1937 the discussion of proletarian art disappeared from the pages of the *New Masses*. As early as June 1936 Trotskyist George Novack, writing in the *New International*, sarcastically noted the change in policy: "Sinclair Lewis has been miraculously transformed from a petty-bourgeois writer, who turned his back upon the revolutionary struggle of the proletariat, into a literary hero of the Popular Front."[26]

Successful in its struggle against sectarian literature, the *Partisan* nevertheless did little during the remainder of 1935 to

[25] Georgi Dimitroff, "The Threat of Fascism in the United States," *Communist*, XIV (October 1935), pp. 906, 908.

[26] George Novack, "The Intellectuals and the Crisis," *New International*, III (June 1936), p. 83. The Trotskyists opposed the Russian Communists, whom they characterized as Stalinists on the basis that the latter had given up the original goals of the revolution.

translate its verbal victory into a concrete program for the literary renaissance. Nor did it assert leadership of the literary left. Only two issues were published during this transitional period. No more was said about the problem of leftism, and comments on the direction of current letters by Rahv and Phillips were confined to book reviews. Perhaps the only sharp words spoken to other members of the literary left were in Rahv's review of Nelson Algren's new book, *Somebody in Boots.* Rahv was disturbed because no left publications other than the *Daily Worker* had by that time reviewed the book. There were indications, however, that the magazine might accept the new Communist tactics. The October issue of the magazine, for example, featured reprints of three speeches, by John Strachey, André Gide, and André Malraux, before the First International Congress of Writers, an international Popular Front organization.

Thus, during the period immediately after the Writers' Congress the *Partisan* had much the same format as before: proletarian prose and poetry of uneven quality appeared alongside more sophisticated review essays. But the direction of the magazine seemed more uncertain than it had been before, and the editors seemed unable or unwilling to deepen and strengthen their influence on left literature.

The editorial indecision of the magazine during this period occurred simultaneously with informal attempts to give the *Partisan* a more secure status in the literary left, by tying it to the organizations of the Popular Front. Late in 1935 the League of American Writers, still hoping to publish an official magazine, considered merging with the *Partisan.* Members of the executive committee of the League opposed such a move, however, because the magazine was "too left."[27] The *Partisan* was still committed to revolutionary literature and to a Marxian interpretation of culture, whereas the most important left organization of writers had absorbed the less openly radical tactics implied by the Popular Front.

Also during the summer and fall of 1935 plans were being

---

[27] "Report of the Enlarged Executive Committee," Minutes, December 11, 1935, p. 1, LAW MSS.

made in New York to merge the *Partisan Review* with Jack Conroy's *Anvil*. The *Anvil* had been moved to New York, where one of the editors, Walter Snow, assumed the financing and some of Conroy's editorial functions of the magazine. It was apparent that both publications had financial difficulties; if the two were merged, the strong elements of one publication would presumably complement those of the other. This merger was planned in New York and had the approval of Alexander Trachtenberg. Fund raising began in the fall and included benefits, speeches, and theater parties. The combined magazine, when it appeared in February 1936, had a new format, a slightly different editorial board, and a new list of associates, many of them drawn from the old *Anvil*. But the *Partisan Review and Anvil*, now a monthly, was still largely under the control of Calmer, Phillips, and Rahv. Conroy, living in the Midwest, had nothing to do with editorial decisions and contributed only one review before the magazine shut down six issues later. The purpose of the merger, as the first editorial put it, may have been to make the magazine broader in scope and more mature, but it amounted to little more than the absorption of the *Anvil* by *Partisan Review*.[28]

Mike Gold greeted the first issue of the combined "Papa Anvil and Mother Partisan" in the *New Masses* in February 1936 with what amounted to an attack on the critical writing that had typified the *Partisan*. A "terrible mandarinism" had been common to many left-wing writers, he exclaimed, "They carry their Marxian scholarship as though it were a heavy cross. They perform academic autopsies on living books."[29] Gold was particularly disturbed by a sarcastic review of Clifford Odets's new play *Paradise Lost,* written by James T. Farrell for the February *Partisan*. Farrell had attacked the play for being trite and inconsequential. The issue between Gold and Farrell was an important

---

[28] A letter from Walter Snow to Conroy describes in detail the merger of the magazines and supports the idea that it had full party approval. Conroy was not at all happy about the merger. Walter Snow to Jack Conroy, November 6, 1935, Conroy MSS; also interview with Jack Conroy, February 27, 1967, Chicago, Ill.

[29] Michael Gold, "Papa Anvil and Mother Partisan," *New Masses,* XVIII (February 18, 1936), p. 22.

and a familiar one, for it involved two opposing sets of literary assumptions. The *Partisan Review* editors and the orthodox left finally split over the same question. Should literature be judged by political expediency; should the critic applaud the literature of writers who were committed politically to the Popular Front or should he reserve praise for literature that had merit only on its own terms? Implicit in all of Rahv and Phillips's critical essays, this question strangely became more pressing as the Communist literary movement became less and less committed to revolutionary art. Despite Gold's hesitations about the orthodoxy of some of the writings in the combined magazine, no serious break between the *Partisan* and the Communist literary movement was yet implied by his remarks. For the time being disagreements were confined to specific articles such as Farrell's review.

From other sources there was more enthusiasm for the merged magazine. In a letter to the editors, Robert Cantwell, one of the more important proletarian novelists of the day, asserted that the magazine should be able to assume critical leadership of the radical literary movement: "The combined Partisan Review and Anvil has an opportunity to take over intellectual leadership in the field of creative literature such as no other publication in the history of this country has possessed; it can become the dominant influence in the intellectual lives of the serious and sincere writers of this period." But the indecision that had characterized the magazine since the time of the first Writers' Congress prevented this. It was not clear from the first few issues of the *Partisan and Anvil* what direction the magazine would take, nor was it certain whether the editors would shift their allegiance from proletarian literature to the Popular Front.

Two articles in the first issue of the *Partisan and Anvil* stressed points that were important in the developing theory of the Popular Front. One, the reprint of Carl Van Doren's speech to the Book Union, a left-wing version of the Book-of-the-Month Club, emphasized the ties of literature in the 1930s to the most important traditions in American letters. The best American literature, he argued, had always inclined to the left. Writers, particularly after 1929, had "reached to the American subsoil for materials for American literature."[30] This association of traditional American literature and liberal politics with radicalism and antifascism was perhaps the most widely used application of the Popular Front to cultural matters. The overwhelming importance of antifascism was also the subject of an address by Waldo Frank, president of the League of American Writers. The speech, reprinted in the *Partisan and Anvil*, was devoted to an analysis of the shortcomings of modern culture and the intellectual's failure to hasten the rebirth of culture. The result, Frank claimed, had been the threat that German and Italian fascism would destroy culture.

The same issue contained a discussion of revolutionary literature produced up to 1936. Newton Arvin's review of *Proletarian Literature in the United States,* a collection of prose, poetry, and critical writing, praised the book as a symbol of the fulfillment of an old promise of American culture. Arvin, however, attacked an essay by Rahv and Phillips (reprinted from the *Partisan*) for being too scholastic. The editors of the magazine, he conceded, had made points about literature with which the critic could certainly agree, but there was no reason to make such writing so "prosaically analytical."[31]

In the March issue Alan Calmer renewed the war against leftism in a reappraisal of proletarian literature. He suggested that all Marxists stop fighting among themselves and agree to a broad set of critical principles. In the face of attacks by bourgeois critics, left-wing writers, he felt, should agree to eliminate all traces of leftism, which had made early radical literature sectarian and uncreative. Those critics, such as Granville Hicks, who were guilty of a dogmatic application of politics to literature, he claimed, had failed to prove the right of "Marxism to be literary criticism." If the radical movement were to make any progress, propaganda as a critical concept should be dropped and critics should forget about the slogan "art as a weapon." They should realize that "proletarian" and "bourgeois" were not

---

[30] Robert Cantwell, "To the Editors," *Partisan Review and Anvil,* III (February 1936), p. 31. Carl Van Doren, "To the Left: To the Subsoil," *Partisan Review and Anvil,* III (February 1936), p. 9.
[31] Newton Arvin, "A Letter on Proletarian Literature," *Partisan Review and Anvil,* III (February 1936), pp. 21-31.

meaningful literary terms. Moreover, they should give up the notion that Marxism could be used to disparage the accomplishments of the past.[32] Calmer, in effect, insisted, as the price of peace, that all revolutionary critics agree with the definition of proletarian art advanced by Rahv and Phillips in the first issue of the *Partisan Review* and refined by them in subsequent essays.

Throughout the remainder of the year Rahv and Phillips continued to amplify their attack on vestiges of leftism, but they had still not advanced a positive approach to American left literature. In the last six issues of the magazine there was no attempt, as there had been before, to create the theoretical basis for a cultural revival; rather, they began gradually and cautiously to attack the premises of proletarianism. As the hopes for a proletarian renaissance faded, this critique became more urgently and sharply focused on the original assumptions of radical literature and the intellectual problems that Rahv and Phillips felt it had promised to solve.

The first *Partisan Review* symposium, printed in April 1936, indicated the direction and extent of the editors' doubts about the proletarian movement. The format of the symposium on Marxism and the American Tradition consisted in replies to a general statement written by Rahv and Phillips and sent to a number of writers and critics of diverse shades of opinion within the left literary movement. As in the case of many subsequent symposia, the statement proved of more importance than the answers. The questions were addressed to the difficulties in defining "Americanism" in relation to Marxism and revolutionary literature. This problem seemed to the editors to demand some serious thought by the radical movement. Was Americanism, they asked, a revolutionary tradition passed on from Tom Paine through the populists and the socialists or was it a system of thought, as some Europeans had said, dominated by individualistic materialism? What relation did the American tradition have to radical literature? "Do you think," they concluded, "that our revolutionary literature reflects and integrates the American

---

[32] Alan Calmer, "All Quiet on the Literary Front," *Partisan Review and Anvil*, III (March 1936), p. 13.

spirit or is it in conflict with it? If this conflict exists, do you think this is a failure on the part of revolutionary writers or do the very premises of revolutionary writing prevent the organic integration of the two?"[33]

The tone of the initial statement and the sort of questions asked reveal the depth to which the editors had gone in their re-examination of revolutionary literature. By raising the question of the relation of Marxism to the American tradition, they indicated doubts about the growing assumption in orthodox radical circles that Marxism was the direct heir of the American revolutionary tradition; that, as Earl Browder would say of the Communists, "We are the only true Americans." Within a year Rahv and Phillips had concluded that Marxism had very little to do with the American tradition. In 1937 they wrote that an essential contradiction existed between Marxism and domestic intellectual traditions that could be resolved only through the "Europeanization of American Literature."[34]

The second half of the questionnaire implied that revolutionary literature had failed thus far to integrate Marxism and Americanism. Two explanations were proposed: that the writers themselves had failed or that the premises of the new literature had been wrong. The intensive criticism of the radical literary movement that was to mark the last few issues of the *Partisan* before it suspended publication in late 1936 first took the shape of questions on Marxism and Americanism. They indicated a deep dissatisfaction with the direction of the cultural renaissance and the feeling that proletarian literature had failed and that the Popular Front held no literary promise.

Replies to the symposium on the whole offered little to bolster the argument for a revolutionary literature. A number of authors —Theodore Dreiser, Newton Arvin, Matthew Josephson, and Joseph Freeman—wrote of the vital connection between Marxism and the American tradition and in some cases of the need to

---

[33] "What is Americanism?" *Partisan Review and Anvil,* III (April 1936), p. 3.

[34] William Phillips and Philip Rahv, "Literature in a Political Decade," *New Letters in America,* Horace Gregory, ed. (New York: W. W. Norton, 1937), p. 178.

Americanize Marxist theory. Answers by William Troy, Robert Herrick, and William Carlos Williams, however, challenged this relationship. Troy, for example, argued that even if revolution were a part of the American tradition, it was not the sort of revolution meant by contemporary radicals, but one based largely on individualism. The attempt to link Marxism and Americanism, he continued, involved a sophistry. It was difficult for the artist "who cares anything for his role to achieve a really logical bridge between dogmatic Marxism and literature." Robert Herrick was explicit in his rejection of Marxism: the democratic process was most important to him. Moreover, he stated that the more "Marxian" literature became, the less it would be real literature. William Carlos Williams, in what was to be the most controversial answer, declared that the American tradition was completely opposed to Marxism and that revolutionary literature was in conflict with America's most important ideals.[35]

The next issue of the magazine disavowed such a conclusion. In answer to a number of letters criticizing Williams, an editorial note explained that the position of the *Partisan Review* "is utterly opposed to the direction of thought shown in Mr. Williams' contribution." The editors were by no means prepared to accept Williams's rejection of Marxism, but significantly they did not bother to criticize the answers of William Troy or Robert Herrick. Their own doubts about the validity of a proletarian literature had in any case been implied by the questionnaire itself, and very soon these doubts would become even more explicit.

The May issue of the magazine featured articles, prose and poetry that again pointed in contradictory directions. The introduction of a new department, "Cross-Country," a series of sketches about life in the United States, was an attempt to move closer to the actual experience, the raw material of proletarian literature, that the editors felt was usually lacking in more formal fictional accounts. Noncontroversial also was William Phillips's review of Alan Tate's *Reactionary Essays on Poetry and Ideas*, which took the critic to task for his blindness to the relation between the meaning of a poem and the larger social

[35] William Troy and William Carlos Williams, "What is Americanism?" *Partisan Review and Anvil*, III (April 1936), pp. 13, 14.

context. The essence of Tate's poetic criticism was, Phillips concluded, "some stray insights, a medley of social prejudices and a metrical approach to poems."

Alan Calmer's review essay, "MacLeish and Proletarian Poetry," on the other hand, was a new attack on sectarian left writers. MacLeish's new book, *Public Speech,* the critic argued, had succeeded when most proletarian writers had failed: it achieved a poetic expression that demonstrated the firmness of thought derived from an inner compulsion; it was not propaganda. Above all MacLeish was a poet; in comparison many of the new radical writers lacked a profound devotion to their craft. Their work was often sloppy and overrated. Calmer's most telling criticism of the proletarian movement was his estimate of its effect on the artist: "While Communism has elevated the place of literature in society, the close connection of the poet with the labor movement has affected him in the opposite way: it has emphasized the insignificance of phrase-making as compared with practical activity."[36] The turn away from Axel's castle at the beginning of the decade had been beneficial, he concluded, but it tended to submerge the artist in organizational and journalistic demands.

The June issue of the *Partisan* contained three sharp attacks on leftism in literature by editors Calmer, Phillips, and Rahv. There was no doubt from this and the final October issue that the scattered criticism of leftism, begun early in the magazine (and stemming back even to the days before the *Partisan*), were now aimed toward rejecting proletarian literature and any direct tie between literature and politics. This process, although it involved a serious reappraisal of the basic premises of revolutionary literature, first exhibited a growing interest in radical but unorthodox European writers who had been influenced by Marxism, particularly Malraux and Silone. The editors soon concluded that these two authors came closest to capturing the reality and complexity of proletarian culture and most persuasively depicted the problems of a revolutionary consciousness.

---

[36] Alan Calmer, "MacLeish and Proletarian Poetry," *Partisan Review and Anvil,* III (May 1936), p. 20.

Alan Calmer's praise for a *Note on Literary Criticism* by James Farrell was particularly controversial. Farrell's book had belittled the critical work of Gold and Hicks and of more party-oriented Communist critics while praising the work of Rahv. In fact, Farrell accepted a number of the original arguments advanced by the *Partisan* in its struggle against leftism. Worse, Farrell had openly dueled over the book with Isidor Schneider and Granville Hicks, whom he called elsewhere a "critical vulgarian." Calmer felt that Farrell's work indicated a new direction in American proletarian letters. The old sectarian criticism still lingered, but surely, he insisted, "There is no longer any excuse for its persistence."

Phillips's defense of André Malraux's *Days of Wrath* was also a denunciation of the proletarian movement. Malraux's novel, he felt, was revolutionary in every sense, but particularly because of its psychological intensity. American writers and critics by comparison had been hypnotized into a belief that the revolutionary novel was a "trumpet-call to concrete action" and a reconstruction of "a fabulous Christian world where political virtue triumphs over political evil, where neon signs point the moral, and conversion is swift and miraculous."[37]

Rahv's review of T. S. Eliot's new play *Murder in the Cathedral* was perhaps the least orthodox of the three articles. Rahv admitted that there were fascist implications to the poet's current positions on cultural problems, yet he insisted that each of Eliot's poems be considered as a work of art in itself. Even if left-wing critics failed to see it, there was, after all, a distinction between life and literature, between the poet and his work. Rahv concluded that Eliot's poetry could not be ignored by young revolutionary writers; rather, they could learn from its variety and complexity and from its contemporaneity.

Most of the ideas in these important essays had been expressed in previous issues. But the intensity of the writing and the application now of criticism to specific cases made the implications of Calmer, Rahv, and Phillips's theoretical objections to leftism more obvious. These essays did not indicate an abrupt break with the Communist literary movement, but they did

---

[37] William Phillips, "The Humanism of André Malraux," *Partisan Review and Anvil*, III (June 1936), pp. 16, 18.

reveal a deep discouragement with the basic ideas that had defended proletarian literature.

One aspect of the format for the last issue of the *Partisan Review and Anvil* changed significantly. The editorial board was reduced to Calmer, Phillips, and Rahv; no associate editors were listed, and all pretense was dropped that the publication represented a merger of two magazines. In the past many of the men whose names appeared in the editorial lists had little if anything to do with the functioning of the magazine. The listing of these names, whether to reward a particular author or, in the first issues, to increase the prestige of the magazine, was nevertheless a sign of the *Partisan's* radical credentials. Their absence in the last issue was a sign of the growing separation between the magazine and the remainder of the Communist literary movement. For the first time the magazine carried no advertisements from Communist publications.[38] This evidence supports the contention of Rahv and Phillips that they seriously considered converting the magazine at this time into an independent, non-Communist radical publication.

There was little beyond this in the last issue to indicate the disillusionment of the editors with proletarian literature. An article by Louis Kronenberger discussed the function of criticism in a world where intellectuals had shifted their emphasis from enriching culture to preserving it. Harold Rosenberg's review essay "Poets of the People" attacked the Popular Front and the new emphasis on the tradition of literary populism, reaching back to Whitman, from which Carl Sandburg and Vachel Lindsay had derived their poetic forms. The article rejected the assumption that socialism derived from American traditions such as populism and that literary radicalism could claim Whitman as a direct ancestor. Nevertheless, Rosenberg ended with a call for a new effort by critics to infuse the American tradition with Marxism in order to make it a force for world socialism.

Very important was the publication of Ignazio Silone's "Two Syllables," a portion of his book *Bread and Wine*. Silone was regarded with suspicion by Communist intellectuals, and the

---

[38] Philip Rahv and William Phillips, "In Retrospect," *The Partisan Reader* (New York: Dial Press, 1946), p. 680.

Partisan editors, by printing him, demonstrated their refusal to accept all of the judgments of the left movement. But the magazine had previously printed authors who were unpopular in party circles, such as Farrell and John Dos Passos. Thus the final issue of the magazine indicated no immediate and final break with the Communist intellectual movement. Moreover, the *New Masses,* especially during and after 1935, had become increasingly temperate in its literary judgments. Thus arguments against leftism even began to appear there after 1935. This change was due in part to the Popular Front, which dictated against alienating authors who supported the political aims of the Communists. Significantly, the *New Masses* was gradually giving up its interest in proletarian literature, but the *Partisan Review* continued to make this issue primary in its discussion of the radical cultural movement. The intensity of their attacks on leftism increased, even though this tendency was diminishing as the whole movement lost momentum. Rahv and Phillips had actually won their argument about sectarian literature, but to the Communist literati this was a dead issue by the end of 1936. The *New Masses* abandoned proletarian literature, but not because it had been convinced by the *Partisan Review* of its theoretical errors. On the contrary, the new cultural attitudes of party intellectuals were determined by the shift of the Communist movement away from revolution.

One of the primary reasons that the *Partisan* suspended publication in October 1936 was financial difficulty. Like other little magazines it was unable to pay for the costs of printing and mailing from subscription and advertising revenues, nor could it provide large editorial salaries. Raising money was always the second occupation of the editors. This was accomplished by a number of means; contributions, fund-raising parties, and lectures. After the termination of the John Reed Clubs, Rahv, Phillips, and Calmer did most of the fund raising. To support themselves during this period Rahv and Phillips both had jobs with the Federal Writers' Project and Calmer worked for International Publishers.[39]

---

[39] Rahv and Phillips, "In Retrospect," *Partisan Reader,* p. 680, and interviews with Phillips and Rahv. See also David Lawrence, "Who Slew Proletcult?" *Vanguard,* IV (November 1937), p. 10.

One solution to the financial problems of the *Partisan* was offered in a new proposal to unite the magazine with the League of American Writers. Such a merger had been a possibility since the American Writers' Congress a year before. In the fall of 1936, however, the League offered the editors concrete plans. In May 1936 the organization agreed to lend the magazine $100. In September Rahv was elected to the executive committee of the League, and the possibility of official affiliation became even stronger. A League executive meeting elected a subcommittee that included Malcolm Cowley, Alexander Trachtenberg, Henry Hart, and Isidor Schneider to discuss with the editors "League participation in publishing *Partisan Review*." The basis for the negotiations was decided at the next meeting; included were proposals that the League purchase subscriptions of the magazine for its members and that the *Partisan* devote a quarterly issue to League activities. The League in turn would be given the right to appoint two members to the magazine staff subject to the approval of the present editors, and it would help raise money to pay off the *Partisan*'s debts, which apparently were substantial. Although the plan was rejected by the magazine, it was reported as late as the middle of October that the editors were reconsidering at least a temporary affiliation.[40]

The reluctance of the *Partisan* to accept any official connection with the League of American Writers indicates the unwillingness of the editors to continue publication of the magazine on anything like its former basis, but their consideration of the plan showed them still vaguely attached to the Communist left. Discouragement with the radical literary movement that had so often been hinted at during 1936 was openly stated two months after the magazine suspended publication. In December William Phillips in a review for the *New Masses* of a collection of contemporary writing asserted that there were "few signs of any important movement growing out of a new generation of writers." "Have all our critical guarantees that proletarian literature would expand and mature to the point of dominating

---

[40] "Minutes of the League of American Writers, Executive Committee Meeting," May 13, September 8, September 21, and October 15, 1936, LAW MSS.

American literature," he asked, "been just so much professional optimism?"[41] The revolution in American letters promised by the proletarian movement seemed a dull failure.

The suspension of the *Partisan Review* coincided with the realization by the editors that the literary movement they had hoped to mold and lead had, in fact, evaporated. Moreover, the news during the summer that many of the original Bolshevik leaders such as Kamenev, Zinoviev, Radek, and Bukharin had been accused of treason struck at one of the foundations of the belief in the proletarian literary movement—at the validity of the Soviet experiment and at the radical tradition identified with American Communism.

The failure of the cultural revolution cut a fundamental tie between the *Partisan Review* and the majority of the radical movement; the belief in a renaissance was shattered. The Communists had apparently shed their revolutionary ideas and were moving toward middle-class respectability and political compromise. To the *Partisan,* the death of proletarian literature left the problems of the modern writer and intellectual with no adequate Marxian solution. Moreover, it now seemed imperative to undertake an intensive examination of those developments in the Communist political movement that had been responsible for the misdirection of cultural events. Within a few months the former editors of *Partisan Review* were engaged in an autopsy of a defunct literary movement, which carried them back before the birth of proletarian literature to the problems of its initial conception.

---

[41] William Phillips, "Marking Time," *New Masses,* XXI (December 22, 1936), p. 23.

Chapter 5

The New Generation

Who in the world of bourgeois letters had
ever heard of or given a hoot for Rahv and
Phillips, for example, amateur literati who mishandled a magazine that started out with all
the auspices and forces to make it a success.

V. J. Jerome, *Daily Worker,* 1937

Partisan Review aspires to represent a new and
dissident generation in American letters; it will
not be dislodged from its independent position
by any political campaign against it.

F. W. Dupee, *Partisan Review,* 1937

The greatest literature of our day will surely
have at its heart precisely this, the artistic
re-creation of the great process going on among
the people of the creation of a broad democratic front and the defeat of fascism.

Earl Browder to the League of American
Writers, 1937

Our League, I should say is the heir of the
old Progressive movement that won so many
writers in years gone by. The movement failed
and because we hope we shall not fail, we
have got to be "tough-minded," as the patriot
fathers were, and the missionaries of old.

Van Wyck Brooks, 1937

The year that elapsed between the suspension of the *Partisan
Review* and the revival of its sequel in 1937, like each year of

the late 1930s, was crowded with immense political and intellectual change. The flare of each world event momentarily illuminated a picture of approaching catastrophe, often so brilliantly as to make it impossible to distinguish the direction of American culture. The stagnation of the literary renaissance and the beginning of the Popular Front made it seem less imperative to create a new culture than to preserve the old. In the glare of politics, cultural change seemed swift and final. Radical intellectuals, believing that they had clear consciences on this score themselves, demanded of their government, even of Western civilization, an irrevocable opposition to fascism that would match the intensity and purity of their own commitment. However, singularity of purpose, which might be useful to the moralist, clashed with practical politics, and no movement that had any significance politically could live up to the urgent demands placed upon it. The Loyalist government of Spain fought the anarchists and Trotskyists; the Stalinists in Russia pilloried the heroes of the revolution; and the New Deal spent itself in verbal fury against the Supreme Court to preserve its modest reforms. The simplicity of antifascism was confounded by political necessity, and imaginary Maginot lines crumbled before the invasion of reality. Having invested politics with the task of preserving culture because of the desperation of the times, not all intellectuals were prepared to take the risks to expose culture in the way that such a choice implied. The conflict between reality and idealism inspired a growing suspicion that the forces that lined up to do battle with fascism were themselves impure and even dangerous, and this realization presented a range of choices. One could either take a stand that compromised principle or retreat to a world of detached moralism. To refuse to accept political compromise had serious implications: if practical politics had once infected the cultural renaissance in the early 1930s, would it not be true also that practical politics would even destroy politics itself? By accepting this conclusion, the faults, not the virtues, of any political movement such as the Communist party seemed most important. On the other hand, if one believed that the Communists were the only true opponents of fascism, as many intellectuals at the time did, any questioning of the motives of the movement, any dissent could be construed as a dangerous diversion from the important task at hand. Either way, theoretical politics—since few intellectuals were involved in real politics—became a science for making moral choices.

Two events in 1936 and 1937 bore into the radical literary movement and split open the intellectual amalgam created by the theory of proletarianism and the assertion of political and cultural unity through the coming renaissance. Had the radical intellectuals been able to fix a constant gaze upon the cultural environment, unmoved by political events, perhaps such a separation would not have come so violently. But the intrusion of the Moscow Trials and the Spanish Civil War diverted the discussion from literature to politics, where the issues were irreconcilable. To the Communists the Spanish Civil War was the test of the Popular Front and the first and most vital confrontation on the battlefield between fascism and the liberal and leftist elements that united against it. The political commitment of the artist reached its greatest intensity when writers joined the International Brigades to fight with Loyalist troops in Spain. The Moscow Trials, beginning in 1936 and extending through 1937, were another sort of test for the political involvement of the intellectual. Stalin's purge of suspiciously independent intellectuals and powerful political enemies made disastrously clear the extreme risk of political activity. Even Malcolm Cowley, who accepted the validity of the trials and wrote an ambitious defense of their procedure, confided to Edmund Wilson in early 1937 that he "went dead" at the news of the trials.[1] A traitor's death for the heroes of the Russian Revolution implied that the larger meaning of the intellectual's death in the fight against fascism in Spain might in fact be suicide committed for a dubious cause. The two events raised questions about the Soviet Union itself, not just about Spain or the nature of revolutions. If the trials were unjust, then it became possible to believe that the struggle in Spain was fruitless; worse, it might be a fight to pre-

---

[1] Malcolm Cowley to Edmund Wilson, May 14, 1937, Malcolm Cowley MSS, The Newberry Library, Chicago, Illinois; hereafter cited as Cowley MSS.

serve a government dominated by the same deformed revolutionary spirit that ruled the Soviet state.

To the editors of the *Partisan Review* the events of 1936 and 1937 cast fundamental doubts on the integrity of Communism. This process was first evident in their reassertion of the theoretical purity of Marxism through their temporary identification with Trotskyism. But in the long run it meant the beginning of a piecemeal rejection of Marxism itself. For Rahv and Phillips, Trotskyism was simultaneously a critique of the Soviet Union and a restatement of fundamental Marxism, because the practical politics of the Trotskyist movement had little attraction for them.

The Moscow Trials in part redefined the attitude of Rahv and Phillips toward politics. The fate of the accused Russian intellectuals recalled to them the disastrous effects of Communist party interference in the proletarian movement. Both were related to the pernicious influence of Stalinism. Politics held their renewed interest not merely as a field for personal activity; politics, they felt, had caused the failure of radicalism. Rahv and Phillips cemented no direct ties with any political movement, and their detachment made it unnecessary to compromise or to submit to political expediency. Thus the break with the Communists in 1937 was for them a final separation from political movements, yet it marked the beginning of a period when politics would be of great importance to them. Now, however, the intellectual, not the working class, would become the central figure of concern. The chastening experience of proletarian art offered substantial reasons to turn away from political literature, for artists had found that the worker was too constricting an audience and the movement too rigid. If anything, wrote Alan Calmer in 1937, the social maladjustment of the young John Reed Club intellectuals had been intensified by the experience with proletarian literature.[2]

During the year that intervened between the two *Partisan Reviews* William Phillips and Philip Rahv openly opposed the Communist cultural and political movement. They moved from

---

[2] Alan Calmer, "Portrait of the Artist as a Proletarian," *Saturday Review,* XVI (July 31, 1937), p. 14.

a hesitant skepticism about the results of the once optimistic literary revival to a certainty that the very premises of that movement had been ill-conceived and that its excesses were caused by the political controls exercised upon it by the Communists. Political guidelines on culture resulted in propaganda and sectarianism. Joining this conclusion with impressions gathered from the Moscow Trials, they asserted that the American Communists had projected Soviet political and cultural policies into their own program, making the party a "miniature Stalinist state." But rather than give up their faith in socialism or in the relevance of Marxism, they shifted their allegiance to Trotskyism, a radical theory that explained and clarified their objections to contemporary Soviet Communism. An American renaissance molded by a proletarian culture no longer had any attraction for them. Only its failure did.

Together with Fred Dupee, recently an editor of the *New Masses*, Dwight Macdonald, who had quit Henry Luce's *Fortune* magazine in 1936, Mary McCarthy, a young poet and vaguely a Trotskyist, and George L. K. Morris, a painter who provided the funds, Rahv and Phillips revived the *Partisan Review* on a new political and cultural basis. Revolutionary culture was to remain at the center of the new publication, but it was revolutionary in a different sense than before. The magazine would be free of any political ties and would be devoted to the most advanced literature, adopting the style of earlier magazines of aesthetic revolt. For the second time in four years Rahv and Phillips felt themselves part of a self-conscious new generation of writers, but this time defined by their schism with the Communists. "Partisan Review," wrote Fred Dupee in the opening editorial of the magazine in 1937, "aspires to represent a new and dissident generation in American letters. . . ."

Born as the dialectical antithesis of the Communist cultural movement, the new *Partisan* at first struggled over the same intellectual ground and responded in many cases to the same political and cultural events as its former comrades. The bitter divorce between the two partners of radical literature, the *Partisan* and the *New Masses*, in no sense terminated their consciousness of each other. On the contrary, the mutual hostility that had occasionally been expressed in both magazines was increased and intensified. A profound and growing distance separated the two wings of revolutionary culture almost from the moment when the editors of the *Partisan* broke dramatically with the Communists by challenging the validity of the Popular Front at the American Writers' Congress in June 1937. Because they shared a Marxist tradition and a preoccupation with the Soviet Union, but adopted a dissident Marxist program, the *Partisan* editors in reestablishing the magazine were, in effect, leading a revolution of intellectuals against the Communist movement. They rejected the Popular Front and its reliance on Soviet power and disavowed the particular American liberal tradition that had become imbedded in the assumptions of the League of American Writers. Traditional American radical letters, now so highly regarded by Joseph Freeman, Malcolm Cowley, and Newton Arvin and carefully nurtured after 1936 by the Communists, seemed to Rahv and Phillips to be an anti-intellectual literature. Its political counterpart, the American populist and progressive movements, appeared to be nativist and debilitating. While the writers and critics grouped in the Popular Front tried to revive a heritage of American liberalism and radicalism, the editors of the *Partisan Review* clung to a view that these traditions were impossibly narrow and bourgeois, a view proclaimed with particular strength in the 1920s.

In two years, from the time of the announcement of the Popular Front to the Second American Writers' Congress in 1937, the Communists had changed from promoting a revolutionary new culture to supporting existing institutions that might oppose fascism. Consequently they aided the Spanish Loyalists and gave informal approval to the Roosevelt Administration in the United States. Conscious of the charge that his movement had abandoned proletarian literature, Mike Gold wrote in 1937 that revolutionary culture had not died, but there had been a "lull, perhaps, while the authors prepare themselves for new tasks." The lull, however, was permanent. Earl Browder's speech before the Second Writers' Congress indicated a new direction in the party's attitude toward literature: "The greatest literature of our day," he declared, "will surely have at its heart precisely this, the artistic recreation of the great process going on among the people of the creation of a broad democratic front and the defeat of fascism."[3] Literature for the Communists meant the aesthetic recreation of the Popular Front. The role of the artist was no longer to be the voice of revolution, but the guardian of liberal and democratic ideals.

However narrow the purpose, to many of the intellectuals who joined the League of American Writers this organization had the broader significance of uniting the writer to progressive politics and of creating a literary movement immersed in a liberal American heritage. By identifying their own work with it, writers like Van Wyck Brooks, Lewis Mumford, and Malcolm Cowley significantly affected the character of the League. The search for a new Americanism, which had always been at the core of Brooks's critical writing, had become by the 1930s a celebration of America's nineteenth-century authors. Brooks's new literary nationalism coincided with the liberal patriotism of the Communist literary program. The vision of a new America that had preoccupied many of the exiles of the 1920s, which was in fact a major element of all three Bohemias of that period, materialized in the nostalgic dream of a liberal heritage. In his desire to find the democratic roots of America, Brooks projected the popular image of the day backward through history to discover that collectivism lay at the very heart of American civilization, not the collectivism exemplified by Russian Communism, but a system of political and economic freedom. Brooks's identification of the League with the movement of which he, Bourne, Reed, and others had been a part represented an abandonment of the position he had held before World War I, a position that dismissed much of the American cultural environment. "Our League," he said in 1937, "is the heir of the old Progressive movement that won so many writers in years gone by. The movement failed, and because we hope that we shall not fail, we have got to be 'tough-minded' as the patriot fathers

---

[3] Mike Gold, "Notes on the Cultural Front," *New Masses*, XXV (December 7, 1937), p. 4. Earl Browder, "Writers and the Communist Party," *The People's Front* (New York: International Publishers, 1938), p. 281.

were, and the missionaries of old."[4] The puritans and the practical statesmen who drafted the American Constitution no longer
seemed the architects of a cold and sterile culture; they were the
forerunners of the democratic system fighting for its life against
fascism.

The call to the Second Writers' Congress was a deliberate attempt to identify the League with the pre-World War I political
and cultural renaissance, with Randolph Bourne's league of
youth, and with John Reed's pagan radicalism: "Today in America there are signs of a literary revival that may resemble or
surpass that of the period from 1912 to 1916. Those of us who
remember the hopeful activity of those years can also remember
how it was cut short by the war. And we can see that the
promise of the 1930s is threatened in a still more definite fashion."[5] To preserve American culture from the brutalities of
fascism, the League appealed to the example of the uncompromising young intellectuals who had opposed World War I, there
they found a precedent for their own program. The literary and
political nationalism of the League drew inspiration from the
desire of many writers to join with an intellectual force capable
and significant in its opposition to fascism—the world Communist movement. But the infusion of the Popular Front with
the tendency of Brooks and others to glorify early American
literature made the League top-heavy with patriotism. One sign
of the League's attachment to liberalism came in 1938 when it
elected President Roosevelt to an honorary membership. Brooks,
who was Vice President of the organization by that time, wrote to
Roosevelt that his writings represented a unique contribution to
American letters.[6] The overt identification of the writers' move-

---

[4] Van Wyck Brooks, "The League of American Writers," *New Republic,*
XCVIII (February 22, 1937), pp. 65-67.
[5] Letter to the Editor announcing the Congress, *Nation,* CXLIV (May 8,
1937), pp. 547-548. Significantly the "Call" was signed by Newton Arvin, Van Wyck Brooks, Malcolm Cowley, Waldo Frank, Jean Starr Untermeyer, Lewis Mumford, and Carl Van Doren.
[6] Van Wyck Brooks to Franklin Roosevelt, April 15, 1938, LAW MSS. Sidney Hook relates in 1947 that he wrote to the President in 1940 to in-
quire about Roosevelt's membership in the League and that, as a consequence, F.D.R. resigned. Sidney Hook, "The Future of Socialism," *Partisan
Review,* XIV (January-February 1947), p. 54.

ment with the Roosevelt Administration and the New Deal created the possibility, later to be realized, that the loyalties of the writers would be stretched between two political centers, America and the Soviet Union.

Elements of the old Bohemia, scattered by World War I, were reconstructed in the Communist cultural movement, which combined the political struggle against fascism with a renewed devotion to American literary history. The Popular Front represented a continuation of the renaissance and revolution before World War I, or at least one tendency within that earlier movement. Among the leading figures in the League were writers who had been active in the first literary renaissance, and they self-consciously identified with the previous period. But the tradition itself, as the writers who began it, had aged and become more conservative. Randolph Bourne's international community of young intellectuals was transformed by the years into a middle-aged society of literary nationalists dependent on the fortunes of a political movement. The rediscovery of America, so important in the work of the writers of the League, became the reassertion of traditional American culture. The Communist literary movement in 1936 and 1937 absorbed a tendency that contained only a withered memory of the prewar Bohemia. Having compromised with the desperate politics of the times, many American writers subscribed to a critical theory that was warmed only by the soft afterglow of the nineteenth century. The unity of radical politics and avant-garde literature of the early 1930s, premised upon the revolutionary character of both, was abandoned. The early tradition of Brooks and Bourne was stood upon its head; the Bohemian community was replaced by the dream of a democratic patriotism.

The cautious optimism about a new American renaissance that was voiced in the call for the Writers' Congress echoed a similar temporary optimism that predicted victory over fascism in Spain. Malcolm Cowley's speech before the Congress, where he related that there were days when he bought ten to fifteen newspapers to discover the outcome of battles in Spain, illustrated the intensity of interest and involvement that many writers felt in the fate of Spain. Recalling these days somewhat later, Brooks wrote that the collapse of Spain represented to him the death of all great causes.[7] For many members of the League the importance of Spain and the urgency of the struggle against fascism smoothed over the implications of the Moscow Trials and muted the shock that Cowley and others confess they felt about events in the Soviet Union. The trials did not seem to interfere at this time with the membership of liberal writers in the Communist intellectual movement, nor did it appear that opposition to fascism or the new literary and political liberalism of the Popular Front was threatened by Stalin's purge. The purge, in some sense, seemed necessary because of Spain. For example, Cowley's long review essay in the *New Republic* in early 1937 of the official transcripts of the trials found a justification for the procedure in the exigencies of history. Trotskyism, since it challenged the Soviet regime, became an ally of fascism because it weakened the forces, specifically Russia, that were devoted to defeating Germany. But the Moscow Trials operated in a subterranean fashion, much as the trial of Sacco and Vanzetti and the Great Crash of 1929 had. They became a symbol of the failure of Communism to members of the League of American Writers, but only after many of these liberal intellectuals had become discouraged with Communism for other reasons.

Trotskyism had its greatest impact on American intellectuals in 1936 and 1937, especially on those who became disillusioned with Soviet Communism because Trotsky, tried and convicted in absentia for treason, became a symbol of the Russian purge. His controversy with the Soviet government demonstrated clearly, but from a radical viewpoint, how far the Bolshevik Revolution had degenerated. Like Stalinism, the Trotskyist movement provided a political core about which a number of dissident American intellectual traditions were gathered. Those writers and critics who responded to the lead of the banished revolutionist and the small band of followers who formed the Fourth International in competition with the Soviet's Third

---

[7] Malcolm Cowley, "Seven Years of Crisis," LAW MSS, p. 13, and Van Wyck Brooks, *From the Shadow of the Mountain* (New York: E. P. Dutton, 1961), p. 85.

were cosmopolitan and international in their tastes, as Trotsky himself was. If the League of American Writers, caught up in the political fortunes of Soviet Communism, became a vehicle for the rediscovery of traditional American literature and liberal politics—of an insular cultural vision—the Trotskyist intellectuals, in particular the editors of *Partisan Review,* demanded a culture based primarily on the literary and intellectual innovations of modern European literature. The antipathy between what were two poles of American criticism thus ran from politics through culture.

The American Trotskyist movement appeared after a split in the Communist party in the late 1920s and remained of slight importance until the middle of the 1930s. Even in comparison to other radical parties its membership was small, but its influence among intellectuals, not unlike that of the Communist party, was greatly disproportionate to its size. In 1935, partially because of the movement's isolation, Leon Trotsky advised his American followers to enter the Socialist party. Sidney Hook, a professor of philosophy at New York University and a future close friend of the *Partisan Review,* helped to arrange a meeting toward this end between James Cannon, head of the American Trotskyists, and Norman Thomas, leader of the Socialist party. Hook advised the Socialist leader that intellectuals who had been influenced by Trotskyism—Louis Hacker, Max Eastman, John Dos Passos, Lionel Trilling, Lionel Abel, and John Chamberlain—would be welcome additions to the Socialist party. In return, the entrance into the party would give the Trotskyists a firmer American base at a time when the Communists were determined to discredit them completely.[8] Once in the Socialist party, the Trotskyists secured a degree of prestige with the liberal community, which aided them in defending Trotsky against the accusations of the Moscow Trials.

The origin of the fascinating group of intellectuals that Hook spoke of has been traced back to the protests of writers against a Communist effort to break up a Socialist rally in Madison

---

[8] M. S. Venkataramani, "Leon Trotsky's Adventure in American Radical Politics," *International Review of Social History,* IX (Part 1, 1964), pp. 4, 10.

Square Garden in 1934. But the existence of an identifiable group of intellectuals—although not then Trotskyists—goes back ultimately to Columbia University during the mid-1920s where Lionel Trilling, Felix Morrow, Meyer Schapiro, Louis Hacker, and Herbert Solow were schoolmates. Despite many political fluctuations, this group provided a sort of nucleus toward which other intellectuals who were influenced by Trotsky gravitated. Immensely articulate and active, these young men plunged into publishing and political organization. After college several of them wrote for the *Menorah Journal,* a publication of the Inter-collegiate Menorah Society and devoted to Jewish culture. Solow became an assistant editor of the magazine, and Trilling, Clifton Fadiman, as well as Kenneth Fearing were frequent contributors. By the end of the 1920s the journal had absorbed the radicalism that was beginning to influence other publications in New York. Together with Elliot Cohen, the managing editor of the magazine, Solow formed the National Committee for the Defense of Political Prisoners as a part of the Communist International Labor Defense. The height of this group's commitment to the Communist cause came in 1932 when, together with many other intellectuals, most of the group supported the candidacy of William Z. Foster for President. At the same time Solow and Louis Hacker, together with Lewis Corey and Max Lerner, worked on the editorial board of the Encyclopedia of the Social Sciences.

By 1933 several members of the group had begun to question the motivations of the Communist movement and to criticize its policy on labor defense and its political stance in Germany that they suspected of indirectly aiding Hitler. As a result, several of the intellectuals in the Committee for the Defense of Political Prisoners resigned and were branded by the party as Trotskyists. Further widening the break and bringing it to public attention was the Madison Square Garden riot of 1934. In protest twenty-five intellectuals addressed an open letter to the Communist party, and among them were Trilling, Schapiro, Clifton Fadiman, Felix Morrow, Elliot Cohen, and George Novack.

The Trotskyist opposition, the Communist League, was the chief beneficiary of this first important defection from the Communist movement. Solow, Novack, and Felix Morrow were closest to this faction, but many of the others also considered themselves Trotskyists. In 1934 the merger of the Trotskyists with A. J. Muste's American Workers party brought the Columbia group together with V. F. Calverton, Sidney Hook, James Burnham, and James Rorty. Once more a labor defense organization was founded, this time called the Non-Partisan Labor Defense, which operated until 1936. One of the most important products of this new intellectual grouping was the publication during 1937 of the *Marxist Quarterly*, edited by Burnham, Corey, Hacker, Hook, Novack, Schapiro, and others. Significantly, many of the contributors to the short-lived journal were part of the old Columbia group or presently taught at Columbia.[9]

A further important action of this group was their work for the American Committee for the Defense of Leon Trotsky, formed in 1936 and headed by John Dewey. It was at this point that the Trotskyist movement had its greatest impact among American intellectuals and that the *Partisan Review* editors began to look to the lone revolutionary in exile for political insights. At first, the Dewey committee worked to obtain political asylum for Trotsky, who since the late 1920s had been an unwanted visitor in numerous European countries. Partly because of its efforts and those of Lazaro Cardenas, President of the Mexican Republic, the exiled Bolshevik leader found sanctuary in Mexico. In 1937 the committee aided the defense of Trotsky even further by sending a group, including John Dewey, Carleton Beals, Suzanne LaFollette, and others, to Mexico to hear Trotsky's reply to the charges that he was guilty of treason and fascist collaboration with the enemies of the Soviet Union. Trotsky's defense was a brilliant exposition of revolutionary Marxism and, like much of his contemporary writing, simultaneously a radical critique of the Soviet regime. The defensive posture of his movement during 1936 and 1937 and its subse-

---

[9] Interview with George Novack, December 27, 1966, New York, and George Novack, "A Representative Figure Dies," *Militant* (December 14, 1964). See also the *Menorah Journal*, *Labor Action*, the *Militant*, and the *Marxist Quarterly*.

quent aggressive counterattack on the foundations of Stalinism made Trotskyism perfectly suited to intellectuals who were discouraged and angered by the Soviet Union, but who remained loyal to Marxism. Central to Trotsky and the people he influenced was the degenerate nature of Soviet Communism. In the Trotskyist movement, opposition to the Soviet regime was part of the definition of radicalism. To the *Partisan* editors, Trotskyism was an answer to the question of what had gone wrong with Communism; it explained from a Marxist viewpoint what had happened to distort and twist the revolution.

One of the most bitter opponents of Trotskyism in any form was Mike Gold. Despite the belligerency of his feelings, he accurately observed in one of his frequent attacks on the sect that the attraction of this critique of the Soviet Union for the intellectual derived in part from its nonpolitical character—because it was a "nay-saying trend."[10] The isolation of Trotskyism together with its intense reassertion of basic revolutionary Marxism attracted Rahv and Phillips, who had become convinced that party politics, specifically Communist politics, had interfered with and destroyed the literary renaissance that once seemed so promising. Compared to the secluded, provincial bureaucrat who ruled the Soviet Union, Trotsky was a man of intellectual brilliance, a cosmopolitan figure, a European, and a man of action. It was precisely Trotsky's intellectuality, his greatest difference from Stalin that made him important to Rahv and Phillips. His theoretical description of Stalinism overshadowed the revolutionary appeal of his miniscule Fourth International, and his theory, always devoted to practical political ends, was ultimately turned to bolster an argument for the separation of politics from other activities engaged in by the intellectual.

For Dwight Macdonald, who joined with Rahv, Phillips, Dupee, Mary McCarthy, and George L. K. Morris to revive the *Partisan Review* in 1937, Trotskyism was more than a radical critique of Stalinism. Macdonald's early life and career were quite different from that of Rahv or Phillips. Macdonald was

---

[10] Mike Gold, "Notes on the Cultural Front," *New Masses,* XXV (December 7, 1937), p. 2.

born in 1906 into a family that on both sides had been native-Americans for a number of generations. Both his father and grandfather were lawyers, and his father received his law degree at New York University. Following his father, Macdonald attended private school at Phillips Exeter Academy and then went on to Yale University.[11] At Exeter he showed an early interest in publishing. His very exclusive "Hedonist Club" put out two issues of a magazine, *Masquerade*, which was noted, as he recalls, for its "extreme preciosity." From Exeter he went to Yale, where he continued his interest in literature. A young fellow student from Chicago, Fred Dupee, who became a close friend, recalls that together they worshipped Proust, Joyce, Anderson, Spengler, Henry James, and Irving Babbitt: "We were in search, very vaguely, of order and orthodoxy."[12]

With Dupee, Geoffrey T. Heller, and George L. K. Morris, also a Yale acquaintance, Macdonald published a small literary magazine, *The Miscellany*. Dupee wrote somewhat facetiously, that in the two years of its existence (1930 to 1933), the magazine managed to attack some of the best poems and novels of the 1920s. A quality of dilettantism did characterize the early magazine at times, and Macdonald's remarks on T. S. Eliot in the middle of a long review essay on Robinson Jeffers provide a good example. Compared to Jeffers, he wrote, Eliot was a "sophomore writing down verses for the 'Lit.'" At the same time, even in these early writings, elements of Macdonald's later interest in the broader questions of culture and politics were apparent, despite his esoteric literary tastes. In an article on the modern theater in 1930 he wrote that the ebb of the theater was a response to the disruption of society and tradition: "Today the disorganization of society and the decay of tradition have had much worse effects on the theatre than on, say literature." Much more important to Macdonald, however, was the new and immensely exciting artistic medium—the film. For the

---

[11] *New York Times,* September 17, 1926. Norman Levy, "The Radicalization of Dwight Macdonald," unpublished Master's Thesis, University of Wisconsin, 1966.

[12] "Fred W. Dupee," Stanley J. Kunitz, ed., *Twentieth Century Authors,* 1st Supplement (New York: H. W. Wilson, 1955), p. 291.

Symposium, in 1933, he examined intelligently and at length the problems and accomplishments of a number of Hollywood directors, contrasting them with the Russian director Eisenstein, to find that they were skilled technicians, but little else. "The explanation," he concluded, "is simply that the Hollywood director has nothing to say."[13] Technical brilliance, compromised by intellectual insipidness, made Hollywood to Macdonald the symbol of a broken artistic promise, a symbol equivalent to the image he used later to characterize politicians as pragmatic automatons.

The devolution of Macdonald's journalistic career from the detached prose of his *Masquerade* and *Miscellany* essays to the tough, highly partisan articles that he wrote for the Trotskyist *New International* beginning in 1938 occurred primarily while he was a staff writer and editor for Henry Luce's *Fortune* magazine. After a brief encounter with the business world as a member of the executive training squad at Macy's department store in New York, and after refusing a job with the store, he joined the new Luce publication in March 1929. It was during this period, he relates, that he became increasingly skeptical about American capitalism: "My undergraduate suspicions were confirmed—the men running our capitalist system were narrow, uncultivated and commonplace. . . ." Written almost twenty years later, this remark nevertheless vividly catches an essential quality of Macdonald's radical commitment in the 1930s. He saw politics essentially as a function of culture, and he frequently judged the quality of politics by the intellectual power that either surrounded it or was absent. That the best minds did not operate the government or even influence it, that the American system of democracy was pragmatic, became painfully apparent to Macdonald, whose intellectual bent led him to read voluminously in the theoretical works of Marx, Lenin, Engels, Trotsky, Strachey, and Berle and Means during the late 1930s.

---

13 Dwight Macdonald, "Robinson Jeffers," *Miscellany,* I (September 1930), p. 22, "The Modern Theatre, An Inquest," *Miscellany,* I (June 1930), p. 7, and "Notes on Hollywood Directors," *Symposium,* IV (April 1933), p. 159.

The Trotskyist movement, and particularly Trotsky himself, appealed to Macdonald's half-aristocratic, half-anarchistic critique
of capitalism and his highly intellectualized radicalism. The
splinter group was attractive to him, above all, he relates, "because it was led by Trotsky, whose career showed that intellectuals, too, could make history."[14]

Macdonald's demand for intellectual and theoretical integrity
was stiffened during his years with *Fortune*. A writer for a Luce
publication, he recalls, was supposed to devote his talents entirely to his job on the magazine. Writing for other periodicals
was frowned upon. Circumscribed by this unwritten regulation,
the staff writers on the magazine fought to preserve their articles
and their ideas intact against the editors who altered them
to fit the conservative politics of the publisher. In the early days
of the Depression, a short time after Macdonald joined the staff,
Luce relaxed his grip on the direction of the magazine and, in
the face of economic catastrophe, allowed articles on broader
subjects than the success stories of entrepreneurs or the celebration of big business. But unlike their employer, many of the
writers were becoming leftists after 1932: "Their discoveries,
whatever their political views originally, made them increasingly left wing." Macdonald's description of his work for the
magazine before 1936 conveys the feeling that he and the other
staff writers had been successful in their attempt to revolutionize the direction of the magazine. On the other hand, his
most bitter remarks about the magazine, after he had left, concern his realization that he had been exploited as a writer and
that Luce had in the long run taken advantage of minor conces-
sions to liberals on the staff: "One of the sad things about being
a liberal on Fortune is that one comes to realize that one's vic-
tories merely enable Fortune to establish credit for editorial independence which may be drawn against later to justify some
piece of right-wing propagandizing." Specifically, Macdonald
broke with the magazine because the editors rewrote his three-

---

[14] Dwight Macdonald, *Memoirs of a Revolutionist: Essays in Political
Criticism* (New York: Farrar, Straus & Cudahy, 1957), p. 8, 15.

part article on U.S. Steel, apparently in compliance with the wishes of the company.[15] The depth of discouragement with his work at *Fortune* is revealed in his comparison of Luce's journalism to Hollywood motion pictures. To Macdonald, Hollywood was the epitome of the corruption of mass art, just as he had come to realize that Luce's publication represented the mindless adulteration of journalism.

While on *Fortune*, Macdonald revealed other qualities that help to explain his interest in Trotskyism. In an article on the Communist party and radical splinter groups he was obviously intrigued by the ability of the Soviet Bolshevik party to take power despite its comparatively small membership. He touched several times on the related point that the American Communists had made an impact on American society that was immensely disproportionate to their size. And even in 1934 he expressed some sympathy for Leon Trotsky. Macdonald's liking for theoretical politics, his belief in the relevance of small political groups, his fascination with the tempestuous intelligence of Trotsky, and his growing radical faith all contributed to making him an active member of the American Trotskyist movement from 1939 to 1941.[16] While writing voluminously for the *New International*, the theoretical journal of the movement, he reached a somewhat different community of intellectuals through his articles for the *Partisan Review*, which he helped edit from 1937 to 1943.

Macdonald, who had saved some money and whose wife had a trust fund, had few financial problems after he left *Fortune* in June 1936. He was now free to engage in political activity and journalism. From this time he drifted quickly to the left politically, although the Moscow Trials deflected him from a growing sympathy with the Communists. His Yale friend Fred Dupee introduced him to Rahv and Phillips, who by this time were deeply disenchanted with Stalinism and interested in re-

---

[15] Dwight Macdonald, "Fortune," *Nation*, CXLIV (May 8, 1937), pp. 528-530.
[16] Dwight Macdonald, "The Communist Party," *Fortune*, X (September 1934), p. 69. Macdonald and his wife took the party names James Joyce and Elsie Dinsmore when they joined the Trotskyist movement. Interview with Nancy Macdonald, December 30, 1966, New York.

viving the *Partisan Review* on a new basis. Together these men moved toward the orbit of the Trotskyists.

Fred Dupee, who joined with Macdonald and the former editors to make the *Partisan* an organ of anti-Stalinism and avant-garde culture, was born in Chicago in 1904. He first attended the University of Illinois, but then went to Yale, where he met Macdonald. Dupee relates that he shared with Macdonald an interest in twentieth-century literature and that T. S. Eliot, particularly, was a major influence on his intellectual development. Although he has since disparaged the work he did for the *Miscellany*, some of Dupee's writings at this time are a clue to his later literary tastes. He wrote of Dostoevski, for example, that "More than any novelist of his time, or perhaps any time, he is endowed with those virtues which we have come to admire, to demand in literature." Because during the early 1930s he was interested primarily in European literature, he shared few of the assumptions held by his proletarian contemporaries about a working-class renaissance. In 1932 he wrote to the *Symposium* that he had found it impossible to review *1919* by John Dos Passos, a book that had received wide acclaim in radical circles. In explaining his inability to deal with the work he said: "The book is loathsome to me—bogus modernism in technique—stale incidents—stale attitudes—hundreds of pages of dreary literal writing about lyric brawls and college friendships. . . ."[17]

Dupee was also different from many of his fellow writers in the 1930s because he spent the early years of the decade in Spain, North Africa, and Mexico. When he returned, the literary climate had shifted, largely to the left, and most of his friends had become radicals. Dupee's own involvement in radicalism was not merely a reaction to the Depression, the world political crisis, or the spreading influence of Marxism in literary circles, although each of these was important. He recounts that another factor, his early interest in Eliot, was influential, for it made the shift to Marxism easier. Eliot in his poetry and criticism had

---

[17] Fred Dupee, "Dostoevsky," *Miscellany*, I (July 1930), p. 11. Biographical material is from Kunitz, *Authors*, 1st Supplement, p. 291. Fred W. Dupee, "Letter to the Editor," *Symposium*, III (July 1932), p. 387.

made the literary world conscious of the meaning of modernity and tradition, just as Marx had seemed to do in politics. Convinced of the political integrity of the Communists, particularly after reading John Strachey's *Coming Struggle for Power*, he joined the party. His activities as a member were diverse. He became literary editor of the *New Masses*, but instead of working in the Greenwich Village branch of the party, as many other intellectuals did, he was assigned to do organizing in the New York waterfront district.[18]

While an editor of the *New Masses*, he met Rahv and Phillips, who had both been writing book reviews for the magazine since the *Partisan* suspended publication in late 1936. Dupee's stay with the *New Masses* was short, however, largely because he had never been interested in the proletarian literary movement and because his tastes were too cosmopolitan and nonpolitical for the magazine. Toward the end of his editorship it was apparent that he was also becoming discouraged with the movement politically, for he demanded the "freedom of expression" to criticize the Soviet Union and the Communist Party. The publication of André Gide's important but disparaging comments on his trip to the Soviet Union provoked the incident that caused Dupee to split with the party. He insisted that the French writer's work be treated with the respect due a major author, but more orthodox members of the magazine staff disagreed. After an argument he left the publication in June 1937.[19]

Dupee's friend James Burnham, another Chicago-born writer and a fairly recent convert to Trotskyism, convinced Dupee about this time to read the works of Trotsky. Burnham, who was a frequent contributor to the *Partisan Review* after its revival in 1937, studied at Princeton and Oxford and in 1929 began teaching philosophy at New York University. Like Dupee and Macdonald, Burnham was unimpressed by the proletarian cultural movement. The *Symposium*, which he edited with Philip

---

[18] Interview with Fred W. Dupee, September 22, 1965, New York. Dupee related the influence of Burnham on his thinking. See also "Radical Intellectuals," *Time*, XXXV (May 27, 1940), p. 96.
[19] Interview with Dupee.

Wheelwright from 1930 to 1933, did not belong to the radical magazine revival and absorbed only piecemeal the radicalism that had invaded the literary world. At first the publication was devoted entirely to theoretical discussion of culture, reflecting its attempt to be "a journal for philosophic discussion." Nevertheless, its pages were open to radicals, even proletarian critics such as William Phillips and Harold Rosenberg. Shortly before the magazine suspended publication in 1933, Burnham and Wheelwright published an editorial, "Thirteen Propositions," supporting the need for revolutionary change in America but disavowing the Communist party. This swerve toward radical politics, but in the direction of an independent Marxism, occurred at almost the same time as Rahv and Phillips were becoming part of the proletarian movement. Yet in 1937 the former editors of the *Partisan Review* had arrived at a theoretical position much like that of the *Symposium* in 1933.[20] Close to the *Partisan Review* theoretically, the *Symposium* was a predecessor of the later magazine because of a remarkable continuity of writers for the two publications. In the early 1930s Burnham, Dupee, Macdonald, Phillips, Harold Rosenberg, Sidney Hook, William Troy, and Paul Goodman all contributed to the *Symposium*; by 1937 three of this group were editors of the *Partisan Review*, Burnham and Hook were close political friends, and Troy, Rosenberg, and Goodman were frequent writers.

Mary McCarthy, the fifth editor of the revived *Partisan*, became associated with Trotskyism, as she relates it, not because of her interest in politics, but through a series of more or less accidental incidents. Although a Westerner—she was born in Seattle in 1912 and brought up there and in Minneapolis after her father died—she went to Vassar College and after her graduation moved quickly and easily into New York literary circles. At Vassar, she recalls, her vague thirst for royalism (since there was no royalty to satiate it) was replaced by belated interest in the *cause célèbres* of the Communists—the Sacco-Vanzetti and Tom Mooney cases. After college, she began reviewing books for the *New Republic* and, like many young writers of her day,

---

[20] "Thirteen Propositions," *Symposium*, IV (April 1933). See also James Burnham, "Marxism and Aesthetics," *Symposium*, IV (January 1935).

lived at the fringes of the radical literary movement. Impressed with the Communists, she could never bring herself to join the party. The hesitations that made her falter before this step were reinforced by her uneasiness about the movement, although her literary tastes and her disdain for party writers were probably her most important reasons for not joining.

Mary McCarthy's Trotskyism was at first more accidental than ideological. She relates that her name was added to a list of prominent intellectuals supporting the defense of Trotsky merely because she had defended his right to a fair hearing. These comments, made at a cocktail party, earned her a place on the Defense Committee, but, more important, they aroused many of her Communist acquaintances to advise her for her own good to end her support of Trotsky. Clearly, this was the wrong approach, for to her defending an unpopular cause was like standing up for an avant-garde artist. Thus a dislike for the popular, along with her doubts about the movement in the first place, initiated perhaps her most serious political commitment. Moreover, as a man of wit and intelligence, Trotsky was an immensely appealing figure.

Her politics never ran so deep and furiously as the politics of the other editors, even though she considered herself a Marxist. But like the others she borrowed elements from a conception of avant-garde literature. Suspicious of popular culture, she was naturally wary of a cause so widely esteemed as the Popular Front. Even her recollection of the early writing that she did for the *Partisan* adopts political jargon: "We automatically suspected any commercial success, any success d'estime; this, I fear, was my guiding critical principle. I remember how uneasy I felt when I decided that I *liked* Thornton Wilder's Our Town. Could this mean that there was something the matter with me? *Was I starting to sell out?*"[21]

While making a new set of literary friends, Rahv and Phillips lingered at the edge of the Communist movement for much of the year during which the *Partisan Review* was suspended,

---

[21] Mary McCarthy, "My Confession," *Encounter*, II (February 1954), pp. 44-49, 56, and Mary McCarthy, *Sights and Spectacles, 1937-1956* (New York: Farrar, Straus & Cudahy, 1956), p. x. My italics.

even while they were planning to revive the magazine on a new basis. Their independent influence within the Communist left had evaporated after the magazine failed, but they occasionally contributed reviews to the *New Masses* until the spring of 1937. In the course of these reviews and in several essays written jointly the two former editors drifted, almost reluctantly, into open disagreement with the orthodox left, although the final separation from the movement was delayed by their hesitation to make a final split. In part, this inertia resulted from their fear that the Communists dominated the New York publishing world and that, as dissident Marxists, they would have little opportunity to be heard. When the break finally came, it had been made inevitable by a long series of minor disagreements with the Communist literary movement.

Some of the reviews they wrote for the *New Masses* were orthodox. William Phillips's appraisal of Sherwood Anderson's *Kit Brandon,* for example, rehearsed an old criticism of bourgeois art by attacking the author's overdependence on Freud. For the new radical journal *Science and Society* Rahv and Phillips offered a discussion of "Some Aspects of Literary Criticism," but concentrated on the problem of a lack of a critical tradition. There was nothing controversial in their proposal that the function of art was to make "life significant by giving form, meaning, and continuity to human experience."[22]

It was primarily Philip Rahv, who had been closest to the Communists from the beginning, who drew the wrath of party officials. In a review of John Steinbeck's *Of Mice and Men,* under the inflammatory title "Insidious Innocence," Rahv dismissed the book as weak and sentimental; worse, it had few characteristics of a proletarian novel. Rahv's attack on the book from the sanctity of proletarianism flew straight in the face of the Popular Front, which was actively courting writers such as Steinbeck who might be sympathetic to the Communist program of antifascism. In the next issue of the magazine a letter to the editor took Rahv to task for his demand that literature be revolutionary, explaining that since Steinbeck's book would ob-

---

[22] Philip Rahv and William Phillips, "Some Aspects of Literary Criticism," *Science and Society,* I (Winter 1937), p. 218.

viously become a best seller, it was the duty of the *New Masses* to praise it. Rahv's reply to this was an angry defense of his views and a sharp attack on contemporary criticism, but it was too strong an attack to have been prompted by this letter alone. The argument, he wrote, illustrated the "vicious and debased literary standards that prevail in American literature."[23] There could be little mistake that Rahv's remarks were aimed at the Communists, and apparently it was this review and reply that most angered party literati. Despite disaffection and anger on both sides, Rahv's reviews continued to appear in the magazine until May 1937, although he made no attempt to broaden his condemnation of the degenerate standards of American literature or single out the factors that might have brought about this situation.

As the reviews of the editors of the *Partisan* appeared less frequently in the *New Masses* and then stopped, Rahv and Phillips's writing for the *Nation* became more important. Before he broke with the party, Rahv began to send his more serious work to non-Communist journals. His review of Ignazio Silone's *Bread and Wine*, printed in the *Nation*, indicated the beginnings of a new critical stance. Silone's controversial book, he wrote, "strikes into new areas, coming to grips with problems so modern that fiction has scarcely touched them." The novelist's unique contribution was to consider the sorts of moral values and problems that proletarian literature had avoided.[24] Rahv's feeling for this book was deeply personal. His writing about it exhibits a sense of discovery, because through the influence of authors such as Silone and Malraux he worked his way out of the maze of proletarian fiction to a new understanding of the avant-garde literature of Europe.

Rahv and Phillips finally and dramatically smashed the ties between themselves and their former literary comrades at the Second Writers' Congress, which was held in June 1937 in New York. From this schism they created a new literary center, conceived as a new generation, that would challenge the Commu-

---

[23] Philip Rahv, "Reply," *New Masses,* XXIII (March 30, 1957), p. 21.
[24] Philip Rahv, "The Revolutionary Consciousness," *Nation,* CXIV (April 10, 1937), p. 412.

nists in radical politics and literature. Aside from this split, the implications of which were not immediately apparent, the Writers' Congress was relatively successful. The League was solidified as a Popular Front organization, and minor opposition did not seem critical. More important were the numbers of important writers, including Ernest Hemingway and Archibald MacLeish, who addressed the gathering. Van Wyck Brooks, Erskine Caldwell, and Upton Sinclair among others were elected regional Vice Presidents. The Congress, to increase its influence, now pledged the League to spread itself geographically, as well as ideologically, for of the 353 delegates, 270 came from the New York area.

There was criticism from other sources, however. James T. Farrell greeted the Congress with an article in the *Saturday Review of Literature,* which questioned the accomplishments of the League in cultural matters and made a prophecy of doom for proletarian literature, a prediction largely borne out by the convention. The great hope of the first Congress, he wrote, the prediction of a great proletarian revival, had not been realized, and the promise of the young intellectuals was unfulfilled. Most of their recent work had been inconsequential, even though the conditions for the creation of good literature had not changed substantially. What Farrell observed was even more obvious at the Congress itself. Proletarian literature was scarcely discussed, and many of the novelists and poets who were spotlighted at the first Congress were upstaged by more important, established writers. Proletarian literature was pushed aside in favor of the artistic recreation of the Popular Front. Joseph Freeman's address summarized much of the thinking at the Congress on this issue: "Even if you begin as Hemingway began with a simple emotional desire to transmit experience, to find and convey the truth, if you follow the search for truth to its logical conclusions, you will end where Hemingway has ended now, in the People's Front."[25]

Experience for some, however, did not lead to the Popular Front, especially for Rahv, Phillips, Dupee, Macdonald, and

[25] Joseph Freeman, "Remarks," in *The Writer in a Changing World,* Henry Hart, ed. (New York: Equinox Cooperative Press, 1937), p. 235.

Mary McCarthy who invaded the Sunday morning "craft commission" meeting, chaired by Granville Hicks, an old enemy of
the *Partisan Review*. The planned format of the commission
was disrupted by a verbal scuffle, and the published notes of
the meeting relate that "the time was consumed in an attack
upon the congress by a small group of six which culminated in
Dwight Macdonald's remark that he was against the united
front and 'for Trotsky.' These attacks were, of course, attacked,
and the meeting seems to be typified by the answer of Mr. Hicks
to Joseph Freeman's question, 'Can't I say one word about
criticism?' 'No, Joe,' replied Mr. Hicks, 'that's one thing we can't
discuss.'"[26] The assault on the Congress centered around
Trotskyism rather than proletarian literature, which had to this
point been Rahv and Phillips's major interest. Until then there
had been no public indication that Rahv and Phillips were
Trotskyists, nor were they in any organizational sense. The direction of the battle with Communists was determined in the
main by Macdonald, but the relative unimportance of proletarianism also indicates that it was a dead issue to Rahv and
Phillips by the time of the Congress. Instead, Trotskyism, the
Moscow Trials, and the exclusiveness of the Popular Front had
become important.

Rahv and Phillips's alliance with Macdonald on any issue
was unforgivable to the Communists, for the former writer for
Fortune was quickly becoming a well-known sympathizer with
Trotskyism. In May 1937 he had replied to Malcolm Cowley's
defense of the Moscow Trials in the *New Republic*. After de-
flating Cowley's arguments he pledged that he would join the
Committee for the Defense of Trotsky. Even after the Congress
Macdonald continued his harassment of the League. In a letter
to the *Nation* he complained, with a certain ironic innocence,
that people of his political persuasion, opposed to fascism, were
not tolerated in the united front. The wide differences between
antifascists, he continued, posed the question of how much freedom the writer sympathetic to socialism should have in commenting on Soviet art and politics. Must the writer shift "al-

---

[26] *Ibid.*, p. 225.

legiance to liberal-democratic literature" because he accepted the People's Front?[27] Identified with Macdonald, Rahv and Phillips were now suddenly renegades from a movement that they had abandoned slowly and painfully.

Completely out of the movement after June, Rahv and Phillips continued to write for the *Nation* along with Dupee, McCarthy, and Macdonald, the group that would revive the *Partisan*. The Communists, however, still smarted from the loss of their former comrades, and their anger was increased by a number of reviews that Rahv wrote for the *Nation*. For one, he called Walter Duranty's favorable sketch of the Soviet Union cheap and as artificial as Hollywood. Later he scoffed at a Russian book on America, which seemed to him particularly naïve in its celebration of the American machine. Just as serious was his discussion of *Europa in Limbo,* by Robert Briffault. Although the book had been praised by Communist critics, Rahv wrote that the author in his didactic zeal emptied "all relations of their human content and turns them into angry sermons on class morality."[28]

Marshaled by Granville Hicks and Mike Gold, the Communists critics counterattacked in the pages of the *New Masses.* Hicks used the appearance of Horace Gregory's collection, *New Letters in America,* which included an essay by Rahv and Phillips, to belittle the two young writers. The former editors of the *Partisan,* he wrote condescendingly, had discovered consciousness and intelligence and were now recommending them to American writers. He lamented that this was the only critical work included in the volume: ". . . the essay is the mixture of platitude and pedantry to which we have become accustomed if not inured. Since Phillips and Rahv first entered upon their joint apprenticeship in criticism, their ideas have seemed not so much false as unimportant." Hicks's dismissal of the editors as insignificant was merely a rhetorical device for preoccupation with,

---

27 Dwight Macdonald, "Letter to the Editor," *Nation,* CXLIV (June 19, 1937), p. 714.
28 Philip Rahv, "Europa in Melodrama," *Nation* CXLV (October 2, 1937), p. 354. James Farrell relates that this article infuriated Rahv's former comrades.

literary Trotskyism and its adherents dominated the annual literary supplement to the *New Masses* published in early December. Mike Gold's "Notes on the Cultural Front" was devoted almost entirely to an attack on this aberration from the Popular Front. A current of anti-intellectualism, always near the surface in Gold's writing, emerged as the dominant tone of the article. His most impressive condemnation of Trotskyism was to say that it was politically isolated and therefore attractive to intellectuals. In reply to the claim that proletarian literature was dead, an argument that, he noted, had its origins in the bourgeois *Saturday Review of Literature*, he answered that the movement was not defunct nor was it devoid of talent. Authors were merely preparing themselves for new tasks.[29]

Gold's defense of proletarian writers was accompanied by a more direct attack by Hicks on the literary Trotskyists who were currently appearing in the pages of the *Nation*. Sometimes favorable to the Soviet Union, the magazine suffered from intellectual schizophrenia, he wrote, particularly in its book review section, edited by Margaret Marshall. Here such well-known opponents of Russia as Rahv, Phillips, Macdonald, and others were given important books to review. Rahv, "despite his general incompetence as a literary critic," he said, was responsible for a number of unkind words about the Soviets.[30]

These outbursts indicated that when it reappeared in December 1937 the *Partisan Review* would find hostility in the literary world, where, Rahv and Phillips even felt that the intellectual environment, particularly book and periodical publishing in New York, was dominated by the Communists. The first editorial of the new magazine was somewhat cautious on this point, but concentrated on the efforts it felt the Communists and their sympathizers would make to isolate the new magazine and thereby quarantine its intellectual contagion: "Every effort, in short, will be made to excommunicate the new generation so

---

[29] Granville Hicks, "Review and Comment," *New Masses*, XXV (September 28, 1937), p. 23. Gold, "Notes on the Cultural Front," *New Masses*, XXV (December 7, 1934), pp. 1-4.
[30] Granville Hicks, "A 'Nation' Divided," *New Masses*, XXV (December 7, 1937), p. 11.

that their writing and their politics may be regarded as making
up a kind of diabolic totality. . . ." The editors feared that if
such efforts were successful, few writers would be willing to
contribute to the new magazine. Even as late as 1938 Philip
Rahv, in discussing the influence of the Communists in publishing, concluded that they had penetrated the editorial staffs of
magazines, book review sections of newspapers, and the offices
of publishing houses. "The result," he stated, "has been that a
kind of unofficial censorship is now menacing the intellectual
freedom of those left-wing writers who are known to be opposed
to the bureaucratic dictatorship in Moscow and to its representatives abroad."[31]

When plans for the revived *Partisan* were made public in the
fall of 1937, the Communists began a campaign against the new
magazine that confirmed the editors' prediction that they might
be isolated from the entire literary left. Mike Gold, writing in
October in the *Daily Worker*, turned his best working-class prose
against Rahv and Phillips in a column titled "A Literary Snake
Sheds his Skin for Trotsky." The two editors, he wrote, "who
formed a sort of Potash and Perlmutter combination," had
turned to Trotskyism after they discovered that they would not
be allowed to lead the radical cultural movement. A week later
another article in the *Worker*, "Trotsky Schemes Exposed," recounted that Rahv and Dupee had both been expelled from the
Communist party for their collaboration with "known Trotsky-
ites" at the June Writers' Congress. These literary turncoats, the
editorial continued, planned to dishonor the old *Partisan Review*
by stealing its name and turning it into a counterrevolutionary
cultural publication. Then, covering its left flank, the article
swiped at the old *Partisan* for having opened its columns during 1936 to "known renegades." The following day in the *Worker*
V. J. Jerome cited the praise for the new magazine in bourgeois
circles that had appeared even before the first issue had been
published: "Who in the world of bourgeois letters," he wrote,

---

[31] Fred Dupee, "Editorial Statement," *Partisan Review*, IV (December
1937), p. 4, and Philip Rahv, "Where the News Ends," *New Leader*,
December 10, 1938, p. 8.

"had ever heard of or given a hoot for Rahv and Phillips, for example, amateur literati who mishandled a magazine that started out with all the auspices and forces to make it a success."[32]

Rahv and Phillips replied to a similar attack on them in the *New Masses* with a letter which the magazine, surprisingly, printed. The two editors maintained that they had always been opposed to the literary tendency represented by the *New Masses* and that the new *Partisan* was merely a continuation of the old publication that had fought sectarianism once from inside the movement, but now, by necessity, from without. The hostility of the *New Masses*, they observed, was also a projection of previous attitudes, and they cited the statement of Granville Hicks in 1934 when he had "called publicly for its liquidation."[33] The *New Masses*, however, insisted that the new magazine was fundamentally different and that old disagreements were those of allies who agreed, at least, on basic political principles. The new magazine was Trotskyite and therefore completely different.

This skirmish between the editors of the *Partisan* and Communist authorities is confused by the language of the argument and by the fact that each side, looking back at the earlier *Partisan Review*, saw a different magazine. But in another sense the clash is revealing because it demonstrated the concern of each group for the other. The break between these two representatives of the radical movement was neither smooth nor complete, nor did it indicate the end of the involvement by the *Partisan* editors with the implications of Communist politics. Significantly, each side adopted a conspiracy theory about the other, which from this point on was always present, but which at the moment worked merely to intensify the ideological difference between former partners in the left. When the new *Partisan Review* appeared in December 1937, it was under the disapproving glare of a significant element of the literary world; it was a revolutionist among rebels.

---

[32] *Daily Worker*, October 12, October 19, and October 20, 1937.
[33] William Phillips and Philip Rahv, "Letter to the Editor," *New Masses*, XXV (October 19, 1937), p. 21.

The bitterness between the *Partisan Review* and the left derived in part from a fundamental theoretical shift by Rahv and Phillips, which had been latent for a long time, but which emerged abruptly at the Writers' Congress and during the summer of 1937. The failure of proletarian culture illustrated to them two crucial shortcomings—more than shortcomings, almost a conspiracy—against the success of revolutionary literature. And the merger of the radical literary movement with political liberalism and early American literature through the League of American Writers, they felt, betrayed the reactionary character of Stalinism. The class struggle in America had been intensified; it had been Europeanized by the adoption of Marxism; American literature, however, remained cloistered by the artist's dependence on a pragmatic past. The anti-intellectualism of American letters, they felt, echoed in the work of regional poets like Carl Sandburg, and provincialism dampened the new culture. The attempt "to create literature in one country," they explained (consciously identifying America's literary efforts with Stalin's political theories), had resulted in the strengthening of the very tendency the movement had set out to explode. Only the Europeanization of American literature offered a resolution to the contradiction between the artist's revolutionary consciousness and the stagnation of American art.[34] Radical art must still meet revolutionary ideology, but in the consciousness on the part of the writer of the clash between the old and modern culture and in his ability to convey this moral struggle. Stripped of a dependence on a political movement, the artist, the intellectual, alone was the meeting place for radicalism in art and politics.

Another, ostensibly different, reason for the failure of proletarian literature offered by Rahv and Phillips actually reinforced their growing concentration on the intellectual rather than the proletarian as the radical man. The vulgarities of sectarianism, they came to believe, were due not merely to vestiges of an American tradition but were inherent "in the corruption and totalitarian essence of Stalinism itself." The direct mixture of

---

[34] Philip Rahv and William Phillips, "Literature in a Political Decade," *New Letters*, pp. 175-178.

politics and literature, the very basis of proletarian literature, had undermined the renaissance that was possible in the early 1930s.[35] When the *Partisan Review* was revived, Rahv, Phillips, and the other editors were convinced that the magazine must be based on the "conviction that literature in our period should be free of all factional dependence." Although there was some timidity to say so, the two editors had concluded that "proletarian literature is the literature of a party disguised as the literature of a class."[36]

Separation of politics from literature became the cornerstone of the writing that characterized the new *Partisan;* yet this separation was not an absolute break, for Rahv and Phillips, especially, thought of literature as an element caught in the complex issues of culture and of the artist as an intellectual endowed with special social characteristics and behavior. By reflecting the problems of the culture through the consciousness of the intellectual, Rahv and Phillips developed a notion that was implicit in earlier essays. The estrangement of the artist from society, his special psychological problems, the difficulty of living two lives, citizen and artist, became their chief concerns. The modulation, as Lionel Trilling has called it, between radical politics and avant-garde art occurred in the consciousness of the intellectual. Practical politics and art were entirely divorced, but literature and politics in a philosophic sense, as a moral stance toward the social context, remained intimate. The estrangement of the intellectual was the justification for his withdrawal from real politics, but it was also an explanation for his ability to rise above the mundane and reunite art and politics into the vision of a revolutionary culture. The alienated man became the radical man. Trotsky, isolated in Mexico but astoundingly aware and perceptive of problems in the Soviet Union, a brilliant social commentator, was a man to be admired, to be emulated, but perhaps not to be followed. By

---

[35] Rahv and Phillips, "In Retrospect," *Partisan Review Reader,* p. 681. See also William Phillips, "Art and Society," *Art Front,* III, Nos. 3 and 4 (1937), pp. 23-24.

[36] Dupee, "Editorial Statement," *Partisan Review,* IV (December 1937), p. 3, and Philip Rahv, "Proletarian Literature; A Political Autopsy," *Southern Review,* IV (Winter 1940), p. 625.

1937 Rahv and Phillips had arrived at an intellectual position that was significantly like that of Randolph Bourne twenty years before. Cultural change could be initiated by an international community of intellectuals, and the vanguard of that community would be the Trotskyist intellectuals whom Rahv and Phillips published in their revived magazine.

The new *Partisan Review* like its predecessor was of a divided mind. The grouping of Phillips and Rahv with Macdonald and Dupee was never entirely without friction, nor did the interests or intellectual styles of the new editors interlock precisely. The political juncture of Macdonald with the former editors was the meeting of two intellectual paths, coming from and ultimately leading in different directions. The conception of the new magazine was not precise, nor did it result from one single set of assumptions. Two distinct views of the magazine, superimposed one upon the other, created a new dimension, and the different commitments of the editors generated the excitement that was typical of the periodical in the following years. Whereas Macdonald enthusiastically plunged into the politics of the Trotskyist movement, Rahv and Phillips continued to deepen and purify their devotion to literary criticism. The result was a tenuous but dramatic merging of two images, the alienated intellectual and the political activist, attached to a profound but minute and politically irrelevant movement.

Chapter 6

Part I   The Intellectual
as Revolutionary

To speak of modern literature is to speak of
that peculiar social grouping, the intelligentsia,
to whom it belongs.

Philip Rahv, 1939

To be at odds with his times—there lies the
raison d'étre of the artist.

André Gide, *Partisan Review*, 1939

The evolution of the *Partisan Review* from a minor literary and
political journal, notable mainly for its repudiation of the Communist cultural movement, to its postwar eminence among intellectual periodicals occurred within the uncertain context of
world conflagration when civilization itself seemed near extinction and the culture of the fittest, the most powerful, threatened
to prevail. From the obscurity of a "new generation," the magazine developed the complicated relations with other intellectuals that transformed it into a cultural center, elevating it to
leadership among an important body of intellectuals. Commenting on the role to which the magazine aspired, William Phillips
wrote in the 1940s: "For many of its readers who are scattered
all over the country it has served as a focal point in their attempts to orient themselves in the world of modern art and
politics. Thus the magazine has come to possess the significance

188

and authority of a stable cultural institution."[1] Even more as-
sertively, editors Rahv and Phillips in 1953 described the ideal
Partisan reader. In effect they demanded that the reader subscribe to a broad program of politics and art: he must be interested in new fiction, art, and criticism, must be knowledge-
able of the fate of modern society (including the menace of
Communism and "nativist" demagogues like McCarthy), and
must feel "above all that what happens in literature and the
arts has a direct effect on the quality of his own life."[2] The
authority of these statements rests on the accomplishments of
the period from 1937 to the end of the war. Their explanation
is complex, sometimes contradictory, but always an integral part
of the cultural history of the United States during those years.
When Rahv and Phillips commented in 1944 that the magazine
had from the first "lived the life of its times," they were reflecting upon the intellectual buoyancy of the publication and
their own ability to rise above dangerous crests of thought or
ride with the main current.

In its ascendancy, the *Partisan* was in no sense the dominant
cultural organ of its times, much as its detractors might accuse
the editors of aspiring to be academicians, for American culture is too complex in dimension, too variegated to permit such
a development. But the magazine was a center in perhaps the
most meaningful sense—as a periodical to which a group of
intellectuals contributed their most important work, where
ideas were expressed first, and where the problems that confronted intellectuals in literature and politics were examined. In
1947 Philip Rahv noted this phenomenon in a letter to Arthur
Schlesinger, Jr. whose article on socialism from the *Partisan*
was being passed around the State Department: "I am very
pleased to hear of the response to your piece in Washington.
One thing that one could say about Partisan Review is that
the pieces in it do get read by the right people."[3]

---

[1] William Phillips, "A Statement and a Perspectus," *Partisan Review*
Papers, Rutgers University, New Brunswick, New Jersey. Hereafter cited
as *Partisan* MSS.

[2] William Phillips and Philip Rahv, eds., *The New Partisan Reader* (New
York: Harcourt, Brace, 1953), p. vi.

[3] Philip Rahv to Arthur M. Schlesinger, Jr., September 4, 1947, *Partisan*
MSS.

As any institution, the *Partisan* exhibited patterns of thought and certain consistent attitudes toward culture and politics, even if it did not develop precisely a cogent, recognizable style. From a rebellious offshoot of Communist literature to a stable cultural institution was an enormous distance negotiated with great difficulty. One of the most important factors that enabled it to do so was the continuity of editors (Rahv and Phillips remained throughout the period, and Macdonald left the magazine in 1943 after six years), which enabled the magazine to develop an inner life of its own.[4] Moreover, the constant deliberation over two problems defined in the early 1930s, called up recurring questions that disturbed other artists and writers. Concern for the role of the intelligentsia in America and for what was defined as the intelligentsia's greatest mistake, its brief affair with Stalinism, were transfixed into permanent patterns of thought.

The radicalism of the magazine was an immense advantage to its growth as an institution, and whether or not the *Partisan* accurately gauged the causes for this phenomenon, it justly believed that the Communism of the intellectuals was not an historical quirk, a blind reaction to the economic depression, but at base an expression of profound malaise about American culture and society. Its anti-Communism, given form at first through Trotskyism and a reassertion of Marxian purity, was complicated by a restatement of the fundamental dichotomy between the intellectual and society. This estrangement, the editors at first feared, would be overcome only at severe cost, as in Russia where intellectual life was regulated by strict political controls and art was synonymous with politics, or quite possibly even as in America where the pressure of onrushing war threatened to force allegiance to a society whose values were determined by nationalism. But in another way, anti-Communism was crucial, for no magazine of whatever stature in the United

---

[4] Mary McCarthy was an editor for only three issues, although she continued to contribute a "Theatre Chronicle" with some regularity. Art critic George L. K. Morris, the fifth editor, had little to do with political and literary issues, his main interest being painting. Morris did, however, provide much of the financing of the magazine until 1943. Rahv estimates that this was about $3000 a year. Interview with Philip Rahv.

States could have remained Communist and emerged from World War II still clinging to the pulse of the culture. The postwar obsession with Communism characteristic of an important segment of American intellectuals gave credence to the statements of those who had once been Communists. It was felt that one's experience of ideological and spiritual darkness was a qualification to speak of the effects and the larger meanings of the political underworld. Thus the *Partisan Review* attained some importance solely by virtue of its second birth in 1937. The editors of the magazine concluded that the Communist experience of the writer had fed upon his estrangement from society: his political compromise reflected his personal dilemma. The vulgarities he committed against art in the name of revolution indicated that his choice of politics was wrong and that his politics must take a new form suited to his own sense of alienation. The radicalism of the *Partisan,* defined first by its split with the Communist movement, demanded no sacrifice of the role of artist or intellectual, no compromise with revolutionary necessity. On the contrary, this new radicalism was expressed in terms of the peculiar problems of the intellectual.

In becoming a cultural center, the *Partisan Review* also acquired many of the characteristics of a new Bohemia. In its concern for the special problems of the writer and artist it proposed a fundamental tie between art and the general culture; it promoted the influx of ideas from Europe; above all, it asserted the notion of a community of intellectuals who shared certain broad interests in culture and politics. Premised upon its quarrel with Communism and upon the proposition that the intellectual was cut off from middle-class society, it organized a kind of "international" of intellectuals, devoted to the preservation of avant-garde culture. It felt confident enough, in fact, to move among European writers and to claim that in the judgment of such people "Partisan Review is broadly expressive of the higher levels of American culture as the Nouvelle Revue Française was expressive of French culture in the nineteen-twenties and thirties."[5]

---

[5] Phillips, "A Statement," p. 3.

At the same time that the *Partisan* editors wrote manifestos and theoretical discussions of the problems of the modern intellectual and explored the politics of Trotskyism and Communism, they managed to attract a number of important young authors, both American and European. During the years after the revival they published such writers as Auden and Robert Lowell with whom they disagreed on political or religious issues. Stories by Delmore Schwartz, Katherine Anne Porter, and Lionel Trilling were matched with the writing of Europeans, particularly Kafka, Silone, and Victor Serge. In poetry also the magazine leaned to the avant-garde, publishing Elizabeth Bishop, Allen Tate, Gertrude Stein, and others. By 1940 the *Partisan* was successful enough, and its stand for twentieth-century literature clear enough, for T. S. Eliot to choose it to print his poem "East Coker" and, in 1941, the "Dry Salvages," two of the *Four Quartets*. The various forms of fiction printed by the magazine share little in common aside from a rather consistent high quality, but as the magazine's critical writing became more involved with such literary innovators of the twentieth century as Eliot, Kafka, Joyce, Proust, Yeats, and others—as the editors turned back to the era of the symbolists, the surrealists, and the exiles—the poetry and prose that they printed was less likely to belong to the genre of American writing exemplified by Frost, Steinbeck, or Sandburg. Farrell and Dos Passos, who were both political friends of the *Partisan* (Farrell wrote frequent essays and reviews), rarely published their fiction in the magazine after its first few issues. Marxist realism, even the naturalism so evident in the early magazine, was banished and replaced by writing that corresponded more to that printed in the *Dial* during the 1920s. The rediscovery of the avant-garde was accompanied by a sharp swerve away from realism, and by an exaggeration of the gulf between the two styles. The direction of these new literary concerns was indicated even in the first issue in December 1937, when Mary McCarthy's first "Theatre Chronicle" attacked Maxwell Anderson with the worst epithets of the avant-garde. He was a rustic; he was popular: "Mr. Anderson's mind is like a musty, middle-western law-office of thirty years ago, full of heterogeneous books, on the law, on American history, on philosophy, and the morocco-bound complete works of William Shakespeare."[6]

Although the editors of the *Partisan Review* printed a number of authors with whom they disagreed on matters other than literature, these disagreements tended to be in one direction, for the magazine's anti-Communism generally excluded pro-Soviet writers just as its tastes excluded naturalism. This exclusivity did not always result from their own censorship, but rather from the facts surrounding the magazine's revival. A campaign to discourage pro-Communist authors from printing in the *Partisan* had been mounted by the Communists even before the magazine first appeared. In one case, at least, this was successful. In an advance notice the *Partisan* announced that William Carlos Williams had agreed to be a contributor, but the *New Masses* countered that Williams had actually refused to let his writing appear in the new periodical. In a letter to the *Partisan* Williams confirmed what the *New Masses* had said, explaining that he had no special interest either in their magazine or in the *New Masses,* but that he had made a choice in favor of the latter "since I found the *New Masses* violently opposed to you on political grounds, so much so that they refused to print me if I remained a contributor to *Partisan Review.* . . ."[7] Thus the political antipathy between the *Partisan* and the Communists, their vastly different literary tastes, and the fact that such differences were important to intellectuals, helped exclude pro-Communists from the new magazine.

As it reassessed the major aesthetic movements of the twentieth century, the *Partisan Review* turned back to Paris, the old center of the avant-garde, and to the culture that had been produced in that city. The war threat to France and its fall to Germany in 1940 took on special meaning aside from any military or political significance. Clement Greenberg, who became an

---

[6] Significantly, the *Partisan* printed an article by Marianne Moore, "The *Dial*: A Retrospect," *Partisan Review,* IX (February 1942). In 1938 John Dos Passos wrote a long series of personal letters from Spain to the *Partisan* editors. Partisan MSS. Mary McCarthy, "Theatre Chronicle," *Partisan Review,* IV (December 1937), p. 56.

[7] William Carlos Williams to the editors, November 16, 1937. Williams had agreed to submit a poem, September 8, 1937. *Partisan* MSS.

editor of the magazine for a short time beginning in 1941 (after
Fred Dupee left for a position at Columbia University), expressed the desperate mode of thinking that viewed the avant-
garde—socialism even—as a conservative force, capable merely
of preserving the culture whose capital had been Paris. "Today," he wrote in late 1939, "we look to socialism *simply* for the
preservation of whatever living culture we have right now."
The magazine's vicarious participation in the fate of European
writers caught before the forces that were ransacking the cultural centers of the past reached its height at the start of the
war. In the summer of 1940 the magazine, particularly Dwight
Macdonald and Nancy Macdonald who was then business man-
ager, organized the *Partisan Review* Fund for European Writers
and Artists to collect money to aid the "hundreds of anti-fascist
writers in Europe" who were trying to escape the war and find
asylum in the United States. Among those helped by the fund
was Victor Serge.[8] Personal identification with European writers
and artists grew out of the *Partisan's* commitment to international culture, its rejection of what it argued was American nationalism, and its assumption of the burden of preserving international culture, and all involved the magazine even further
in the most important issues confronting the intellectual, thus
making it a center for the discussion of these issues.

The fall of France was in a sense the final step in the rise
of New York as a competing cultural center. Harold Rosenberg's
essay in the autumn of 1940, which explored the implications
of the capture of Paris by the Nazis, lamented its death as an
international city. Paris had once been the "Holy Place of culture"; but for a decade "the whole of civilization has been
sinking down, lowering Paris steadily toward the soil of
France. Until its restoration as the capital of a nation was completed by the tanks of the Germans."[9] The decline of international culture continued to be a major preoccupation of the
Partisan Review and heightened the responsibility the editors

[8] Clement Greenberg, "Avant-Garde and Kitsch," *Partisan Review*, IV
(Fall 1939), p. 49; interview with Dwight Macdonald, and interview with
Nancy Macdonald.
[9] Harold Rosenberg, "On the Fall of Paris," *Partisan Review*, VII (November-December 1940), p. 448.

felt for the fate of civilization. Early in 1941 the magazine printed a list of prominent European intellectuals, their locations, their political allegiances, and their reactions to the war. "As the war continues," the editors wrote, "reshaping the structure of European society, scattering writers and artists throughout the world, it seems useful to try and set down the most recent available information on what has happened to the more significant representatives of European culture." Even well into the war this interest in European writers did not dim, and the *Partisan* continued to print articles, letters, and comments on the cultural life of France and the life of exiled writers.

It was not only the *Partisan Review* that noted a shift in the balance of international culture. In 1939 Malcolm Cowley remarked in a speech before the League of American Writers that New York was basically a European city and that international culture was beginning to flourish there as it had flourished in Paris. "Every world city," he said, "is more or less cut off from its own country. In New York I think that is especially true."[10] To Cowley, the coming of the war and the flight of European writers to sanctuary in the United States recalled the international community of writers that invaded Paris during the 1920s.

New York did not only represent the most important commerical center of American culture. It was also a port to the East, with much traffic in European literary and social movements and receptive to the ideas of Old World culture. Moreover, it was the center of American radicalism; this, too, was seen by the editors as a tie to Europe. When Philip Rahv was criticized for writing that "The literary left-wing movement is particularly native to New York, for its underlying philosophy, Marxism, is a product of European thought," the editors replied that this was a fact of intellectual life obvious to the point of banality.[11]

---

[10] Malcolm Cowley, "Writers in Exile," Speech before the Writers-in-Exile-Session of the League of American Writers, June 4, 1939. LAW MSS. See also the "Exiled Writers Issue," *Saturday Review of Literature*, XXII (October 19, 1940).

[11] Unpublished essay by Philip Rahv incorrectly quoted in the *New Masses* and corrected by the *Partisan: Partisan Review*, IV (December 1937), p. 74.

The importance to the magazine of its New York setting was revealed from the results of a questionnaire sent out to subscribers in 1941. It was found that more than 35 per cent of the magazine's subscribers lived in New York City and more than one half were spread out over the East Coast. This preponderance of New York readers matched the ties of the magazine to the cultural institutions of that city. Moreover, many of the contributors (like the readers) were employed in publishing or teaching in the immediate area. During the period from 1937 to 1943 some of the most important political articles, aside from the essays by the editors, were written by Sidney Hook and James Burnham, both of New York University. The *Partisan's* informal ties to the faculty of New York's other leading educational institution, Columbia University, were even stronger, for it provided the greatest number of regular contributors, including Lionel Trilling, F. W. Dupee, Meyer Schapiro, Ernest Nagel, Richard Chase, and Louis Hacker, among them some of the leading Trotskyist intellectuals. An important indication of the potential influence of the magazine revealed also by the questionnaire was the youth of its subscribers. In 1941 more than one-half the regular readers were in their twenties, some 25 per cent in their thirties, and only about 17 per cent over forty. The results of the survey, which must have been gratifying to the editors, revealed that the *Partisan Review* was, insofar as it could be determined, a magazine read by young intellectuals located primarily in New York and on the East Coast.

In early 1940 the editors, recognizing the implications of the changes that they had made in the *Partisan Review,* cast about for a new name. Because of "many misunderstandings of the magazine's purpose and character," they sought to rename their periodical *The Forties.* The attempt was only halfhearted, however, for after a deluge of complaints by readers the old name was retained. The proposed change did not mean that the *Partisan* would abandon politics (when the *Partisan* was tied to the Communist party, it had completely avoided political comment), nor that it would suddenly be devoted to purely literary issues (as a Reed Club publication, it was almost exclusively literary). The proposal indicated, on the one hand, that the magazine sought to avoid entangling alliances with political parties, to bury its Communist past. On the other hand, it intended to commit itself more completely to an exploration of the problems of the intellectual and the fate of culture. Of course, not all efforts of the magazine were consciously aligned with this larger purpose of creating an intellectual center. For example, in 1940 the editors sent free copies of the magazine to Sing Sing prison. Nor did all the editors agree precisely on the function of the journal. But in general the magazine was directed to the radical intellectual community of New York.

The political independence of the magazine was a strong factor in its rise to influence among intellectuals who after 1937 were rapidly becoming discouraged with Communism. The first issue of the magazine in December 1937 declared "unequivocal independence" and disclaimed "obligation to any organized political expression." Because of the initial attacks on it by the Communist press, the magazine was at first wary about making any strong political statements, and since William Carlos Williams among others had refused to publish in the *Partisan,* there was a certain hesitancy to write anything too openly hostile to the Soviets. Moreover, some friends of the new magazine advised a cautious policy. This reticence showed up in the question of whether or not to publish a section of André Gide's "After-Thoughts on the Soviet Union." In November 1937 Rahv wrote to Gide that the magazine had decided not to publish his article. Commenting on the Communist campaign to isolate the *Partisan,* he noted that "unfortunately, a large and fairly influential section of the American intelligentsia supports the Party in its campaign and refuses to write for us."[12] The editorial board split over this decision not to print Gide, but by the second issue of the magazine those who favored publication of the article had prevailed. In early 1938 the editors again wrote to the French author, explaining that they had reconsidered their original stand: they would now publish the article, since

---

[12] Edmund Wilson to Fred Dupee, December 2, 1937, *Partisan* MSS. Dupee and Macdonald both relate that they wanted to print Gide, but that Rahv and Phillips were at first reluctant. Macdonald and Dupee interviews. Philip Rahv to André Gide, November 25, 1937, *Partisan* MSS.

questions of the political effect of the work had been carefully considered and, in spite of the anger of the Communists, it was felt the piece should appear. Gide's article itself was a testimony of personal disillusionment more than it was a systematic analysis of the faults of the Soviet Union. But what must have been most irksome to the Communists was the French author's disgust at the tactics used to woo him during his visit: the best rooms, the formal dinners, private railroad cars; all of the ostentatious efforts to please him were repulsive and "conjured up the idea of privileges, of difference, where I thought to find equality."[13]

The *Partisan's* political inhibitions won it no friends among the Communist literati, who were angered at any opposition to the Soviets. On the other hand, its reticence inspired some critical remarks from the Trotskyists. The American members of the Fourth International commended the magazine's break with the Communists, which they saw as a hopeful sign, but they argued for a much more aggressive stand against the Stalinists. It seemed to them that the *Partisan's* separation of politics and art was a wise theoretical and tactical position up to a point, but not to the extremes to which the magazine proposed to carry it. The relation of art and politics should neither be "one of despotism and servile dependence, as the Stalinists demand, nor one of toplofty indifference, and alienation as the Partisan Reviewers think necessary."[14] Already the Trotskyists were suspicious of the *Partisan Review* and for reasons that from their point of view correctly foreshadowed the future. But for the time being they were also highly pleased at the defection of an important segment of intellectuals from the Communist literary movement and with their informal ties to the Fourth International.

From another corner of the radical movement, Malcolm Cowley took sides, if somewhat belatedly, against the new magazine in the pages of the respectable *New Republic*. Both

---

[13] Letter (no author) to Gide, January 6, 1938, *Partisan* MSS. André Gide, "Second Thoughts on the USSR," *Partisan Review,* IV (January 1938), p. 24.
[14] "Partisan Review," *Socialist Appeal,* December 4, 1937.

the *Partisan*'s anti-Stalinist politics and the poetry that it printed were unfortunate, he wrote. The editors' struggle with the Communist party press had deranged their values and forced them to commit the very literary crimes charged against their opponents. Rahv and Phillips's reply was a sharp defense of their magazine. The *Partisan*, they claimed, had never attempted to be nonpolitical, for its revival was premised in part upon the necessity of fighting the Communist influence in culture. Moreover, the magazine did not print only established writers as Cowley had charged. Cowley's retort, as critical as his first article had been, was a more thoughtful attack on the direction of the new magazine. Politics to the *Partisan*, he wrote, meant a retreat from practical life into a "red ivory tower," an esoteric world corresponding to the "white ivory tower of the Symbolists." Cowley and the Trotskyists agreed at least on one point: the politics of the new magazine was too detached from meaningful struggle. One could not live by "revolutionary faith alone."[15]

Because of its sensitivity to critics of its revolutionary credentials, the *Partisan* also felt it necessary to answer comments in *Poetry* magazine to the effect that the revised magazine was not revolutionary. On the contrary, wrote the editors, the *Partisan Review* was committed to revolution, but "as for the role of literature in the revolutionary process, we are frankly skeptical of the old imperatives."[16] This series of attacks and rebuttals grew out of one of the guiding premises of the magazine which contradicted the major assumption of radical writers of the 1930s. By rejecting the notion that literature and politics were functionally related and that literature must reflect the political imperatives of the moment, the *Partisan* brought upon itself a flurry of criticism from more orthodox leftists.

As the criticisms of the new magazine by the Fourth Internationalists suggested, political ties of the *Partisan Review* to the Trotskyist movement were vague. Trotsky himself was dubious

---

[15] The editor of the *Partisan* tried to get Edmund Wilson to reply to Cowley publicly, but he only sent Cowley a private letter: Dwight Macdonald to Edmund Wilson, November, 1941?, *Partisan* MSS, and Malcolm Cowley, "Red Ivory Tower," *New Republic*, XCVII (November 9, 1938), p. 22.

[16] "Riposts," *Partisan Review*, IV (February 1938), p. 62.

about the magazine, particularly because of its failure to strike
more sharply at the Communists. Quite understandably, he declined to contribute to the publication when the editors invited
him to participate in a symposium, "What Is Alive and What Is
Dead in Marxism?" In a letter to Rahv in the summer of 1938
he spoke of that necessary element of "fanaticism" that must be
adopted to make an effective struggle against Stalinism.[17] Until
the summer of 1938 Trotsky had been skeptical of the new
magazine. He had been unwilling to authenticate it by contributing any of his own writings and thus refused a number of
invitations from the editors to send them articles and reviews.
For one brief moment the magazine did move closer to the
Fourth International—when it printed a manifesto, "Toward a
Free Revolutionary Art," coauthored by Trotsky, under the signatures of André Breton and Diego Rivera in 1938. Attacking
fascism and the degeneracy of the Soviet regime, the manifesto
called for the overthrow of the Soviet bureaucracy, for the complete freedom of the artist, and for the creation of an International Federation of Independent Revolutionary Art. The publication of a letter on revolutionary art written by Trotsky and
solicited by the editors was another sign of the temporary in-
timacy between the *Partisan* and the Trotskyists. "Art and Politics," was a biting attack on the Soviet Union and on the art of
Stalinism which, he wrote, symbolized the decline of the proletarian revolution. So close an ally of truth was each piece of
art that it contained an element of protest against reality:
"Every new tendency in art has begun with rebellion."[18]

Close ties to the Fourth International were only brief. The attempt of Breton, who had broken with the Communists in 1935,
to create a new federation of radical artists under the aegis of
the Trotskyist movement was a failure. After 1938 the *Partisan*
drifted slowly from its insecure mooring in the Fourth International; despite Macdonald's membership in the American party
beginning in 1939, Rahv and Phillips at least never accepted

[17] Isaac Deutscher, *The Prophet Outcast, Trotsky: 1929-1940* (London:
Oxford University Press, 1963), pp. 431-432, 480.
[18] Philip Rahv to Edmund Wilson, August 31, 1938, *Partisan* MSS, and
Leon Trotsky, "Art and Politics," *Partisan Review*, V (August-September
1938), p. 3.

all of Trotskyism, even in their most sanguine moments. There was a meaning to the activity of 1938 which went beyond politics, however. The conjunction of Breton, Trotsky, and the *Partisan Review* implied much more than an alliance against Stalinism. The *Partisan's* interest in Breton, who symbolized a major literary tradition from the previous decade, pointed to its rediscovery of avant-garde art of the 1920s and its belief that much of that art was radical in form and in content.

The organization of a League for Cultural Freedom and Socialism in June 1939, with Macdonald as acting secretary, was another, later attempt to organize intellectuals into a political grouping under the ideological guidance of Trotskyism. The statement of the league, printed in the *Partisan*, attacked fascism and Communism, but it also cited pressures in America by governmental and private institutions that sought to bend the intellectual to a new form of nationalism, risking regimentation and the debasement of the arts. The organization pledged itself to complete freedom of expression, opposition to fascist tendencies in America, and the liberation of culture through the liberation of the working class. The Communists reacted to this and other attacks on them with a manifesto of their own and gathered the signatures of 400 American writers beneath the statement that the Soviet Union was in reality a bulwark of democracy. The answer of Macdonald's league, again printed in the *Partisan*, was a fresh attack on war preparation in the United States, but it was also a challenge to the League of American Writers to repudiate Soviet foreign policy that had culminated in the Nazi-Soviet pact of 1939.[19]

A competing and ultimately more important organization of intellectuals than Macdonald's league was also founded in the early summer of 1939, largely through the efforts of Sidney Hook, with John Dewey as chairman. This Committee for Cultural Freedom, in one sense a continuation of the Dewey Commission on the Moscow Trials, announced its presence in manifestos in the *New Republic* and the *American Mercury*. It took no stand for revolution or socialism, but directed its attention solely to

---

[19] "Manifesto," *Partisan Review*, VI (Fall 1939), pp. 125-126. Rahv, Phillips, Dupee, and Macdonald signed, among others.

forces of totalitarianism abroad—fascism and Communism—
and their manifestations in America. Totalitarianism, they proclaimed, was already enthroned in Germany, Italy, Russia, Japan,
and Spain and now threatened the intellectual freedom of
America. The most significant aspect of the committee's statement was the equation of Germany with Russia. Because of
this stand, it received hostile notice in the *New Republic* and
the *Nation,* an indication of the bitter feelings aroused over the
issue of the Soviet Union. The *New Republic* was scornful of the
group for its supposed Trotskyism, for tying Russia to Germany,
and for failing to take note of forces in America working to
destroy intellectual freedom. John Dewey's answer in the next
issue correctly pointed out that the *New Republic* had distorted
the Committee's position. But the magazine defended itself:
Communists, after all, were not as bad as fascists.[20]

The *Nation's* response was milder, but in many ways more interesting. Editor Freda Kirchwey, in an article entitled "Red
Totalitarianism," wrote that Communists might be guilty of
duplicity and have many other serious faults, but they could
not be opposed in the same manner as fascists. The meaning of
the formation of the Committee, she continued, was essentially
political, despite its disavowal of politics, because of the role
played by Sidney Hook, whom she identified as a writer for the
Partisan Review. Hook's replies to the *Nation* and to the *New
York Times,* which had written that the Committee had been
formed to oppose other organizations that did not take a stand
against the Soviet Union, were essentially the same: the Committee merely opposed totalitarianism wherever it appeared.[21]
But whatever Hook's disclaimer, the Committee, in fact, was
concerned mainly with Communism.

The identification of the Committee for Cultural Freedom
with *Partisan Review* through Sidney Hook and of the League

---

[20] *New Republic,* XCIX (May 31, 1939), pp. 89-90, and John Dewey,
"Letter to the Editor," *New Republic,* XCIX (June 14, 1939), pp. 161-
162.
[21] Sidney Hook, Letter to the Editor, *Nation,* CXLVIII (June 17, 1939),
p. 710. Sidney Hook, Letter to the Editor, *New York Times,* May 17,
1939. A Committee for Cultural Freedom eventually became the publishers of the *Partisan,* but it was not the same committee.

for Cultural Freedom and Socialism through Macdonald reflected two different and competing tendencies in the editorial
policy of the magazine even as early as 1939. The Dewey-Hook
organization was essentially nonradical, and its most important
stand, since almost everyone was opposed to Nazism, was its
repudiation of the Communists. Macdonald's group, however,
still subscribed to Marxism and revolutionary change. Since it
was involved with both groups, the *Partisan Review* was in a
position to lead an important segment of radical intellectuals in
a direction in which they were in fact already headed—toward
a repudiation of Communism and the Soviet Union—and, significantly, the magazine offered two styles of anti-Stalinism,
revolutionary and nonrevolutionary.

From the first days of its revival the magazine clearly recognized the primary political issue of the day for the intellectual
—not Spain as some argued, not even the Moscow Trials, but
the sojourn of writers and artists in the American Communist
movement. In 1937 it was far ahead of the major group of intellectuals that would eventually reject Communism; thus it
achieved a reputation for having been right first. The mixture
of nonrevolutionary anti-Communism and Trotskyism, which
ultimately proved to be incompatible, created explosive issues
between editors Rahv, Phillips, and Macdonald, which were
aggravated by the intrusion of the war and the necessity to deal
with more immediate priorities. But until 1943 the editors clung
tenaciously to the magazine as a forum for compromising their
growing cultural and political disputes.

From its first issue the magazine assumed the characteristics
that would contribute to its rise as a cultural center and an intellectual meeting ground for the discussion of politics and
literature. Like the old *Masses* in 1912, it combined art and politics in a new and influential way; like the *Seven Arts* it pledged
itself to an international community of intellectuals. But unlike
its two predecessors, it was devoted to the rediscovery of twentieth-century literature. It preached a new politics that rejected
many assumptions of the 1930s but remained caught up in the
language of that decade. When Clement Greenberg wrote of
the two important factors that had contributed to a general little

magazine renaissance in the early 1940s, his remarks were particularly apt for the *Partisan Review*. The decline of Stalinism and the influx of writers and artists from Europe had contributed to the stability of small magazines. Thus the moral collapse of Stalinism and the physical collapse of Europe promised to revive American writing.

As the *Partisan Review* stretched its influence among intellectuals, as it attracted an influential group of contributors, it developed from the experience of the editors a new orientation toward literary criticism and politics. Unlike other journals of its kind, the *Partisan* reflected the different tastes of its editors not only in their selection of essays and creative writing. It was also the vehicle for their literary and political expressions; often their work overshadowed the writing of other contributors. The political alliance against Stalinism and the belief that literature and politics must be separated had originally bound together the dissimilar personalities of Rahv, Phillips, Dupee, and Macdonald. This unity persisted until 1943 when the issue of World War II, which Rahv and Phillips supported and Macdonald opposed, shattered the editorial tranquility, and Macdonald left the staff. Leading up to this break were five and one-half years during which the editors, each in his own fashion, developed, extended, and refashioned the political and cultural assumptions that had once made for unanimity. Two distinct poles emerged, one represented by Rahv and Phillips, the other by Macdonald. By the time that dissension over politics became intolerable, the literary and cultural interests of the editors had also grown apart. Rahv and Phillips headed toward a more exclusive interest in literary criticism centered in the great experimental writers of the twentieth century: Proust, James Kafka, Joyce, and Eliot. Meanwhile Macdonald developed a new style of political journalism and a form of cultural muckraking, which examined the faults and virtues of popular culture, the film and popular novelists and explored the presumed degeneration of mass taste.

The new literary sensibilities of Rahv and Phillips were still concerned, even obsessed, with the experience of writers with Communism and with the fate of the intellectual in modern society. Alienation became the key concept in their examination of modern literature, which defined the great artist as inherently radical by virtue of his art. And the 1920s now seemed to be a period that most clearly understood and expressed the problems of alienation. The art it produced and the expatriation it inspired became to the editors symbolic of the continuing difficulties of the intellectual in society. It was not Rahv or Phillips who first expressed this idea in the magazine, however, but William Troy. In the midst of an article on D. H. Lawrence, Troy alluded to an idea which became essential to the magazine. Since Lawrence had criticized the mass production of ideas and emotions and the regimentation of man, "he was a revolutionist . . . in the sense that every Bohemian artist under the bourgeois regime has been a revolutionist."[22] The artist and the intellectual could by the nature of their acts of creation be considered revolutionists.

Philip Rahv sketched the outlines for a new theory of creative and radical alienation in an essay, "Trials of the Mind," published in early 1938. Rahv's identification with the intellectuals on trial in Moscow and his attempt to share in their fate—a feat of imagination that was reflected in almost every section of the essay—made his writing intensely painful. Almost every idea had the cogency of an aphorism. "It is not only the old Bolsheviks who are on trial," he wrote, "we too, all of us are in the prisoner's dock. These are trials of the mind and of the human spirit. Their meanings encompass the age." In his depression about the headlong plunge of civilization into war, he challenged the belief that man could really control history, as once optimistically predicted by the *Communist Manifesto:* "We were not prepared for defeat. . . . But now, amidst all these ferocious surprises, who has the strength to re-affirm his beliefs, to transcend the feeling that he had been duped?" The failure of capitalism had been long assumed, but the failure of Communism was a chilling shock and left the intellectual stripped of hope and belief in progress, with only himself and his own talents to rely upon. Driven to envision a sort of perverted Lockean world, where brutality and violence ruled the mind, it seemed to Rahv that the intellectual's only birthright was to be a spiritual

---

[22] William Troy, "The Lawrence Myth," *Partisan Review,* IV (January 1938), p. 8.

guardian of culture: "Culture is their only real property. They are the guardians of values, on the one hand their cultivators and on the other hand their exploiters."[23] The only way to understand the reality of the world was to see it as tragedy, where to act out one's fate was to achieve freedom. War, the Moscow Trials, and the failure of the revolutionary movement exposed the reality of the intellectual's role—to save civilization.

William Phillips's essay, the "Esthetic of the Founding Fathers," written at about the same time, also focused on the implications of the early 1930s and was, in its larger meaning, as pessimistic as Rahv's article. Like much of Phillips's early critical writing, the argument was spread between the widely separate poles of Marxist political theory and literary criticism. Although he repeated early ideas, the widening circles of his doubts took him further from the radical center in which he had once believed. The failure of the Communist literary movement, now apparent to all, he felt, had no natural causes, nor could its errors be ascribed to youthfulness. Its excesses were inspired by the political stands and the factional requirements of the Communist party. The Stalinist error was precipitated in part because the party had hurried to occupy the field of radical aesthetics, something that Marx, Engels, Lenin, and even Trotsky had never tried to do. No literary criticism that sought to incorporate the economic and sociological insights of Marxism, which attempted to apply to theoretical aesthetics what had been learned in other fields, could be exorcised from the writings of the "Founding Fathers" of Communism. Radical literature failed because from the first an active force was working consciously to counter it, a force almost determining its failure.

Phillips was now more skeptical and hesitant, yet very close to the same point at which he had begun his critical writings. Theoretical and detached, he was still searching, with less success than ever now, for a valid use of Marxism. But, he concluded, that area had narrowed to a small point occupied solely by the artist himself. He argued, Marxist criticism was invaluable, once the critic realized that literature was a body of perceptions,

---

[23] Philip Rahv, "Trials of the Mind," *Partisan Review*, IV (April 1938), pp. 3-11.

ideas, feelings, and values and acted upon this assumption to weigh and test art as an individual reaction to society. Here, Marxism could help judge values and understand historically and imaginatively what values the artist "rescues from society."[24]

More important than this strenuous attempt to justify a Marxist-based criticism was Phillips's assumption about the role of the writer and the critic. To him, the writer was the focal point of literature, and literature was a mode of perception, an expression of the relation between the writer and society. This argument cried out, still voicelessly however, for a theory of psychology that would delineate the process of literary creation itself. But Phillips's Marxism, still extremely important to him, prevented the psychological implications in his critical thinking from becoming dominant at this point. Moreover, the curious phrase in which the writer is pictured as saving value, curious because it assumed so much, showed the direction of his thought. Criticism could share in literature's imaginative possibilities when it sought to affirm those values that literature saved. Once society possessed a value, perhaps in the same way it might possess an artist, that value would be compromised. Values, in other words, needed to be rescued from society, and that was precisely the function of the writer and the critic.

What Phillips intended in these remarks was made much clearer in his discussion of Thomas Mann two months later. Phillips was intrigued by Mann's portrayal of the artist as "the archetype of European man," as the intellectual pitted against new barbarisms such as fascism. He wrote of the intellectual as the guardian of culture, a role that unfortunately had been compromised as war approached. Most intellectuals, Phillips noted, had forgotten their vital function in society—"to safeguard the dreams and discoveries of science and art, and to champion some political movement insofar as it fulfills the requirements of an intellectual ideal."[25] Mann seemed well aware of this

---

[24] William Phillips, "The Esthetic of the Founding Fathers," *Partisan Review*, IV (March 1938), p. 21.

[25] William Phillips, "Thomas Mann: Humanism in Exile," *Partisan Review*, IV (May 1938), p. 3. This discussion of Mann was extensive during the first year of the magazine's revival.

predicament; nevertheless, because of his failure to expose the roots of society's decay—its social structure—his program merely represented the "agony of an individual conscience." Phillips's focus on values and his reliance on Marxism made him skeptical of the vision projected by Mann. To Phillips, the intellectual must be an aloof commentator, yet paradoxically responsive to every tremble of society, and above all committed to the preservation and enrichment of the culture. To be true to himself and to history, the intellectual must be alienated.

At the same time Rahv was also reaching for a new critical foundation. He found it in the combination of his new political stance with a reevaluation of avant-garde art. As unlikely a figure as Dostoevski seemed now to offer important insights into the current dilemma of the intellectual. No one, Rahv asserted, could read Dostoevski and discover the truth about the Moscow Trials. Yet his novel *The Possessed* was immensely relevant to the experience of the 1930s because it spoke of the same intellectual problems that Stalinism had raised: "Of all the novels of Dostoevsky, it . . . now seems closest to us." The motivations and actions of the revolutionaries described in the novel suggested to Rahv the surprising corruption of the revolutionary ideal that followed Lenin's death. Dostoevski had been a political reactionary, he admitted, but not a conservative, and his insights into modern society were often similar to those of revolutionaries. Just as Silone's portrayal through the consciousness of his characters of the clash between modern thought and tradition had once deeply impressed Rahv, so in the Russian author this style seemed to be perfected. To demonstrate Dostoevski's current relevance, Rahv borrowed an element of historical theory developed by Trotsky, the "Law of Combined Development," which explained that historical movements, once in progress, could advance beyond their original limitations; thus ideas arising from a set of narrow assumptions could be transformed by the process of expression into something quite different. Dostoevski was a reactionary; he appealed to a Romantic tradition, but he had insights that even in the late 1930s were as yet dimly perceived: "Reactionary in its abstract content, in its aspect as a system of ideas, his art is radical in sensibility and subversive in performance."[26]

Rahv's use of political terminology to make what is perhaps the most important point of the essay is no accident. On the contrary, it recalls an older idea, once applied to proletarian literature but now transformed and no longer in league with any political movement—the notion that literature, especially good literature, was revolutionary. Rahv had thus returned, in one sense, to attitudes expressed in the 1920s by the surrealists who hailed Dostoevski and to the critical ideas often advanced in such publications as *Broom*. A new sort of literary-political combination emerged from Rahv's concentration on sensibility and performance, rather than abstract ideology. And by this measure the most frustrating problem that faced the early *Partisan Review* could be solved. Perhaps, using this standard, even T. S. Eliot could be considered a radical: "It is coming to be something of a revolutionary act simply to print serious creative writing," the editors wrote in reply to letters that had criticized their publication of Eliot in 1941.[27]

But Rahv did not immediately lose his old interests or concern for his early attachment to Communism. Despite its disappearance, proletarian literature, which he and Phillips had once considered a form of avant-garde literature, preoccupied his critical writing for some time. In a review of Hemingway's *To Have and to Have Not* he pointed out that the novelist's failure to move from individualism to collectivism was hampered by his use of older styles of imagination that had appeared in his earlier books. Emancipation from elementary bourgeois illusions was no great achievement, wrote the critic, unless this led to a deeper more perceptive understanding of man. The effect of the pervasive radicalism of the 1930s did not create for Hemingway the environment for a great new expression; it merely forced him, along with others, to try to make a political point. But the implications of this were more serious than occasional bad

---

[26] Philip Rahv, "Dostoevsky and Politics," *Partisan Review*, V (July 1938), p. 35.
[27] Reply by the Editors, *Partisan Review*, VIII (November-December 1941), p. 519.

novels. In an article for the socialist weekly, the *New Leader,* in late 1938 Rahv used his toughest prose, a style of polemic learned in the early 1930s, to examine the effects of Communist influence in the arts. Depicting their inroads in publishing houses as a kind of conspiracy, he wrote that the result was an unofficial censorship that menaced anti-Communist writers, a "G.P.U. of the mind."[28] Intellectuals had been attracted to the mantle of Soviet power worn by the American Communist party, he asserted; but they remained in the movement for fear of being persecuted by the party and cut off from its organizations and from the curiously respectable lives they currently led. This analysis of Stalinism in the arts had none of the subtlety or understanding that his earlier articles possessed, or that his own experience would have indicated. Having lived through conversion and deconversion, which were for him complicated, difficult processes, he showed here no willingness to apply his own experience as a measure of understanding. Now, far away in time and particularly distant from the premises of proletarian literature, he wrote of the movement as if it were ruled by psychological disorders, by a need to submit to power and a fear of exile. Thus he exaggerated certain truths and perceptions that he had about the whole movement.

But Rahv was of two minds. Having laid the proletarian movement to rest once in the *New Leader,* he returned to make a "political autopsy" of it shortly afterwards for the *Southern Review.* In this analysis he engaged in a more complex discussion, sensitive to the original motivations of intellectuals who joined the movement. Yet even here the same acid prose etched his conclusions. The triumph of left-wing literature in America had seemed inevitable in the early 1930s: "And, on the whole, in looking back on those early years, the expectation of this triumph appears to have been based on plausible enough grounds."[29] But this literature, he concluded, was moribund from the first because of its exploitation for party purposes by the Communists. It had finally been destroyed by the Popular Front.

[28] Philip Rahv, "Where the News Ends," *New Leader,* (December 19, 1938), p. 8. The G.P.U. was the Soviet secret police.

[29] Philip Rahv, "Proletarian Literature; a Political Autopsy," *Southern Review,* IV (Winter 1939), p. 617.

Later, in 1939, Rahv systematized many of the insights that he had scattered in his earlier writings about the meaning of the 1930s. He was deeply disturbed by the support of many intellectuals for the war effort; indeed, recalling the earlier period when Randolph Bourne and a few courageous others had braved the militarist barbs of their fellow intellectuals to oppose war, he asserted that the meaningful literature of the postwar period had arisen from an abhorrence of war. War, he felt, siphoned off the creative energy of the culture to run the machinery of patriotism. The belief that 1939 might mark the end and the failure of a once potentially significant era seemed to haunt Rahv. He argued that there was no younger generation, and no new ideas during the decade aside from social revolution. Paradoxically, social revolution had fastened itself by means of the Popular Front to "ideas historically transcended generations ago and highly congenial to the present order of things." The immersion of revolutionary literature in a solution of politics had in the long run worked to dissolve revolution into reaction: culture had begun to reflect the two great catastrophes of the era—the victory of fascism and the degeneration of the Bolshevik Revolution.

Rahv's identification of political literature—by this he meant proletarian literature and the writings of the Popular Front— with political reaction was a final step in sloughing off his former beliefs about the possible role of literature in the revolution. The literature of the Communist movement was caught up in a revival of American nationalism and in the aesthetic recreation of the Popular Front, and both nationalism and the Popular Front from Rahv's radical point of view were reactionary forces bent upon war.

Liberated from his old conclusions, he was now free to examine what appeared to be the key to understanding modern literature and possibly a source for a new sort of radicalism— the intelligentsia. "To speak of modern literature," he wrote, "is to speak of that peculiar social grouping, the intelligentsia, to whom it belongs." Essential to any social examination of modern literature was an examination of the "special role and changing status of the intelligentsia. . . ." In America, he continued, the emergence of the intelligentsia had been completed after World War I, and its elemental expression had been one of antipathy to its social surroundings. There had been a choice—to be alienated from society or from oneself—and the artist had chosen estrangement from his environment. The experience of the 1930s had done very little to change this condition, and the same questions of integrity and existence raised before were posed by the new social catastrophe: "The dissident artist, if he understands the extremity of the age and voices what it tries to stifle will thus be saved from its sterility and delivered from its corruption." Once again Rahv used a concept of property to define the role of the intellectual; in fact, he repeated the exact phrase that he had used a year earlier: culture was the intellectual's "only real property." Technical and spiritual culture was the intellectual's real estate, and he earned a livelihood by preserving the old and by creating new forms of consciousness. In effect the intelligentsia had replaced the proletariat for Rahv as a revolutionary class.[30] In the process of this exchange, the connotations of terms shifted. The precise meaning of revolution became more ethereal, and intellectual literature fell into the place shaped originally for proletarian literature. There was also the sense of fighting against enormous odds. Currently, with academicians, accommodators, and vulgarizers in control of the arts, the few sensitive writers who remained now looked back to the previous decade as a golden age of experimentation and innovation. Through the bleak twilight of the 1930s, Rahv distinguished not the liberating masses of the Communist International, but a small band of intelligent men dedicated to preserving themselves and their culture, striding carefully around the pitfalls of patriotism, skirting compromise, and in the fading light even more conscious and careful in their task, whose features evoked a memory of the 1920s.

Fred Dupee's writing also emphasized the pressures that had been placed on the independence of the intellectual by the experience of the 1930s. Reviewing André Malraux's book on

---

[30] Philip Rahv, "Twilight of the Thirties," *Partisan Review*, VI (Summer 1939), pp. 6, 10, 15. See also Philip Rahv, "What is Living and What is Dead," *Partisan Review*, VII (May-June 1940).

Spain, *L'Espoir,* he reexamined the similarity between Malraux and Silone, which had been previously noted by Rahv and Phillips but appeared now to be merely a temporary conjunction. Malraux's proposed elite of technicians corresponded to Silone's priesthood of the moral elite: both implied the failure of Communism. Yet Malraux had compromised himself by attaching himself to Stalinism and, even worse, his novels suffered from conformity to the People's Front. Silone's work, on the other hand, illuminated "as with the flash of a giant metaphor" the bankruptcy of Stalinism.[31]

Dupee's examination of European culture—particularly English writing—extended through the early period of the revived *Partisan.* In the summer of 1938 he wrote two articles on the British cultural scene, both concerned with the effects of the approaching war as a threat to the intellectual community. He found that in England, as in America, there were magazines devoted to the fight to save culture, among them *Scrutiny* and T. S. Eliot's *Criterion.* But on the literary left in Britain he found no unchallenged literary movement, such as proletarian literature had been in the United States. The current atmosphere of gentle reformism, of vague idealism, which had seeped into American radicalism, had also overflowed into British letters. Poets such as Auden and Stephen Spender would eventually find themselves, he predicted, writing for the whole society again and for the bourgeoisie against whom they had once revolted.

For the editors, particularly Rahv and Phillips, the symposium, "The Situation in American Writing," printed in the summer of 1939, revealed a continued questioning of many of the assumptions that they had held during the 1930s and indicated an effort to reorganize the basis of literary criticism. The slant of the questions, the form of expression, pointed to a very different set of critical values. "Would you say, for example," they asked a number of critics and writers (none of them proletarian writers), "that Henry James' work is more relevant to the present and future of American writing than Walt Whitman's?" Interestingly, John Dos Passos, Allan Tate, James Farrell, Katherine Anne Porter, and Wallace Stevens, all of those asked except Louise

---

31 Fred Dupee, "André Malraux," *Partisan Review,* V (March 1938), p. 27.

Bogan, felt that this question was either irrelevant or too limiting. "Would you agree that the corruption of the literary supplements by advertising—in the case of newspapers—and political pressures—in the case of the liberal weeklies—has made serious literary criticism an isolated cult?" Again, few responses seemed to agree with the assumptions behind the question. In much the same vein the editors asked if writers revealed any allegiance to class, religion, or region. Did they write mainly for themselves or for a specific audience? Again most of the respondents parried the question, for few had any specific audience in mind. A final question that divided the contributors related to the obligation of the writer to society as war approached. Among those who opposed a war, Katherine Anne Porter, Kenneth Fearing, and others argued that the writer must not be drawn into the social and intellectual compromises that war often necessitated.[32]

The questions, like the "representative list of American writers" (which included none of the leading figures of the Popular Front), assumed the existence of a new critical pantheon, a new group of literary deities. Whitman, the thunderous old god of the proletarians, had been cast out in favor of Henry James. The assumption of the ordinary proletarian writer that one must produce for a specific audience was denied. It was hinted that only such journals as the *Partisan Review* were of independent mind and could contribute serious criticism. Finally, the apparent direction of American liberal letters with its movement toward nationalism was renounced.

The evolution of new critical attitudes and revised literary tastes was most striking in Rahv and Phillips. Rahv bemoaned the fact, unacknowledged or unrealized by many other critics, that from 1930 onward American literature had declined. In an

---

[32] "The Situation in American Writing," *Partisan Review,* VI (Summer and Fall 1939). James Agee's reply to the questionnaire, which the editors refused to print, attacked the questions and the premises of the symposium, particularly the role that he felt the *Partisan* had assumed. "God help 'American' or any other 'literature,'" he wrote, if the *Partisan Review* represents its highest expression. James Agee, *Now Let Us Praise Famous Men* (Boston: Houghton Mifflin, 1939 and 1940), pp. 352-357. Macdonald relates that he wanted to print the reply. Interview with Dwight Macdonald, September 20, 1965, New York.

article for the *American Mercury* entitled "The Slump in American Writing" he noted that no new school of writing existed to
breathe life into literature, no young avant-garde writers attacked older, established authors. Rather, à kind of infection of
the American literary mind had been spread by the changing
status of the American intellectual. Rahv argued that in their
politicization during the last decade writers had absorbed the
mental habits of their allies—the political bureaucrats and the
cultural Philistines. He concluded that this revealed a significant
split in the American mind, much like the division made between Whitman and James in the symposium of 1939. But both
Whitman and James, he wrote, despite their differences, were
devoted to experience as a final judge. In modern American
literature this appeal to experience, this commitment to action
and to the public life, had perpetuated a split between the inner
and the outer life, while the alienation of the American intellectual from meaningful participation in society, his self-chosen
role of bystander, had only stimulated his desire for experience.
The sole important character missing from the American novel,
the intellectual, was also the only character capable of mending
this schism. When compared to the writing of Silone and Malraux, the radical literature of the 1930s in America was plagued
by this lack of depth and by an inability to understand the
implications of political ideas. American writers, even those as
skillful as Steinbeck, were unable to reproduce more than a
slice of life. Americans had failed to experience life at the level
of history. But Rahv predicted that this cult of experience was
coming to a close, because international intellectual forces, not
native ones, would in the future dominate the course of American culture.[33]

This argument can be traced back to Rahv and Phillips's appraisal of leftist literature, "Literature in a Political Decade,"
published in 1937. The American writer suffered from insularity
and provincialism. To this Rahv had now added a class analysis

---

[33] Philip Rahv, "The Cult of Experience in American Writing," *Partisan
Review*, VII (November-December 1940), p. 424. In a later essay Rahv
would alter and rename the split "Paleface and Redskin." See "Paleface
and Redskin," *Image and Idea: Fourteen Essays on Literary Themes*
(Norfolk, Conn.: New Directions, 1949), pp. 1-3.

of the intelligentsia and a more complex understanding of American and European literature. His criticism of American culture for its failure to approach the complexity and psychological perception dictated by European standards evolved into an important insight into the major tradition of American literature. Proletarian literature and the part that the Communist party played in driving it to ruin were of little importance compared to the prose and poetry of naturalism, for which he now voiced his long-felt antagonism; he defined proletarianism as just one branch of naturalism. Rahv's grounds for condemning the literature of the 1930s seemed to have shifted, but in part he was only responding to a shift in the radical literary movement. The Communists, after embracing proletarian literature, had reversed themselves and aligned their movement with a major group of writers who were busy with the revival of traditional American letters. Thus Rahv was merely following this change, cutting away at the arguments of each stage, but from basically the same position—his devotion to avant-garde literature.

In 1942, writing again on naturalism, Rahv predicted that although this style had held sway during the decade of the 1930s, it was now exhausted and in rapid decay. The artist of the avant-garde, he felt, was once more looking closely at his own image, listening to the inner promptings of his conscience, and no longer feared to "lay hold of the instruments of mystification." Rahv had used the term "mystification" in almost the same context once before when he described the process by which the alienated artist, in this case Henry Miller, was forced into a narcissistic attitude to use the self in order to possess a world full of abstractions. But perhaps Rahv's most revealing use of the term "mystifications" was when he employed it to describe the effects of the Moscow Trials on the intellectual life of the decade.[34] By understanding his own role as an intellectual, the

---

[34] Philip Rahv, "On the Decline of Naturalism," *Partisan Review*, IX (November-December 1942), p. 483. See also Philip Rahv, "The Artist as Desperado," *New Republic*, CIV (April 21, 1941), pp. 557-559. Rahv also used this idea particularly with Kafka. See "Franz Kafka: The Hero as Lonely Man," *Kenyon Review*, I (Winter 1939), 60-74. Philip Rahv, "Koestler and Homeless Radicalism," *Image and Idea*, p. 156.

writer could comprehend the great catastrophes of the 1930s and his own relation to them.

Naturalism was declining, Rahv argued, because it sought to reflect precisely a world incapable of reproduction, a world crippled by a crisis in the interpretation of reality. The growth of psychological science, particularly psychoanalysis, disassembled the experience, which naturalism sought but failed to reproduce. In the light of his own experience of the decade, his own shattered beliefs and trials of the mind, Rahv combined insights gathered from Marxism and from a social and psychological analysis of alienation into a theory of criticism that placed the artist at the center of culture and made him the subject matter of writing. This new theory built a theoretical structure to interpret the major works of the twentieth-century avant-garde in terms of a society in which the intellectual was an alienated social being, a revolutionist against the bourgeois community and against its favorite forms of literature.

William Phillips's article, the "Intellectuals Tradition," was a theoretical discussion of many of the problems that Rahv had examined. Phillips argued that it was generally admitted that alienation was a major problem in modern art, but that implications of this fact had not been understood, particularly the alienation of the intelligentsia as a class. Marxism offered little insight into this problem because it stressed the correspondence between a work of art and its historical context. The effort to make Marxism a critical theory, he wrote in what was ironically an apt description of some of his own earlier work, would lead "to endless theoretical maneuvers as its exponents attempted to hold on the values of literature in the very act of denying them." Continuity existed not between art and the social context, but between art and the artist. Thus the protagonist of modern art "has been the figure of the artist himself, through his successive phases of assertion, alienation, and survival."[35] Modern art had come into being with the formation of an intelligentsia as a distinctive group, "thriving on its very anxiety over survival and its consciousness of being an elite." Phillips then

---

[35] William Phillips, "The Intellectual's Tradition," *Partisan Review*, VIII (November-December 1941), pp. 481-482.

compared the intelligentsia to the medieval church, asserting that both classes functioned to preserve their own culture and traditions. Such a social role brought with it enormous pressures and difficulties. This made understandable the inability to develop and sustain a tradition of a detached, self-sufficient group of intellectuals, which was the most distinctive feature of American culture and, at the same time, its greatest failure. By contrast, the intelligentsia in Europe was an active and self-conscious elite. The glorification of America flowing from the pens of nationalistic writers who supported war was more evidence of the weakness of the intellectual's tradition in America and his desire to lose himself in respectability.

Phillips's essay in some regards complimented Rahv's various discussions of the direction of the avant-garde, but with its sweeping theoretical statements it was more limiting and more strict in its definition of what was useful in tradition and what was not. Nevertheless, both Rahv and Phillips in concentrating on the art of the intelligentsia—obviously an important one— used a class analysis drawn from Marxism combined with psychological insights derived from Freud and others.[36] Thus their literary criticism sprang from two centers but was never bound exclusively by either. The crucial problem first expressed in the dilemma of how to preserve bourgeois art while remaining committed to the destruction of the bourgeoisie through revolution was solved by entirely reformulating the question. It was no longer an issue of "bourgeois" art, for in the late 1930s Rahv and Phillips came to believe that no great art was really bourgeois in a bad sense, but rather that the great art of the twentieth century belonged to the intelligentsia, a separate class, and potentially a radical class in its opposition to society, with its own sense of loyalties, of anxieties, and even of property.

The shift in literary tastes that was strikingly apparent in the new *Partisan Review* was motivated by the fascination of the editors with an entirely new group of writers and by their rediscovery and restatement of the meaning of avant-garde art. Besides Malraux and Thomas Mann, Ignazio Silone was

---

[36] Rahv and Phillips both began to read Freud and other psychologists in earnest at the end of the 1930s, although they both relate that they had been superficially acquainted with psychoanalysis before this time. Interviews with Philip Rahv and William Phillips.

important, especially in the first years of the revived magazine. Lionel Abel in the first issue discussed the novelist's *Bread and Wine,* restating the basic moral theme of the book and citing its importance in understanding the political experience of the 1930s. Two issues later, Silone contributed a curious, short but disturbed "Childhood Memory" dealing with the custom of weaning children in Italy. The piece was not particularly profound or important in itself; it was published, rather, because of Silone's importance and of his relevance to the life of the magazine.

In March 1938 Rahv wrote to Silone explaining that the magazine planned a symposium on the cultural implications of the Moscow Trials; would he be interested in contributing some remarks? Although nothing came of the symposium, the *Partisan's* continued interest in Silone was evidenced when it published "The School for Dictators," part of his forthcoming book on fascism. By 1942 the magazine's enthusiasm for the Italian author had cooled somewhat. Phillips, reviewing his latest novel, *The Seed Beneath the Snow,* criticized the author's tendency to find salvation in rural and religious Italy. The highly intellectualized moral tensions that Silone had so skillfully isolated in his previous works were incapable of portrayal at the almost instinctual level of life of the Italian village. Silone's chief attraction, Phillips conceded, was the fact that he had "given literary status to the crisis of our times."[37]

More indicative of a revised set of literary tastes was the writing of the editors, especially Rahv, on Franz Kafka. In two articles, for the *Kenyon Review* and the *Southern Review* in 1939, Rahv demonstrated a great sensitivity and sympathy for Kafka's art. Both essays leaned heavily on psychology for literary analysis and both made much the same point—that in Kafka the system of Western individualism, of bourgeois man, and of rationalism had come to a dead end. Kafka's heroes were prototypes of the unadjusted man.[38] Attention in the *Partisan* itself was directed to publishing Kafka's works. Three stories,

[37] Philip Rahv to Ignazio Silone, March 3, 1938. *Partisan* MSS. William Phillips, "The Seed Beneath the Snow," *Partisan Review,* IX (November-December 1942), p. 529.
[38] Philip Rahv, "Hero as Lonely Man," *Kenyon Review,* and Philip Rahv "The Death of Ivan Ilyich and Joseph K.," *Southern Review,* V (Summer 1939), pp. 174-185.

"Blumfield, an Elderly Bachelor," "In a Penal Colony," and "Josephine the Songstress," appeared in 1938, 1941, and 1942.

The new cast of literary players drawn from the lists of twentieth-century writers also included men like Gide, Joyce, Eliot, Proust, and several of the surrealists. Thus the magazine became a kind of continuation of the old *Dial*, which had published many of the works of these early authors. It devoted extensive articles and review essays to a reconsideration and an analysis of these writers, thus performing the task that the *Dial* had not completed—of introducing the European writers into the context of American culture in terms of a theory of the cultural elite to which these authors belonged. Great modern literature, they asserted, could be understood only in terms of the intelligentsia for whom it was created.

In American literature, the editors also turned to the past, but unlike many of the critics associated with the Popular Front, they were most interested in Henry James. The Henry James revival, common to a number of left-wing critics including Dupee, Rahv, F. O. Matthiessen, and Newton Arvin, is one of the most interesting phenomena of the late 1930s. To the *Partisan* editors, James's importance was manifold: he was a Europeanized American, a novelist intrigued by nuance in culture and psychology, but above all he represented an American tradition involved intimately with the avant-garde art of the twentieth century. Of all others, he had perhaps contributed most to creating ties between European and American culture.[39]

Another expatriate American, T. S. Eliot, was also central to the intellectual life of the *Partisan*, as he had been from the beginning. But now, instead of presenting an unresolvable dilemma to the editors of a political reactionary and a literary radical, he was seen more and more as a genuine radical. Lionel Trilling, reviewing Eliot's *Idea of a Christian Society*, made a point that seemed to absolve Eliot from his political stands: in the face of the strenuous demands on all intellectuals at the end of the decade, Eliot's total commitment to the intellectual life was admirable. Any criticism of Eliot's religious faith, his supposed "surrender" of the intellect (an accusation usually

[39] Philip Rahv, "The Heiress of All Ages," *Partisan Review*, X (May-June 1943). Interview with Fred Dupee.

made by Marxists who, Trilling argued, were guilty of these very faults themselves) was specious. Eliot's vision of the Christian state, his "community of Christians," represented an intellectual elite devoted to the conscience of the nation, and here it was that the poet was important to contemporary cultural life. The magazine, always critical of certain aspects of Eliot's writings, especially his religiosity, nevertheless felt him to be a kind of cultural hero.[40]

The similarities between the writers who were most important to the *Partisan Review*, aside from their stature, is not to be found in their political ideas, their literary styles, their attitudes toward culture, or even their artistic medium, but in the fact that they were considered to be the principal modern writers of the intelligentsia; hence, for Rahv and Phillips, the true avant-garde. R. P. Blackmur, a frequent contributor to the *Partisan*, wrote of this group that what united them was their psychological expatriation, their alienation from any nationality, and their estrangement from modern society. In their rediscovery of the 1920s and avant-garde art and in their emphasis on the intelligentsia as a class, Rahv and Phillips sometimes drew too wide and sweeping conclusions to describe the period when such art flourished. Alienation, at least in the sense in which it was described by the *Partisan Review*, was not characteristic of all avant-garde artists, nor did expatriation necessarily imply disillusionment or estrangement. As with any criticism, this evaluation described the present as well as the past.

Part II   Kulturbolschewismus: The Middlebrow Counterrevolution

While the editors of the *Partisan Review*, particularly Rahv and Phillips, were evolving a new theory and justification for avant-garde art, the Popular Front had associated itself with traditional American art. Important literary figures who participated in the League of American Writers were leading a campaign

---

[40] Delmore Schwartz, "T. S. Eliot as an International Hero," *Partisan Review*, XII (Spring 1945).

against the very act that the *Partisan* was pledged to defend. Thus the antagonism between America's two leading Marxist literary centers, the League of American Writers, and the *Partisan Review* and other independent socialist organs, encompassed issues broader than politics. The *Partisan's* condemnation of what it characterized as *Kulturbolschewismus* (the counterattack against avant-garde art), derived from three sources: the magazine's past association with the Communist movement, its commitment to advanced art, and the attitude, especially of Dwight Macdonald, toward middle-class culture.

Although Macdonald took part in editorial decisions to print Kafka, Gide, Silone, and others and despite the interest in avant-garde writing that he shared with Rahv, Phillips, and Dupee, his major concern was popular culture, particularly the film. His first article for the magazine was an exposé of the *New Yorker*, similar to his attack on *Fortune* magazine a year earlier. In the role of cultural muckraker, Macdonald explored the class bias of the *New Yorker* and drew a sketch of the typical writer for it who extracted a kind of "humor of the inadequate" from his society. Because the magazine was the only major vehicle of humor for the urban intelligentsia, it dominated its chosen field; yet in reality it was the "last of the great family journals. Its inhibitions stretch from sex to the class struggle."[41]

Macdonald's exposé style was highly effective in the collection of newspaper stories that he spliced together to describe the death of Rosa Luxemburg for a piece accompanying a series of prison letters written by the German revolutionist and printed in the *Partisan* in the summer of 1938. But it was the film, above all the Russian film, that held his attention. In a two-part history, published during the summer of 1938, he explored the causes for the precipitous decline in the quality of Soviet film making. After an initial blaze of creativity and innovation, on the threshhold of even greater accomplishments with the advent of sound, the Soviet film industry had degenerated and its aesthetic heart had been stopped by the demands of politics.

---

[41] Dwight Macdonald, "Laugh and Lie Down," *Partisan Review*, IV (December 1937), p. 48. A few months later the *New Yorker* asked Macdonald to write for them and he did. See Dwight Macdonald, "Parajournalism II: Wolfe and the New Yorker," *New York Review of Books*, VI (February 3, 1966), p. 23.

Under pressure from the Five-Year Plan, the Russians turned to new themes and new styles dictated by the forced proletarianization of the arts. In the course of a few years a great art was first broken down and then remolded into a conscious copy of Hollywood, its revolutionary content purged as it became expedient for the leaders of the Soviet Union to present the masses with the gratifying sensation of living in an ideal world. The appointment of Semyan Dukelsky, once of the Soviet secret police as head of the Committee on Cinema, was evidence to Macdonald that "the degradation of the cinema under the present regime may be said to have reached its logical and inevitable conclusion."

Within six months Macdonald again pondered the degeneration of the Soviet film, this time from a slightly different direction. The decline of this art form, he concluded, was a reflection of the decline of the new Soviet society which had survived only a few painful years. The fault was not that the great Russian directors were propagandists or that they made their art too political; on the contrary, they had originally drawn great inspiration from politics. It was the attempt to pattern films after Hollywood, to depict Soviet society as an ideal socialist state, that had introduced escapism into Russian films. What really bothered Macdonald, however, was that the Russian masses, like the American public, enjoyed degenerate art. Temporarily, at least, he dismissed the problem: "The reason for this is not that the masses are backward . . . but that they have been taught to like it."[42] Macdonald's final word for the *Partisan* on the Soviet film decline was a review in 1942 of Eisenstein's *The Film Sense*, which once more lamented the misdirection of a great art form. By this time Macdonald seemed resigned to the tragedy of Eisenstein who had adapted his art and debased his talent before political pressures that had crushed other forms of Soviet expression: "I think we had better get used to such shocks," he wrote, "there are probably more unheroic tragedies to come."[43]

[42] Dwight Macdonald, "Soviet Cinema, 1930-1938," *Partisan Review*, V (July and August-September 1938), p. 60, and Dwight Macdonald, "Soviet Society and its Cinema," *Partisan Review*, VI (Winter 1939), p. 88.
[43] Dwight Macdonald, "Film Chronicle," *Partisan Review*, IX (November 1942), p. 506. After this, most of the film writing was done by Paul Goodman.

The major part of Macdonald's cultural writing, however, was more political than were his discussions of Eisenstein. Like Rahv and Phillips, but for different reasons, he strongly opposed the League of American Writers and the tradition of literary patriotism that that group offered. Even after the League's influence was shattered because it shifted its position to oppose the war against Germany after the signing of the Hitler-Stalin pact in the summer of 1939, Macdonald still saw nationalism in American letters as a grave threat.

Until the League's demise in the early forties the *Partisan* followed its activities closely. Because the magazine had crystallized as an anti-Stalinist, avant-garde cultural journal at the 1937 American Writers' Congress, it is not surprising that it published an analysis of that convention. Philip Rahv's ironically titled "Two Years of Progress" spoke of the moral degeneration that had infected the League and transformed it into an organization to defend the status quo. "Within the short space of two years," he wrote, "the 'revolutionaries' of 1935 had substituted the stars and stripes of New Deal Marxism for 'the red flag of the new materialism.' "[44] Rahv's major criticism of the League was that its political stand was reactionary and its literary tastes insipid. It was an organization that sought to lead American intellectuals into support of a war against fascism, and for capitalism a war that Rahv opposed at the time. Like Bourne and a few others in 1917, the editors of the *Partisan Review* drew back from supporting America's entrance into the war at least until after 1941. After that only Macdonald continued his opposition.

Before the Hitler-Stalin pact, the prowar attitude of the League seemed to the editors a betrayal of Marxism and a fatal concession to the middle class. The political costs of such a position were well understood, and perhaps most forcefully expressed, in Sidney Hook's essay, "The Anatomy of the Popular Front." This political tactic did little else, he wrote, than deliver left-wing elements to the control of the most right-wing groups within an alliance; all else was rhetoric. To the editors of the

---

[44] Rahv, "Two Years of Progress," *Partisan Review*, IV (February 1958), p. 24. Granville Hicks, writing after he had left the party, said that he would have changed only two or three pages in his book, *I Like America*, written while in the party. Hicks, "Communism and the American Intellectuals," *Whose Revolution?*, p. 96.

Partisan, the cultural repercussions of such a political position
seemed even more severe, partly because they had always been
more concerned with the effect of political radicalism on culture
and partly because the patriotic fervor voiced by intellectuals
seemed to be leading toward something like fascism in culture.
The hysteria that occasionally glimmered below the surface in
writers who participated in the League seemed to forewarn of
a serious intellectual crisis.

In the summer of 1939 the League of American Writers was
at the height of its influence; its membership had risen sharply
during that year and it seemed more strongly than ever committed to nationalism in the arts. However, the League's major
attraction, its opposition to fascism, was suddenly exploded with
the signing of the Hitler-Stalin pact. Now it switched to oppose
a war against fascism. It branded the coming European struggle an imperialist struggle and urged intellectuals to help preserve American democracy.[45] A rash of resignations from the
organization followed in the wake of this accommodation to
Soviet policy; some were immediate like Thomas Mann's, others
such as Granville Hicks's and Malcolm Cowley's came after slight
hesitation. After Cowley had retired, he wrote to the League
that the policy of the organization seemed determined to weaken
the country's power of resistance. It seemed no longer
an opponent of facism, but a partner with American reactionaries who favored isolation. Cowley was rather typical in
his motivations for quitting, for he felt that the League had
betrayed its original commitments. Even the *Partisan Review*
editors reacted to the change of League policy, sending a letter
to the organization signed by John Dewey, James Farrell, Louis
Hacker, Sidney Hook, Phillips, Rahv, Dupee, and others, which
challenged the League to repudiate Soviet foreign policy: "Until
August 21, 1939, the League of American Writers functioned as
the most active political organization among American writers
and intellectuals."[46]

---

[45] Franklin Folsom, "Report for the Period Between the Third and Fourth
Writers Congresses, 1939-1941," p. 6 LAW MSS. "In Defense of Peace,"
Statement of the League of American Writers, June 12, 1940, p. 1, and
"In Defense of Culture and Peace," Resolution #1 presented to the Amer-
ican Writers' Congress, June 1941. LAW MSS.
[46] Malcolm Cowley to Franklin Folsom, June 29, 1940, Gaylordsville,

The self-destruction of the League (it was defunct by the end of the war) did not end the attachment of a group of major American intellectuals to the politics of pragmatism and the culture of nationalism. It merely removed an organization that promoted such attitudes. The same writers who suffused the League with literary patriotism, intellectuals such as Van Wyck Brooks and Archibald MacLeish, continued to plead for Americanism in the arts. In response the *Partisan Review* mounted a defense of international culture and political independence and of noninvolvement in the propaganda of war.

One of the first analyses of the Brooks group in the *Partisan Review* was Meyer Schapiro's review of Lewis Mumford's book, *Culture of Cities*, in which the critic singled out the author's vagueness and his misunderstanding of politics. Mumford's book, he wrote, was softheaded, for it overlooked the class origins of the state and substituted taste as a test of political theories for a more scientific examination of class relations. Lionel Trilling noted a similar kind of vagueness in Ernest Hemingway, which had come about as a result of his conversion to the same liberal political tradition. In the novelist's work this tradition had been an immensely destructive force: "Insofar as we can ever blame a critical tradition for a writer's failures, we must, I believe, blame American criticism for the illegitimate emergence of Hemingway the 'man' and the resultant inferiority of his two recent major works."[47]

Fred Dupee's discussion of the "Americanism of Van Wyck Brooks" in 1939 was the first of a number of direct confrontations with what would later be known as *Kulturbolschewismus*. Dupee had high praise for Brooks's early work, for his stress on the importance of an emerging intelligentsia, and for his appreciation of the importance of the new psychology. Unfortunately, like a number of other critics who began by questioning the prevailing American cultural standards, he ended by affirming them, by turning back to the early days of American literature to praise the works of an emerging national culture.

Connecticut, pp. 2-3. LAW MSS. Copy of a Letter to the Secretary of the League of American Writers, October 5, 1939, p. 1. LAW MSS.

[47] Lionel Trilling, "Hemingway and His Critics," *Partisan Review*, VI (Winter 1939), p. 57.

In 1941, immediately before America's entrance into the war, cultural nationalism reached a new height, and the *Partisan's* response was more aggressive. Archibald MacLeish, then employed by the State Department, made a strong attack on intellectuals who did not support the war. In his speech, "The Irresponsibles," he enunciated one half of what the *Partisan* called the "Brooks–MacLeish Thesis." The magazine's reaction to this implicit attack on them and all others who had not picked up the banner of Americanism, was the severest sort of denunciation of MacLeish. Morton Zabel's "The Poet on Capitol Hill" slashed at MacLeish's attitude toward dissenting intellectuals: "An indictment of writers and scholars equal in severity to this has seldom been heard in public places in modern times. . . . Perhaps the maledictions of Hitler and Goebbels alone have surpassed it within living memory." The remainder of Zabel's article questioned MacLeish's poetic credentials and his moral and artistic right as a writer to dictate to other writers on their duties toward culture. What MacLeish feared, he concluded, was to be "isolated from his stays and props in society."[48] MacLeish seemed to fear, in other words, the alienation from modern society that many of the major artists of the avant-garde had accepted as one of the facts of existence.

The major weight of the attack on the Brooks–MacLeish thesis was carried by Dwight Macdonald. To Macdonald, an official approach to art smacked of the worst excesses of the decade and pointed to totalitarianism in the arts. In much the same way as he became obsessed with Eisenstein's personal degeneration, he fixed upon Brooks, MacLeish, Mumford, and others who were using politics, he felt, to mask an attack on a tendency in literature that they disliked. In a paper, "Primary Literature and Coterie Literature," Brooks had distinguished between great literature of Western culture, the optimistic, affirmative writing, and literature of the aestheticians, of Eliot and those writers who conceived of their art as belonging to a coterie. In an article drawn from these remarks Brooks explained that a great writer was a great man writing, and "A great man writing is one who

---

[48] Morton Zabel, "The Poet on Capitol Hill," *Partisan Review*, VIII (January-February and March-April 1941), pp. 3, 140.

bespeaks the collective life of the people, of his group, of his nation, of mankind." To Brooks, a writer's most useful possession was an American memory giving him access to a tradition that would provide stability, health, and purpose.[49] Brooks's dismissal of Eliot and practically all of modern literature enraged Macdonald. With the best of intentions, he wrote, Brooks had become "our leading mouth piece for totalitarian cultural values." The gravity of Macdonald's charges and the anger in his choice of words, his accusation that Brooks used methods precisely like those employed in the Moscow Trials, only underscored the seriousness of his concern. To him, this was not an isolated case of wrong thinking, but something akin to the problem of Stalinism in the arts and a tendency that the *Partisan Review* had fought from the first days of its revival. From the beginning, he noted, the magazine had been engaged in a rearguard action against an "official aesthetic," first in the Popular Front and now in the crisis-caused absorption of intellectuals into the propaganda machinery of the government. Those artists whom Brooks attacked and the *Partisan* upheld, Macdonald asserted, were in fact a threat to any reactionary society and therefore a threat to contemporary America.[50] It was important for radicals to defend such men. The creative artist, in other words, was by definition a rebel and his art subversive in any society bent upon war.

Macdonald's anger at the Brooks–MacLeish thesis and his fear of the cultural tendency they represented did not subside after the publication of his attack on them. Rather, he tried to enlist the support of other intellectuals. After Edmund Wilson wrote to him praising his remarks and promising that he would write to Brooks on the matter, Macdonald urged Wilson to take a strong public stand on the issue: "If you approve, as you wrote earlier, of my piece, then I take it you agree it's a serious matter going far beyond Brooks' own personal failings . . . a symptom of growing cultural repression and regimentation. And in that case it would seem the responsibility of writers on *our* side of

---

[49] Van Wyck Brooks, "What is Primary Literature?" *Yale Review*, XXXI (September 1941), pp. 29, 34.
[50] Dwight Macdonald, "Kulturbolschewismus is Here," *Partisan Review*, VIII (November-December 1941), pp. 446, 451.

the fence to stick their necks out now, to speak out publically against this sort of thing. Personal letters don't do the job at all. (You'll recall we had the same disagreement at the time Cowley made his smear attack on P.R. in the New Republic—and I still think the personal letter you wrote him at the time (instead of a public statement) was the wrong tactic.)"[51] Macdonald also tried to use his article as the basis for a symposium on cultural nationalism. Letters were sent to authors seeking their remarks on the Brooks–MacLeish thesis, and eventually a number of replies were printed. The urgency felt about this issue was expressed in the invitations to comment on Brooks. Nancy Macdonald, writing to Glenway Wescott for the editors in November 1941, said: "This is a life-and-death matter, we feel, involving the very survival of our culture. We can think of no differences between writers today great enough to prevent their speaking out together against the 'Brooks–MacLeish thesis.'"

The results of Macdonald's attempt to forge solidarity among artists and writers were disappointing, partly because Pearl Harbor and America's entrance into the war intervened. A number of comments appeared in 1942, but few matched the fervor of Macdonald's denunciation of artistic nationalism. Lionel Trilling, William Carlos Williams, and John Crowe Ransom, among those who answered, were suspicious of Brooks, but equally dubious about Macdonald's call for socialism. Not surprisingly, the most important response was from T. S. Eliot, since Macdonald's article had been an implicit defense of Eliot and the art of the avant-garde, which had repeatedly come under attack in the 1930s. Eliot compared the Brooks thesis to similar sneers at highbrow culture in England; he too, like Macdonald, feared attacks on "culture in the name of culture."[52]

Macdonald's essay, "The (American) People's Century," published in the summer of 1942, was his final statement in the defense against *Kulturbolschewismus*. Ostensibly, the article was an attack on the political goals of the war, on Vice President

---

[51] Edmund Wilson to Dwight Macdonald, November 8, 1941. Dwight Macdonald to Edmund Wilson, November, 1941?, *Partisan* MSS.

[52] Nancy Macdonald for the editors to Glenway Wescott, November 17, 1941, *Partisan* MSS. T. S. Eliot, "A Letter to the Editors," *Partisan Review*, IX (January-February 1942), p. 116.

Wallace's speech about the "century of the common man," but these remarks also provided a pretext for a discussion of the liberal assumptions from which Wallace spoke. The Four Freedoms, the universal literacy and industrialism that Wallace thoughtlessly applauded were really mixed blessings, and the proof existed in Germany and Russia where such elements of "progress" had actually restricted freedom. Instead of appealing to the universal needs of mankind, Wallace's postwar plans for the world really meant refashioning it in America's image. But Macdonald was even more disturbed because he found that Wallace and Henry Luce essentially agreed upon goals for postwar reconstruction. The conjunction of liberalism and imperialism thus seemed complete.[53] Two disturbing elements of American culture were joined: Luce who symbolized the decadent journalism purveyed by conservative capitalism upon the masses and Wallace who was a representative of the optimistic liberalism enthroned in the Roosevelt Administration and encrusted in the artistic tenets of the Brooks–MacLeish thesis.

To Macdonald, the war linked these two tendencies and threatened to make them permanent features of American culture. Thus war was an evil not only in itself, but also as the catalyst for dangerous cultural change, much as it had seemed to Bourne twenty years before. As art became more politicized, it appeared to Macdonald that a political solution, socialism, was more desperately needed. Early in 1939 Macdonald had appealed to the memory of Randolph Bourne and fashioned an essay which brought up-to-date some of the ideas in Bourne's "War and the Intellectuals." Attacking intellectuals for lending support to the coming war, he wrote: "The great objection to the war program of the intellectuals is not so much that it will get us into a war . . . but that it is diverting us from the main task: to work with the masses for socialism, which alone can save our civilization."[54] The key concept here is "civilization." To him the opposition to war and the fight for civilization and

---

[53] Dwight Macdonald, "The (American) People's Century," *Partisan Review,* IX (July-August 1942).
[54] Dwight Macdonald, "War and the Intellectuals: Act II," *Partisan Review,* VI (Spring 1939), p. 10.

for socialism, seemed the same as the struggle against Henry Luce, Henry Wallace, Archibald MacLeish, and Van Wyck Brooks. As America's entrance into the battle drew closer, Macdonald saw his predictions come true: American culture stiffened and grew less pliable under the demands for sacrifice to the necessities of defense.

Thus Macdonald's opposition to the war was as much based on a concept of culture as it was on a Marxian analysis of the struggle as an imperialist war. So long as Macdonald continued to believe in Marxism and the possibility of broad social change, he also held to the possibility of cultural regeneration, of creating great mass art. But as his faith in Marxism evaporated after the war, he gradually transposed the theory of class struggle into a corresponding theory of civilization, finding culture split into three irreconcilable classes, each with its distinct logic and purpose: mass-cult, mid-cult, and high culture. Mass art represented the degeneracy of art, for its primary purpose was to distract. Mid-cult (middle-class) art absorbed and corrupted many of the discoveries of the avant-garde and opposed the direction of elite art much as the Brooks–MacLeish thesis had once done.[55] Macdonald continued to defend avant-garde culture as he had always done, but as before, he rarely wrote about it.

The other editors of the *Partisan* were also disturbed by the Brooks–MacLeish thesis and by growing nationalism in the arts, but they did not share Macdonald's preoccupation with mass art, nor did they see the war or socialism in precisely the same terms. It is true that Rahv and Phillips identified *Kulturbolschewismus* with the excesses of Stalinism. In a letter to Malcolm Cowley in 1944 Rahv made this apparent. Speaking of Brooks and Bernard De Voto, he wrote: ". . . they make the same mistakes that the vulgar Marxists did, only from a (sometimes well concealed) rightist angle: the same extra-literary pressure and presumptions; instead of worshipping the 'proletariat' they worship 'America'—an object of adoration and pomp-

---

[55] Dwight Macdonald, *Against the American Grain* (New York: Random House, 1962), pp. 5, 34, 38, 208.

ous reference which in their sense of it is quite as mythical as the Marxist object."[56] But to Rahv and Phillips, socialism, by the 1940s, was scarcely applicable in this situation; the way to preserve literature depended on the radicalism of the intellectual inherent in his estrangement from bourgeois society. Faced with the threat of war and the possible extinction of culture, the intellectual must return to his task of preserving culture. To Rahv and Phillips the threat from within America never seemed as strong as it did to Macdonald; they feared destruction from without, from Germany, from the Soviet Union, and from the Soviet influence through the Communist party.

Other writers for the *Partisan Review* commented on the constriction of freedom at the approach of war. James T. Farrell was particularly strong in his attacks on Max Eastman, Mortimer J. Adler, Brooks, MacLeish, and Mumford for succumbing to war hysteria. Aside from Farrell's skirmishes with the fellow travelers of literary nationalism, Sidney Hook's preoccupation with a related issue, the revival of nonrational thought, was important to the life of the magazine. Hook's major target was Jacques Maritain, who, he argued, was a totalitarian. The revival of Catholicism urged by Maritain and the possibility that such a movement might be successful, resulted from a demoralization of socialism throughout the world.

In some sense, the war sharpened and defined more clearly the issues that united the *Partisan Review* editors, yet it split them apart in their solutions to these cultural problems. Born as a dissident generation, the *Partisan* editors were devoted to preservation and advancement of avant-garde art, and the war only strengthened the need for clear thinking on this score. Attacks on modern art and literature, on modern thought by neoconservatives like Maritain, by nationalism and Stalinism— all of these forces seemed bent on destroying the culture that the magazine was pledged to protect. Failure to accept the conclusions of experiments in science and psychology, the failure to acknowledge the greatness of experiments in twentieth-century art, indicated to the editors a failure of the nerve of civilization.

---

[56] Philip Rahv to Malcolm Cowley, August 4, 1944, New York, p. 1, Cowley MSS.

The examination of this new weakness in culture in the symposium "The New Failure of Nerve" in 1943 thus became a central document in the history of the magazine, combining a discussion of the forces that threatened the independent life of the intellectual. In 1943 the *Partisan Review* found itself fighting for the survival of the scientific method, for experimentation in the arts, only twenty years after the old *Masses* and the *Seven Arts*, the intellectuals of the young rebellion and of the revolution, had announced the triumph of the scientific life.

Although the editors agreed in their opposition to reactionary forces in the culture, they were badly divided over the program to counter these forces. Rahv and Phillips after 1941 supported the war as the only practical way to defeat fascism, but Macdonald was adamant in his refusal to commit himself to the Allied cause. Thus as the cultural conservatism produced by the war united the editors, the question of the war itself became the issue over which they finally separated.

Chapter 7

The Politics of Collision

> The present crisis, however, has been going
> on for an unheard-of period, and by now the
> tension has become almost unbearable. Day
> after day the thing drags on, generating ever-
> increasing pressures which are deforming all
> social and political forms.
>
> Dwight Macdonald, May 1937

The political alliance between Rahv, Phillips, and Macdonald,
forged in the heat of reaction to Stalinism, could not transform
the vast differences in temperament or in political and cultural
backgrounds that tended to define the preoccupations of each
editor. For Rahv and Phillips Trotskyism was an important stage
in their reconsideration of Marxism, a stopping place in an intellectual journey out of orthodoxy. To Macdonald, Trotskyism
was the radical center itself, not a step in reconsideration, and
his commitment to it was a move toward Marxism. Thus the
revived *Partisan Review* had about it a charged atmosphere re-
sulting from the combination of different chemistries and generated by the positive and negative mixtures of Marxism represented by Macdonald on one hand and Rahv and Phillips on the
other. As Macdonald wrote more on politics for the magazine,
Rahv and Phillips wrote less, and figures like Sidney Hook
tended to express what was approximately their political point
of view. Although Macdonald was a member of the American
Trotskyist movement for a relatively short time, 1939 to 1941,
the first evidence of his discouragement with the movement,
similar in effect to the tone and style of Rahv and Phillips's dis-

234

couragements several years before, was also a reassertion of fundamental purity, in a sense a demand for a deeper and more intense radicalism. Significantly, this occurred almost simultaneously with the outbreak of war, and the great struggle to Macdonald seemed the very negation of what radicalism stood for. As he demanded greater purity in radicalism, the war seemed to embody all that was destructive. Rahv and Phillips reacted to the war in a much different way. To be sure, they opposed the bad side effects of the conflict, the patriotism, the nationalism of the poets and artists of Capitol Hill, but these remained to them side effects and seemed to have as much to do with the liberal nationalism propagated by the Stalinists before the war as with the demands of the world struggle. No revolutionary answer occurred to them, no choice appeared feasible, and after Pearl Harbor they switched to support the war. Thus the sinews of the magazine were stretched beyond their capacity to bind, and after a brief fight over control of the *Partisan* Macdonald quit the staff in 1943.

The implicit anarchism of Macdonald's thought was squeezed and molded into recognizable shape by the immense pressures of a war that he could not support, unwilling as he was to commit cultural values to the test of fire, unable to choose sides in the conflict, and cautious to remain skeptical of any social system or social theory. To him the present role of the intellectual was clear: to transform commitment to society into commitment to social values. Macdonald's choice of a "third camp" position, when one was not feasible, led him, paradoxically, to face the reality of war that others, more hopeful about its results, could not or did not choose to see. Even Trotsky, Macdonald's political mentor had given qualified support to the war before his death, and Macdonald had been highly critical of this position. Macdonald's conception of politics was too demanding, too pure, and, above all, too individual ever to submit itself long to the discipline of a political movement, and even in the rarified atmosphere of Trotskyism he felt choked by compromise and half-truth. His political and cultural values, devoted to the preservation of intellectual integrity, led him away from movements, and eventually away from the *Partisan Review* to *Politics*, the journal that he began editing in 1944; politics came to mean the expression of a deeply personal reaction to the events of political and cultural life.

Macdonald's first writing for the *Partisan* exhibited his early interest in the film and popular culture, but in subsequent articles he edged slowly toward the style that characterized his more political articles after 1940. This emphasis is true also of the writing that he did for the *New International*, the theoretical organ of the Trotskyist movement in the United States. The *New International* had resumed publication in January 1938 after a year's suspension. Its editors, James Burnham and Max Shachtman, made it a magazine of considerable intellectual stature, and by 1939 its circulation had climbed to around 5000, larger than the *Partisan Review's*. Partly because of the influence of Burnham, Macdonald began to contribute articles to the magazine. Against the advice of James Cannon, who was the leader of the movement in the United States, he decided to join the party in 1939. Macdonald's official debut in party circles, his first article for the *New International*, was a bristling attack on Trotsky for his role in putting down the Kronstadt Rebellion in 1921 and for his recent justification of this action by the early Soviet government. Macdonald's stand was important, for it cast him with a group of Trotskyists, including Max Eastman and Victor Serge, who in the winter of 1937 and 1938 had questioned Trotsky's responsibility for this affair. He was thus identified with a dissident group that eventually split off from the parent party. The *New International* was willing to publish his regular column, "Reading from Left to Right," which examined current journalism, but the Trotskyists refused, even in their discussion bulletins, to publish the voluminous theoretical works that he wrote on the Soviet state and on party discipline and theory.[1]

Significantly, Macdonald joined the Trotskyists at almost the same time that deep cracks began to appear in the movement over interpretations of the outbreak of the war in Europe. By October 1939, when he wrote on "Kronstadt Again," the move-

---

[1] Deutscher, *Prophet Outcast,* p. 436, and Harry Roskolenko, *When I Was Last on Cherry Street* (New York: Stein & Day, 1965), p. 158.

ment was badly split. At the National Committee meeting of the party in September, James Burnham had introduced a resolution arguing that the Soviet state was in no sense a "worker's state" (a term indicating proletarian rule), hence none of its actions should be supported. Max Shachtman and others seconded the resolution, and in 1940 this group abandoned the official Trotskyist movement to form their own party, taking the *New International* with them. Macdonald stood with Burnham (who left the new party within a month of its founding) and Shachtman and continued his column. By early 1941 his interests had shifted almost exclusively to explaining the nature of the fascist state and the broader meanings of World War II. Before this time, even before the fighting had begun, he had hinted that this would be a major concern. In early 1939 he wrote: "Today, war has become the supreme reality and meaning of the whole system. . . ." The approach of violent conflict imposed tensions on society that were insupportable: "Day after day the thing drags on, generating ever-increasing pressures which are deforming all social and political forms." The war in its early stages, Macdonald argued, demonstrated with finality the corruption of the Soviet Union and made obvious the terrifying implications of accepting its leadership. The blindness of well-meaning intellectuals who supported Russia, he hoped, would be lifted, because Munich and the invasion of Finland exposed Stalinism as the enemy of the working class. But the effect of such a disillusionment would probably be demoralizing and might obscure an insight that must be preserved: that the war could only be ended by a revolutionary struggle of the international proletariat.

If the beginning of the war exposed to Macdonald the nature of Stalinism, it also clarified the character of Nazism. Macdonald's "Notes on a Strange War," written in the spring of 1940 for the *Partisan*, contained an embryonic statement of his theory of "bureaucratic collectivism," which sought to extend a Marxian-like analysis to what he had concluded was the appearance of a new economic and social system, fascism. The major characteristic of this new state was the increased control of the government over the economy and the weakened control over the state exercised by traditional economic classes—in other words, the ascendancy of the mindless bureaucrats whom Macdonald had always abhorred. This development was true, he concluded, not only of Germany, but also of England and France because of pressures of the war.[2] The only "realistic hope" was for an alternative that did not support England or Germany: socialism was the only third choice.

As the European struggle intensified, Macdonald expanded his theory. The sudden victory of Germany over France, the almost effortless snuffing out of the independence of a once powerful nation, inspired Macdonald to the insight (and here he broke fundamentally with his fellow Trotskyists) that the war was a contest between two different social systems. France and England represented traditional capitalism, and Germany represented a new system that combined all of the worst features of a moribund capitalism with a new and effective use of state power and state economic planning—a deformed and hideous effigy of socialism. The fascist state, born in the suspension between two theories of social organization, emerged from this ideological vacuum as a new sort of society incapable of being defeated in battle except by a true socialist state or a state similar to a fascist one. The war, argued Macdonald, could not be won by a democratic United States, but only by a socialist or something like a fascist America, only by one or the other of the two systems capable of uniting all social groups. The role of the intellectual, he felt, was quite clear: "Only if we meet the stormy and terrible years ahead with both skepticism and devotion—skepticism toward all theories, governments, and social systems; devotion to the revolutionary fight of the masses— only then can we justify ourselves as intellectuals."[3] Perhaps only in detachment, from the remoteness of exile like Trotsky's or the internalized estrangement of the modern writer, could the intellectual perform his true role.

---

[2] Dwight Macdonald, "Reading from Right to Left," *New International,* V (May 1939), p. 153; "The War of the Neutrals," *Partisan Review,* VI (Fall 1939), p. 11; and "Notes on a Strange War," *Partisan Review,* VII (May-June 1940), pp. 170-175.
[3] Dwight Macdonald, "National Defense, the Case for Socialism," *Partisan Review,* VII (July-August 1940), pp. 253, 266.

Trotsky's inglorious assassination in the summer of 1940 by Stalinists in Mexico brought an editorial from Macdonald which touched the depths of his personal commitment to radicalism. Trotsky's death was symbolic, he wrote, of the extinction of hope for the Soviet Union, because only Trotsky might have led the revolution to overthrow the corrupt bureaucracy that ruled there. In an even larger sense, Trotsky's death was symbolic of the dark flood that had engulfed all of Europe. To Macdonald, Trotsky was primarily an intellectual: "a father to many of us in the sense that he taught us our political alphabet and first defined for us the problems to be solved, so that even when, in the manner of sons, we came to reject the parental ideas, our very rejection was in the terms he taught us."[4] It was Trotsky the intellectual, the idealist, the exiled critic of society that appealed to Macdonald and not the leader of the Red Army who had ordered the troops to crush the Kronstadt Rebellion.

Early in 1941, in the *New International*, Macdonald resumed his analysis of the German state. He asserted that the new state had essential similarities with the social system evolved in Russia after the degeneration of the Bolshevik Revolution. Russia was postcapitalist and so was Germany. Russia had destroyed the capitalist market and production for profit and so had Germany. This new "bureaucratic collectivism" was superior to capitalism in perhaps the only thing that mattered, its adaptation to war. Its current successes suggested its permanence. Switching to the *Partisan Review* again, Macdonald added an argument that again sharply divided him from more orthodox Trotskyists: the essence of the new fascist state was dependent on political power, not economic power. In Germany, the Nazis even exploited the bourgeoisie, and as they subverted the old function of classes, they transformed society itself. In an addendum Macdonald retreated slightly on one point, the permanence of fascism. He was no longer certain that the Nazi state would continue at its present level of stability.[5] Nevertheless, he remained convinced that only socialism or another fascist nation

---

[4] Dwight Macdonald, "Trotsky is Dead," *Partisan Review*, VII (September-October 1940), p. 352.
[5] Dwight Macdonald, "The End of Capitalism in Germany," *Partisan Review*, VIII (May-June 1941), pp. 207-208.

could defeat Germany in war. The flip-flop of Macdonald's discussion from the *Partisan* to the *New International* ended in mid-1941 when he stopped writing for the latter magazine and left the party. His theory of bureaucratic collectivism had by that time carried him too far from the Trotskyist center, even though he continued to call for a socialist America.

Macdonald was not the only exile from Trotskyism who used the insights of the "Old Man" to develop a new political theory. Far more important was James Burnham whose work, *The Managerial Revolution,* was published first in a condensed version in the June 1941 issue of the *Partisan Review.* Burnham's theory, like Macdonald's, sought to isolate what was new and common to fascism and Stalinism and to determine in what ways the traditional Marxist approach to history was erroneous. His conclusions strayed even further from orthodoxy than Macdonald's. Socialists, he argued, had been confounded by events of the 1930s and the war—so much so that it made "impossible an even roughly accurate anticipation of future events." Undaunted himself by this elusiveness of the future, Burnham dismissed capitalism and consigned it to a quiet grave, for he was interested in what would follow in its stead. Socialism was not the automatic outgrowth of capitalism, he argued; not at all. Instead, a new form of society had appeared that was governed by a managerial elite and exemplified in Russia and Germany. Thus the Bolshevik Revolution was a variant of the managerial revolution, as was the Nazi take-over in Germany and, to a limited extent, the New Deal in America. Questions of the degeneration of the Soviet Revolution, once this theory was accepted, became specious, he asserted: Stalinism was the direct heir of Leninism. Burnham's apparent admiration for the new class of managers, his argument from inevitability, and his casting aside of precious Marxian distinctions compelled Macdonald to reply. Reviewing Burnham's book in early 1942, he criticized the author's factual errors and his attempt to blur important differences, but most of all his tendency to disembowel the hope for socialism by predicting the inevitable triumph of the managerial revolution. The points raised by Burnham and Macdonald and their similar but distinct views of the new German state occupied the political writing of a number of contributors in the *Partisan Review* for much of 1941.[6]

Macdonald's last contribution to the magazine as an editor was part of the "New Failure of Nerve" series originated by Sidney Hook. Macdonald was pessimistic about the possibilities of guarding the future of democratic values. The war, he felt, was being fought increasingly on nonpolitical grounds: "It is notable that everything possible is done by our leaders to depoliticalize the war." The system of values based on reason and science, democracy and progress, "painfully built up since the end of the middle ages, and which has commanded general assent since the eighteenth century is today threatened as never before." The rise of bureaucratic collectivism endangered all of these values, but also presented revolutionary opportunities with the chance, even the necessity, to reassert the deeper meanings of human nature through social struggle. Socialism was no longer inevitable, he felt, even though it was desperately necessary.[7] But Macdonald was by now very much isolated from the other *Partisan* editors and its major contributors in his belief that it was still possible.

Politics to Rahv and Phillips after 1937, still at the center of their view of society, meant the vehicle for testing the theories of Marxism and for revising their earlier views. In another sense, politics implied anti-Stalinism, for Trotskyism was really only a temporary stance, and neither editor accepted the whole theory or felt compelled to contribute to the party press. The evolution of their political views narrowed the importance of politics and lessened their active interest in movements. One sign of this new meaning of politics was the symposium on what was living and dead in Marxism that the editors planned in early 1938. Letters asking for contributions were sent out, but the series never appeared. A second try at such a discussion occurred with

[6] James Burnham, "The Theory of the Managerial Revolution," *Partisan Review*, VIII (June-July 1941), p. 185, and Dwight Macdonald, "The Burnhamian Revolution," *Partisan Review*, IX (January-February 1942), pp. 83-84.
[7] Dwight Macdonald, "The Future of Democratic Values," *Partisan Review*, X (July-August 1943), pp. 324, 326, 342-344.

the publication of Edmund Wilson's article, "The Myth of the Marxist Dialectic," part of his larger work, *To the Finland Station*. Again, the editors attempted to begin a reappraisal of Marxism, planning to secure comments on the piece by Hook, Shapiro, Burnham, Bertram Wolfe, and others, although Macdonald commented to Wilson that he doubted that they could find anyone to defend the dialectic. Wilson's article, which appeared in the fall of 1938, was a strong condemnation of the dialectic, a characterization of that theory as semireligious idealism and mysticism. Wilson advised discarding the dialectic, since it hinged ultimately on Marx's "Germanism," not on science: it was an element of his thought approximating religious faith.[8]

The symposium idea never reached fulfillment; instead, William Phillips answered Wilson. Phillips's defense of Marx tried to restrict the German revolutionist's original use of the concept of dialectics. Marx was no metaphysician, he argued; he was a revolutionist and a philosopher of social action. Marxism was not inaccurate; only the subsequent generations that had failed to move beyond his original insights were to blame for the mysticism that surrounded this concept. In his anxiety to preserve Marxism, Phillips raised the possibility that Marxism, or most of it, would eventually be discarded as obsolete, by arguing for a narrow interpretation of its original meaning. But one crucial idea, aside from certain political insights, made Marx important to Phillips: his consistent concern for the problem of alienation. Marx never tired of "pointing out the growing self-alienation, in capitalist society, which smothers man's creative impulses." Marxism seemed most relevant to Phillips in its support for the view that the creative man and the intellectual were almost inevitably alienated from bourgeois society. By 1942, Rahv and Macdonald, when asked to contribute to a symposium on the dialectic by the magazine *DYN*, considered the issue dead and their replies dismissed the theory as irrelevant.[9]

[8] Norman Thomas to Philip Rahv, January 18, 1938, and Dwight Macdonald to Edmund Wilson, August 31, 1938, *Partisan* MSS. See also Edmund Wilson, "Myth of the Marxist Dialectic," *Partisan Review*, VI (Fall 1938), p. 80.

[9] William Phillips, "Devil Theory of the Dialectic," *Partisan Review*, VI (Fall 1938), p. 90, and *DYN* (July-August 1942), p. 50.

In the fall of 1938 Rahv wrote that the one beneficial effect of the destruction of the Communist movement was that it would make true socialism possible again: "Once the interests of the mind are no longer confused with the interests of the Soviet bureaucrats, it may again be possible to define political differences without mystification and to revive the original meaning of the socialist doctrine." What socialism meant to Rahv was revealed in his attempt to redefine politics in an article clearly meant for the series "What is living and what is dead in Marxism?" Rahv felt compelled to pose this question, but he recognized that it also meant "taking our ideological lives into our hands." The crisis of Marxism had arisen, he argued, because the social revolution had failed, the Soviet Union had failed, and political reaction had succeeded. The old notion that new values attached themselves automatically to the working class was irrelevant and false, for the proletariat had not fulfilled its predicted role in history: "In its own right the proletariat represents no ideals—it is only in its role as a dynamic and militant force in the struggle to liberate humanity that values can be attached to it." Rahv's rejection of inevitability and the automatic process of history paralleled his dismissal of naturalism, which, he had argued, was the automatic incorporation of reality into art. The distance between this and his proletarianism of the early 1930s was enormous, even greater when it is recognized that Rahv believed that ideals and values did in a sense attach themselves to another class in society, the intellectuals. Rahv agreed with Edmund Wilson that the dialectic should be discarded, and he would also throw out the concept of the dictatorship of the proletariat in its Bolshevik incarnation. Moreover, the highly disciplined political party, a Leninist party, seemed particularly misguided.

Most significant of all, perhaps, was the admiration that Rahv showed for Hook and Burnham, against whom the arguments of orthodox Marxists, he wrote, seemed pitiful.[10] Hook and Burnham, both in the philosophy department of New York University, be-

---

[10] Philip Rahv, "Munich and the Intellectuals," *Partisan Review,* VI (Fall 1938), p. 8, and Rahv, "What is Living and What is Dead," *Partisan Review,* VII (May-June 1940), pp. 175, 177-178.

came increasingly the political spokesmen for one strong tendency within the *Partisan Review* that was opposed to Macdonald. The difference between Macdonald and Hook had been apparent from the days of their rival committees of intellectuals for cultural freedom. But now, because Rahv and Phillips wrote less on politics, Hook and Burnham became more important, even if they did not always express precisely what Rahv and Phillips felt. Furthermore, the influence of James T. Farrell, who remained a Trotskyist, waned until by the mid-1940s he no longer wrote for the magazine. Even unorthodox Trotskyists wrote less for the magazine after this point.

The importance of Sidney Hook added a new dimension to political discussions and disputes in the magazine. Hook's controversial articles and reviews at this time alternated between two broad topics: the retreat from reason that, he felt, was exemplified in Jacques Maritain and others and his own retreat from orthodox Marxism as he identified more elements of revolutionary theory with the Soviet Union that he despised. The latter topic had two major characteristics. One was the recurring analysis, ever more critical, of the Soviet Union. The second was the attempt to discredit the intellectual premises of Stalinism and to discredit those intellectuals who might subscribe to any part of them. During the war, particularly while Macdonald remained an editor, the two topics balanced each other. But one characteristic about Hook's comments on both subjects was especially noteworthy: his discussion of politics in ideological and philosophic terms. His desire to drive ideas back to their philosophic origins matched his tendency to take the ideas of American Communists and sympathetic liberals and expose their similarity to Soviet policy. His schematic discussions overlaid his judgments with moralism. Implicit in his writings was the necessity he felt to choose and the necessity to reject totally the ideas deemed irresponsible or dangerous.

The fight among the editors over support or opposition to the world war, which reflected their different political philosophies, became the issue that shattered the alliance between Rahv and Phillips and Macdonald. In the struggle over editorial policy Macdonald was temporarily seconded by Clement Green-

berg, a literary and art critic brought onto the staff by Macdonald.
Although Greenberg agreed with Macdonald politically and on
important cultural issues, he did not share a deep commitment
to the Trotskyist movement, nor did he contribute to their publications.[11]

Aside from cultural issues, Macdonald and Greenberg also
agreed on the meaning of the war. In July 1941 they signed a
manifesto that opposed the position of other members of the
editorial board and defined clearly the points of difference.
These "Ten Propositions on the War" argued that the struggle
must be opposed by revolutionary socialism, for only the working class fighting against the Roosevelt–Churchill regimes and
then taking power could ever hope to defeat fascism. The working class need not be regimented into a Leninist party; a social
democratic government would suffice. Even if no revolutionary
leadership existed for such a program, this lack was not fatal.
The argument of the manifesto, a condensation of Macdonald's
views on the meaning of the war and the new social system in
Germany, was really an outline of the attitudes that intellectuals
should take toward the war: "The only way this conflict can be
won in the interests of mankind as a whole is by some method of
warfare that will transfer the struggle from the flesh of humanity
to its mind. Such a method is offered only by the cause of the
socialist revolution."[12] Only through socialism, Macdonald felt,
could the war become political and the participation of the intellectual a positive force. Only socialism could restore the human
values and the intellectual integrity to civilization that "bureaucratic collectivism," degenerate mass art, and the tradition of

[11] Greenberg was born in The Bronx in New York in 1919 to parents who
were both Jewish immigrants. After attending Syracuse University he entered his father's dry goods business. From there he went to work for the
United States Civil Service Commission and entered the customs service
of the Port of New York in 1937. Greenberg had a deep interest in art
and attended W.P.A. art classes in 1937, but he recounts that his acquaintance with artistic circles in New York at the end of the 1930s was slight.
While an editor of *Partisan Review*, he "was almost entirely out of touch
with art life." Kunitz, "Clement Greenberg," *Authors*, 1st Supplement,
p. 386, and Clement Greenberg, "The Late Thirties in New York," *Critical
Essays* (Boston: Beacon Press, 1961), p. 230.
[12] Clement Greenberg and Dwight Macdonald, "Ten Propositions," *Partisan Review*, VIII (July-August 1941), p. 278.

banal patriotism had destroyed. The struggle against war meant
to Macdonald the struggle against these things.

Rahv replied to this analyses in the next issue in "Ten Propositions and Eight Errors." His fellow editors, he argued, were
wrong at precisely the most crucial point in their thesis: that
their opposition to the war had any meaning at all. No movement, class, or party, no group of influential intellectuals, supported their ideas; thus no revolution was possible. All of this
was utopianism, Rahv countered, for the war could in fact be
won by democratic capitalism. After the war was over socialists
could turn to socialism. In a rebuttal in the same issue Greenberg and Macdonald refused to retreat before Rahv's logic and
again made a case for the possibility of socialist revolution.
Both positions remained at this point until Macdonald left the
magazine in 1943.

Macdonald's assumptions about the posture that the *Partisan*
should take toward the war were suggested in connection with
a letter to him from Karl Shapiro printed in the fall of 1941.
Shapiro, having been asked by Macdonald to write an "army
letter" for the magazine, replied that he had changed his mind.
He found none of the things wrong with army life that he and
Macdonald expected: no undue patriotic and political pressures,
unfair treatment of Negroes, or poor relations between officers
and men.[13] The column that Macdonald had tried to secure for
the magazine (and which anticipated much of his own writing
for *Politics*) would have been an exposé of the style of life in
the army and the conduct of the war.

The fight over the war, especially heated in late 1941, threatened to consume the magazine after Pearl Harbor in December.
Rather than claw each other verbally, the editors decided to
call a truce: "It is clear," they wrote in early 1942, "that Partisan Review can have no editorial line on the war." Although
discussion of the war on the home front slackened, the flow
from England became important. George Orwell, before the
war relatively unknown in America, was persuaded to write a
"London Letter" beginning in early 1941. These letters proved

---

[13] Karl Shapiro to Dwight Macdonald, *Partisan Review*, VIII (September-
October 1941), p. 439.

to be particularly important in the evolution of the *Partisan* for a number of reasons. First, they supplied Macdonald with reasons for, or at least reinforced, his assertions about the nature of the war, particularly as to British war aims and the possibilities for revolutionary change in England. Moreover, Orwell's letters and replies to his remarks by other English writers recreated in British terms the arguments for and against the war that separated the *Partisan* editors. Finally, the contact with Orwell and Stephen Spender brought the magazine in touch with Cyril Connolly's *Horizon*, in some ways an English counterpart of the *Partisan Review*.[14]

Important similarities between the *Partisan* and the *Horizon* were indicated by the fact that the two magazines were quite conscious of each other. Poet Harvey Breit was correct in part when he called *Horizon* the "Partisan Review's English Brother." Connolly, editor of the English periodical, wrote that *Partisan Review* was "by far the most interesting and progressive literary magazine in America, as well as politically the most far-sighted." But the affinity between the two magazines was perhaps more symbolic than actual. Each magazine grew out of a cultural atmosphere dominated by Communist intellectuals; each developed in somewhat the same direction—toward an emphasis on intellectual not political art. Possibly the best comment on the meaning of *Horizon's* appearance was made by poet C. Day Lewis, who wrote that the format of the new magazine was representative of a large body of opinion among writers in England who felt that the emphasis for the present must be on the artist as artist rather than on the artist as a prophet.[15]

Orwell's early letters dealt widely with two things: the effect of Communism in England at all levels, on intellectuals, statesmen, and the working class, and the potentialities for transforming the war into a struggle for socialism. He was most devastating in his attacks on the implications of Stalinism. The outbreak of war, he argued, had caught the Communist intellectuals unawares; the war, when it came, was not at all like the great

---

[14] Stephen Spender was an editor of *Horizon* and Sonya Orwell a staff member.
[15] C. Day Lewis to the League of American Writers, March 17, 1940, p. 5, LAW MSS.

antifascist crusade that they had expected. Again and again he returned to the point that infuriated British opponents of the war: to be effectively antiwar in England, he asserted, "one has to be pro-Hitler." But at the same time Orwell continued to take note of "revolutionary situations" in England that offered themselves after Dunkirk and during the summer of 1942. Thus Orwell's contributions could be used to support either the position of Rahv, or Macdonald, or both.

In mid-1942 the *Partisan* printed a number of articles discussing pacifism and the war, which took issue with Orwell's harsh formulation that opposition to the war was in effect pro-Nazism. Poets Alex Comfort and D. S. Savage as well as George Woodcock observed that pacifism was not "objectively, pro-German"; on the contrary, it offered the only viable alternative to fighting fascism with fascism. Macdonald's position here was much closer to that of the English pacifists, while Rahv and Phillips in their support of the war were closer to Orwell.[16] The argument between British intellectuals partly echoed and partly replaced the submerged political dispute between the American editors. Thus the extensive debate over the position of English intellectuals released the repressed argument over the war that divided Rahv and Phillips, Macdonald and Greenberg.

The political truce between the editors of the *Partisan* was a sign to more orthodox Trotskyists of implicit support for the war. But reluctance to discuss the war was also related to the possibility that the magazine might be shut down by the government for its position.[17] Irving Howe in early 1942 wrote in the *New International* of the "Dilemma of Partisan Review." Howe argued that by remaining silent on the war the magazine had destroyed its future. In a reply Macdonald found himself defending the *Partisan* on the grounds that it was primarily a cultural not a political magazine, an argument that would return to haunt him the next year. Macdonald was candid, however, about the possibilities of settling the dispute. If the "left wing," meaning himself and Greenberg were to try to take over

16 George Orwell, "London Letter," *Partisan Review*, VIII (July-August 1941), p. 317, and "Pacifism and the War: A Controversy," *Partisan Review*, IX (September-October 1942), pp. 414-416.
17 Interview with Dwight Macdonald.

the magazine, they would either have to destroy it or leave, neither of which would make the *Partisan Review* an antiwar journal. The rebuttal by the editors of the *New International* was in the main a personal attack on Macdonald and his strange career in the Trotskyist movement, where, they claimed, he spent all of his time, "quibbling about theory and organizational principles, none of which he was fully acquainted with then nor understands any better since his departure." They argued that whatever Macdonald might say, the *Partisan Review* was quickly becoming pro-war, for it printed Orwell's letters without comment, while it refused to publish criticisms of the magazine made by James T. Farrell.[18] One argument of the editors sounded a prophecy: Macdonald's career in Trotskyism had ended because the movement was unwilling to let him express unpopular ideas that were contrary to accepted policy. In a little more than a year this same constriction caused him to break with the *Partisan Review*.

A number of factors precipitated Macdonald's resignation from the staff. For one thing he was isolated in his opposition to the war after Greenberg left the magazine in early 1943 to enter the Air Force. This isolation was acutely apparent in the course of the "New Failure of Nerve" series beginning in 1943. The collection of articles, devoted to an examination of the decline of reason evident in philosophic thought in Europe and America, was an extension and a much fuller development of ideas expressed earlier by Sidney Hook and in the issue of the *Partisan* in the summer of 1942 devoted to discussing the new historical theories of decline advanced by Toynbee and Spengler, theories that seemed inspired by desperate political crises.

Sidney Hook's "Failure of Nerve" was a broad defense of science and rationality against the growing currency of the nonrational theories of Kirkegaard, Reinhold Niebuhr, Jacques Maritain, and Aldous Huxley, which placed a large emphasis on evil in mankind and in society and stressed faith over reason in the final analysis of social and human problems. Drawing from important intellectuals associated with Columbia Uni-

---

18 "Partisan Review Controversy," *New International*, VIII (April 1942), pp. 92, 93.

versity, the symposium featured vigorous defenses of science by Ernest Nagel, Richard Chase, and John Dewey. The central document, however, was written by Hook. "The new failure of nerve in contemporary culture," he noted, "is compounded of unwarranted hopes and unfounded beliefs. It is a desperate quest for a quick and all-inclusive faith that will save us from the trouble of thinking about difficult problems."[19] Lurking behind this escape from the scientific method, Hook found two decades of totalitarianism, of economic crisis, and of the failure of socialism. The result of the decline in reason was the false profundity of theologians like Reinhold Niebuhr. Although Hook's arguments in favor of the scientific method are important, the political conclusions that he drew from them are even more significant. In a sequel, published in the next issue, he tied the preservation of rationality and of the scientific orientation to reality, to support for the war, and to support for democracy, welfare, and a planned economy. Those who opposed the war were in grave error; that handful of Trotskyists, "Romantic Revolutionists" like Macdonald, certain socialists, and a few others were confused and misled. The war, he argued, could be a democratic war, and it was the duty of the intellectual to support it. Thus the failure of nerve that Hook described took two forms: the urge toward faith implicit in the neoreligious revival and the implicit utopianism expressed by the last defenders of revolution.

Macdonald defended himself in the course of an article that was part of the symposium. He acknowledged the insights of Hook, Nagel, and Dewey in diagnosing a turn toward obscurantism in American thinking. But these Columbia philosophers, he felt, were overly optimistic about the means of preserving democracy. The allied armies were not the conquering legions of freedom, he replied, but nonpolitical soldiers in a nonideological struggle. Only revolution, now dimmer even to him, seemed to offer any hope for the preservation of values worth the struggle.

Macdonald's ability to tread a course of noncommitment, to

---

[19] Sidney Hook, "The New Failure of Nerve," *Partisan Review*, X (January-February 1943), p. 23.

compromise his strongest views, cut out the heart of the jour-nalistic style that he had developed since leaving Luce. The necessity of holding back his opposition to the war was unbear-able, and he left a situation that he felt he could no longer control. In this way his final separation from Rahv and Phillips is reminiscent of his break with *Fortune*. The immediate cir-cumstance for his resignation was a financial crisis in the maga-zine. During the summer of 1943 the *Partisan* had apparently exhausted its funds, and there was some question about con-tinuing publication on any basis. The editors agreed that if Rahv and Phillips could not raise sufficient funds to continue, Macdonald would take control of the magazine. If they did succeed in raising the money, he would resign. In a letter to Rahv, Macdonald enclosed a proposed editorial announcing the end of the *Partisan Review* in its present form and its revival in a new guise, under the editorship of Macdonald. Macdonald insisted that the editorial include the statement that political as well as cultural differences had been at issue between the edi-tors.

By September the fate of the magazine was settled: Rahv and Phillips were able to continue publication on the old basis, and Macdonald resigned. His letter of resignation was a sharp attack on the magazine, but a candid statement of his reasons for quitting. He had been disturbed, he wrote, by the growing academicism of the magazine, its reluctance to take chances, and its conservatism on vital political issues such as the war. He, alone, among the editors, he claimed, had maintained a Marxist position. The magazine had been hushed on political questions at the very time when political and social comments were in great need. Announcing that he would begin a new magazine on politics, he asserted that by his leaving "from now on Partisan Review will devote itself to cultural issues, leaving the thorny field of politics to others."[20]

Phillips and Rahv replied with equal sharpness, defending the position of the *Partisan*, its Marxism, and its style of political

---

[20] Dwight Macdonald to Philip Rahv, June, 1943?, *Partisan* MSS, and Dwight Macdonald, Letter to the Editors, *Partisan Review*, X (July-August 1943), p. 382.

commitment. Macdonald, they argued, had sought to change the magazine and subordinate culture to politics, the very issue that caused their original dispute with the Communists. Furthermore, Macdonald was wrong in equating all politics with his own special brand of Trotskyism. The policy of the magazine would continue to be the "modulation" of socialist ideas with a varied literary and critical content.[21]

The *Partisan Review* foundered and smashed against the shoals that it had so widely avoided when it had been relaunched six years earlier. The immense changes in culture set off by the war and the evolution of new political and cultural interests by the editors changed the direction of the magazine, until it was once again pointed dangerously at the protruding problem of how to merge politics and culture. During the years, Macdonald had greatly changed his conception of the magazine. He had defined a politics that was so intensely personal as to defy compromise. But Rahv and Phillips also had shifted their views of culture and politics. Now they tended more and more to separate literature from politics to the point where it meant little more (when it was not completely subsumed in literary issues) than the guardianship of the intellectual's political conscience. Literary issues became their central interest, with particular attention to the role of the intellectual as a distinct social and psychological type whose sole property was culture and whose work was avant-garde art. Macdonald, too, was devoted to the preservation of culture, but to him the war threatened destruction of the values he cherished; to compromise on the war meant to compromise his own role as a radical intellectual. No center, however elastic, no institution could modulate these distinct views.

---

[21] William Phillips and Philip Rahv, "Reply," *Partisan Review*, X (July-August 1943), pp. 382-383. Apparently Burnham was opposed also to Macdonald; he wrote to Rahv in 1943 that he was looking forward to the *Partisan* without Macdonald. James Burnham to Philip Rahv, October 5, 1943, *Partisan* MSS.

Chapter 8

The Failure of Nerve

It is when men no longer feel that they have
adequate choices in their styles of life, when
they conclude that there are no longer possibilities for honorable maneuver and compromise, when they decide that the time has
come for "ultimate" social loyalties and political decisions—it is then that ideology begins
to flourish. Ideology reflects a hardening of
commitment, the freezing of opinion into system.

Irving Howe, *Politics and the Novel*

European culture, when it emerged from World War II, wore
its suffering openly: some intellectuals had died, many were
scattered by the conflict into exile; lives were disrupted and
cultural centers split apart. In America the wounds of war were
more often to the mind. The bitter experience of the 1930s,
bitter most of all for the radical American intellectual, clouded
the postwar years with the memory of a decade driven by the
necessity to choose and choose again between good and evil,
a decade when choices promised purity, but produced only
compromise. It had been a time unusual for the seeming clarity
of political and cultural issues, but quite ordinary in the sense
that issues in the long run were not clear and no choice was
easy. "What strikes me most, looking back," wrote Dwight Macdonald, "is the contrast between the scope of our thought and
the modesty of our actions."[1] The aspirations of the 1930s lay

---

[1] Macdonald, "Memoirs of a Revolutionist," *Memoirs of a Revolutionist,*
p. 22.

253

unfulfilled upon the spirit, and compromises made in their name seemed to infect the conscience. The war, if it did anything to the American radical community, now by and large an ex-radical community, swept away the expectations born of the catastrophe of 1929. It demanded attention to reality by destroying the hope for change, a reality that had always existed but was repressed in the name of renaissance and revolution. The society that fought and won the war was not the regimented, fascist-like state that Macdonald had feared, nor was it a society cleansed by a great and successful world crusade for democracy. What emerged was a mediocre society whose senses were dulled to the issues of culture and politics but which was able, nevertheless, to convey an overwhelming sense of permanence. World War II had a very different effect on people than the previous war, wrote John Dos Passos: "the brutalities of war and oppression come as less of a shock to people who grew up in the thirties than to Americans of my generation . . . who were confident that industrial progress meant an improved civilization . . . a more humane and peaceful society." In the period after the war it was obvious to some of the older generation of radicals that the American environment was drastically changed. Floyd Dell wrote of this change in the early 1950s: "Thirty-odd years ago, when I was on trial, I felt that the contest between me and the United States Government with all its powers was a contest between equals, and as a matter of fact I won; but I think the odds against me would be too heavy nowadays. . . ."[2]

Arthur Koestler's call for an "active fraternity of pessimists" who understood the failure of progress, socialism, and history seemed a first step toward making the war and the Depression decade understandable and reasonable. Koestler used the Moscow Trials in his important book *Darkness at Noon* to illuminate the failure of categories of thought that had dominated the period. The vogue of Koestler (". . . his books and articles seem to be discussed everywhere," commented Macdonald, "from liberal cocktail parties to C.O. camps") was evidence that expectations for the future would be lowered and faith in change

---

[2] Dos Passos, "Preface," *First Encounter,* p. 7. Floyd Dell to Elizabeth Lancaster, March 23, 1951, Washington, p. 15, Dell MSS.

diminished. In 1945 Rahv wrote of Koestler that he was the poet
and the ideologue of the "homeless radical" who had emerged
from the war and that his sketch of this new sort of radical
made the "'positive contributions' featured in the liberal press
seem puerile and insane."[3]

To the editors of the *Partisan Review*, the events of the late
1930s and the war years forced a revision of their expectations
for a literary and a political renaissance. The optimism of Bohemia and even the incisive skepticism of the "new generation"
of 1937, two important traditions out of which the magazine
had grown, gave way to less optimistic priorities. The 1930s
had failed, socialism had failed, the literary revolution had
failed, and the portrait of the artist at the end of the war was
the disheartening "portrait of the artist as a middle aged man."[4]
The presuppositions of liberal and radical politics and the faith
in reason and progress seemed confounded by the irrationalities
of war and the brutality of struggle. The *Partisan* editors and
many of their contributors interpreted the failure of politics
and culture as a sign to glance inward at the psychology of the
intellectual and thus extend and refine the discussion of the intelligentsia begun in 1937.

Despite the constriction of hope, many old habits of mind
lingered. It was still necessary to reject liberalism in literature
and nationalistic art. In fact, it seemed even more important
to attack the liberal tenets of politics that had been associated
with Communism, beginning in 1936 with the Popular Front
and extending throughout the wartime alliance with the Soviet
Union. If the world was less a place to fulfill the hopes of a
culture in 1945, it was also for a short time less dramatically
divided. But the old urge to choose, to commit oneself, persisted.
Once the war was over and fascism was destroyed, the Soviet
Union abroad and the Communist party in America suddenly
became the greatest danger. It now seemed imperative to destroy any alliance with them and to create once more a

[3] Dwight Macdonald, "Comment," *Politics*, I (February 1944), p. 4. Philip
Rahv, "Koestler and Homeless Radicalism," *Partisan Review*, XII (Summer 1945), p. 399.
[4] William Phillips, "Portrait of the Artist as Middle Aged Man," *Partisan
Review*, XI (Winter 1944), p. 120.

Manichaean political world where choice was as possible as it had been in the 1930s. But the simplicity and finality of such a political scheme was again complicated, as it had been before, by the uneasiness that the *Partisan* editors felt about the American environment, with its tradition of pragmatic politics and realistic and naturalistic art.

At a time when it was crucial to understand the past, both its literature and its politics, reason seemed less important than it once had, while psychology, providing insights into the personal alienation of the intellectual, appeared to be a key to understanding. William Phillips wrote that what has been designated as the "modern experience" is the "unique combination of neurotic experience with some apparently objective or plausible view of the world, such as we find in writers like Kafka or Eliot. . . ."[5] An appeal to experience or reliance on automatic progress (which Rahv had felt to be characteristic of many American writers) no more explained the political climate of the 1930s to the editors of the *Partisan* than it explained the whole complex of problems to which the avant-garde artist addressed himself. The more subtle science of psychology provided an element of thought that had been underestimated before the war.

After the split with Macdonald the *Partisan Review*, true to his prediction, did avoid ordinary politics. There were no comments opposing the war, little criticism of its conduct, and even less discussion of the Soviet Union than had been typical of the previous Trotskyist period. But by the end of the war the *Partisan* again became absorbed in politics, particularly in examining the implications of the alliance with the Soviet Union, and the remnants of the Popular Front. It was during these years, shortly before and after the end of the war, that the political stance of the magazine was solidified. The *Partisan Review* devoted itself to the politics of the intellectual and helped lead a campaign to destroy the remnants of the Popular Front, which had prospered because of the wartime alliance. The magazine became the conscience and the guardian of the radical intellectual.

---

[5] William Phillips, "Art and Neurosis," *Art and Psychoanalysis* (New York: Criterion Books, 1957), p. xix.

One major thrust of the magazine was directed against what it called the "totalitarian liberal": "one who voices the liberal tradition, yet through his action helps create the totalitarian society. The most common species is the fellow-traveler, the man who feels that Russia is on the 'right road.'" Further evidence of the new attention given to ending the influence of Communism came in a change in the emphasis in works by Sidney Hook. In the spring of 1944 Hook was still concerned with the revival of conservatism, the revival of classicism and religion in education. In an article defending John Dewey and his ideas of progressive education, the philosopher argued that Mark Van Doren's book, *Liberal Education*, was part of a wider cultural retreat from reason. But by the summer Hook had changed his appraisal of the order of threats to American culture. Writing to Rahv, he suggested that the *Partisan* meet Stalinism head-on, Jacques Maritain, his old enemy, and the Catholic Church now seemed to him much less a danger.[6]

The *Partisan Review* interpreted the postwar struggle against the influence of Communism as an immensely difficult one: Stalinism appeared to be as well entrenched as it had been in 1937. In a letter to George Orwell in early 1946 Rahv commented that he doubted if Orwell's book, *Animal Farm*, would receive as favorable a reception in America as it had in England: "Public opinion here is almost solidly Stalinist, in the bourgeois as well as the liberal press. At least that is what it looks like in New York." Similarly, when William Phillips wrote to Arthur Koestler in 1946 asking him to become the magazine's London correspondent, he cited the influence of Stalinism as the central cultural and political issue of the day: "We need hardly tell you that there is a good deal of confusion and ignorance among American liberals on the question of Stalinism. We have done everything we can to explode the Stalinist mythology."[7]

The fear that Stalinism had invaded the centers of journalism and the organs of the liberal intellectual life was an old one,

---

[6] Sidney Hook, "God, Geometry, and the Good Society," *Partisan Review*, XI (Spring 1944), p. 161. Sidney Hook to Philip Rahv, August 15, 1945, *Partisan* MSS.
[7] Philip Rahv to George Orwell, January 11, 1946, and William Phillips to Arthur Koestler, October 9, 1946, *Partisan* MSS.

but in the postwar period this influence appeared to take on a new and ominous quality. Before the war the *Partisan Review* editors had criticized the Communists essentially from a Trotskyist position, for Macdonald, and even Rahv and Phillips, were convinced that the Bolshevik Revolution had decayed and degenerated because of the corrupting grasp of Stalin. The revolution had been betrayed; however, revolution as an ideal still appealed to them. But the postwar politics of the *Partisan Review* was directed against this ideal, for it no longer seemed that the Russian Revolution was even in its earliest stages the great progressive force they had once believed it to be. Moreover, Stalin could no longer be viewed merely as the corruptor of a revolution; somehow it had to be explained how Russia had emerged so successfully and powerfully from the war with Stalin at its head; how it was that the Soviet Union could pose a direct military and political threat to America.

Perhaps the most important article in the revision of thinking about the Soviet Union was James Burnham's "Lenin's Heir," but it was, strangely, an article with which neither Rahv nor Phillips agreed. Burnham's reappraisal of Stalin did not equivocate. Trotsky was wrong: contemporary Soviet Russia did not exhibit the revolution betrayed, but the revolution fulfilled. Burnham disagreed fundamentally with Trotsky that Stalin was a mediocre leader. On the contrary, he argued, Stalin was a leader in the oldest tradition of Russian tyrants, the czars; consequently, he was a great man. It was crucial to realize, he concluded, that "Stalinism is Communism."[8] Burnham's article, much like his managerial thesis presented some years before, was an attempt to demonstrate that a contemporary situation was the inevitable result of its origins, an inexorable unfolding which would continue until the world was covered by the new society. Thus, since Germany, Russia, and to some extent the United States had certain similarities, insofar as they shared these they were part of the same inevitable managerial revolution. In much the same manner he concluded that Stalinism was really Communism and, not allowing for historical differ-

---

[8] James Burnham, "Lenin's Heir," *Partisan Review*, XII (Winter 1945), pp. 70, 72.

ences, that Stalin was great in the way that the Russian czars had been great.

This total rejection of Trotskyism brought an angry rebuttal from Dwight Macdonald, who took time out from editing his own magazine to reply to Burnham. As he had done once before, Macdonald pounced upon Burnham's argument from inevitability, an argument that, he claimed, lurked near the center of the article. Burnham was wrong to assume that Stalin, because he was a great man, was also a continuance of the tradition of Lenin. He compared Burnham to Koestler for trying to withdraw morality and ethics from politics in an effort, it seemed, to prepare American intellectuals for submission and obedience. But Macdonald was most upset by the fact that *Partisan Review* had printed this article without a disclaimer. The implication of Macdonald's rejoinder—that the editors agreed substantially with the article—was, in many ways, unfair, for the *Partisan Review* often printed, without comment, articles whose views were not precisely those of the editors', something that Macdonald undoubtedly would admit in his less polemic moments. On the other hand, Macdonald was right to impute some agreement by the editors with the general direction of Burnham's article, which pointed to a rejection of Trotskyism and a revised attitude toward the Soviet Union based on its postwar power. Rahv and Phillips, although not considering Leninism to be synonymous with Stalinism, saw certain elements of continuity. But more important, Burnham's elevation of Stalin to the category of a great man and his awe at the new Soviet power provided an argument that tended to justify the magazine's greatly heightened fear of Communism.[9] If Stalin were a great man, his movement should be feared, not dismissed.

Phillips, in a reply both to Macdonald and to Burnham, struck out for a middle ground between the two, but occupied terrain closer to the latter. Although he felt that Burnham's theory was essentially wrong, he argued that Macdonald's stand was much too optimistic because he chose a "third camp" position between the Soviet Union and the United States where

---

[9] Dwight Macdonald, "Beat Me Daddy," *Partisan Review*, XII (Spring 1945), p. 181.

none seemed to exist. But Phillips agreed with Burnham at one critical point. He accepted the advice that the left must alter its appraisal of the Soviet Union: the war had irrevocably proven that Russia had the industry, courage, and strength to defeat Germany, when such a victory had not seemed plausible.[10] The meaning of this argument would soon be made clearer, but what was already apparent was the idea that because Russia had survived and had become a great power, it was also a much greater threat to America, and anyone who supported it or attempted to accommodate it was himself a threat to the cultural and political life of the United States. Because of this feeling, the experiences of the intellectual in the Communist movement in the 1930s became lessons to instruct American radicalism.

In the summer of 1946 Rahv indicated that he also agreed at other points with Burnham's thesis. Reviewing the biography of Stalin, by Leon Trotsky, he wrote that Trotsky's theory of the bureaucracy had been demolished; in its stead stood the reality of a new ruling class of a new social order, as inimical to socialism as to capitalism. He agreed that Stalin should be compared with the Russian czars, although he was not prepared to admit that Stalinism was merely a modern projection of Leninism.

The summation of these new views on Russia, the statement of the *Partisan's* basic political orientation, appeared in an editorial printed in the summer of 1946. The editorial, "The 'Liberal' Fifth Column," was an intense and acid denunciation of liberals who favored accommodation to the Russians; it was a piece of writing that seemed to gather strength from a fear of the Soviet Union and its unexpected resiliency and power. Drawing upon idioms from the 1930s, the editorial denounced those Americans who favored the Communists, whose actions resembled a "fifth column." The editorial spread a net and caught in it all those who favored "appeasement": The *New Republic*, the *Nation*, *PM* (the New York newspaper), and even the "Tireless Eleanor Roosevelt," who continued her "tiresome pleas

---

[10] William Phillips, "The Lion and the Foxes," *Partisan Review*, XII (Spring 1945), p. 191.

for 'cooperation' with Russia in order to insure Russian 'security.' " The Communist position was no longer of intellectual interest, for the falseness of it had been already decided. What mattered now was that Communists operated in the interest of Russia: "In a situation of impending or existing hostility between America and Russia, the Communists will be dealt with for what they are, outright foreign agents. . . ." A year earlier Rahv had used the term "fifth column" to describe what was elsewhere called the "totalitarian liberal." But the limits of the concept of the liberal as traitor were expanded greatly in this editorial. In another direction, the editorial also denounced the "timidly conservative" American State Department whom the liberals, it was felt, were attempting to cajole into "pulling Stalin's chestnuts out of the fire for him."[11] The proposal to invest the American State Department with the task of creating an "aggressively democratic policy," that is of depending on the government to spread the social system, democracy, of which the editors approved, was a complete reversal of their attitude during the 1930s when almost nothing of value was consigned to the safekeeping of government, when values were "rescued" from society. Lowered to the soil of American life by four years of war, the *Partisan* accepted the politics of desperation and saw an end to practical alternatives: there seemed only two choices for them, America or Russia, democratic capitalism or Stalinism. The final portion of the editorial rang a slightly ominous note: reactionaries, it argued, were never intelligent in their discernment of differences on the left; thus if reaction came to dominate American political life, it would probably attack all dissension and suppress civil liberties. In a letter a few months later William Phillips made this point in stronger language. Communism, he noted, "is one of the central political and cultural issues today, and the Left must not permit the struggle against Stalinism to be appropriated by the Right."[12]

Once again Dwight Macdonald found the political pronounce-

---

[11] William Barrett, "The Liberal Fifth Column," *Partisan Review*, XIII (Summer 1946), pp. 283, 286, 292. Philip Rahv to Author, March 22, 1966. See also Rahv, "Koestler and Homeless Radicalism," *Partisan Review*, XII (Summer 1945), p. 401.
[12] William Phillips to Arthur Koestler, October 9, 1946, *Partisan MSS.*

ments of his former editorial partners surprising and untenable, and he said so in *Politics*. Responding to this attack, the editors of the *Partisan* extended their net farther and caught Macdonald in the ideological snare of supporting Stalinism: "Since Macdonald has dismissed every possible political opposition to Stalinism, what his position comes down to—in objective terms —is a complete surrender to Stalin." No third position, no alternative seemed at all reasonable to them, nor did they feel that one could mediate between Stalinism and democracy, as some liberals advised. The only alternative was to give support to American policy insofar as it was democratic and oppose it when it did not meet such standards.

Macdonald's rebuttal, again in *Politics*, made the differences between him and the *Partisan Review* sharp and distinct. True, he admitted, he did take a "third camp" position which searched for a choice besides that between the United States and the Soviet Union, but it was not he who evaded politics, but the *Partisan Review*. Furthermore, since he had left it the magazine had scarcely ever discussed politics and had relinquished criticism of Stalinism because the editors supported the war and found it uncomfortable to attack an ally. However one might try to disguise its meaning, he concluded, the editorial was testimony to the *Partisan's* "explicitly making its peace with the status quo."[13]

The disagreement over the meaning of politics which had helped construct a wall of arguments between Macdonald and Rahv and Phillips in 1943 was even more apparent in this exchange. To the *Partisan* editors, politics meant the politics of necessity, dominated by the need to choose sides in a world where two ideas possessed hegemony over two spheres of interest. It was a politics that demanded that they commit themselves—but tentatively—in order to accept responsibility only for approved policies or for those that approximated the democratic standards that they demanded. The compulsion to choose and yet, within the context of a basic commitment, to remain

---

[13] "The Fugitive from Politics: Dwight Macdonald," *Partisan Review*, XIII (November-December 1946), pp. 612, 616, and Dwight Macdonald, "'Partisan Review' and Politics," *Politics*, III (December 1946), p. 403.

detached, came from the belief that neither choice was perfect, but that the alternatives were total evil (Stalinism) and partial evil (democratic capitalism). Above all, the *Partisan Review* watched the politics of the intellectuals: did they reject Stalinism completely or did they try to make some accommodation to it? This question took precedence over all others. Once the commitment to anti-Stalinism was made—for this seemed to them the only possible stand after the war—variations of political positions were important and might be discussed. But one of the historical characteristics of this political position that Macdonald noted was that it rarely advanced much beyond the initial point of departure from Communism. By accepting "reality," by acceding to an unpleasant choice, their position veered toward a philosophy based on the logic of *Realpolitik,* which was held by other American liberals who rejected and even fought a faith in profound change, and discarded the vision of a good society existing outside the context of contemporary institutions.[14]

The magazine, which drew political sustenance from its antagonism to Stalinism and from all of the events of the 1930s that emphasized the evils of the revolution betrayed, was nourished also by a contrary experience of the 1930s which illustrated over and over again the perils of making total peace with America as Brooks, MacLeish, and others had done. One powerful element of continuity was the editors' distaste for liberalism: once they had disliked it because it was nonrevolutionary; later they disliked it because it became nationalistic at the approach of war. Now they rejected it because they were convinced that many liberals were pro-Stalinist. The America to which the editors chose to give their critical support was an America dominated at home by public welfare and economic planning of sorts—all major planks in the liberal platform. But it was primarily the foreign policy of the United States to which the magazine gave its approval, specifically, policy toward the Soviet Union. At home, intellectual liberalism had

---

[14] For example, Arthur M. Schlesinger, Jr., *The Vital Center* (Boston: Houghton Mifflin, 1949), and Reinhold Niebuhr, *The Children of Light and the Children of Darkness* (New York: Scribner's, 1945).

to be purged of the influence of Stalinism; this was the primary task of politics. Macdonald was accurate in describing this political stance as a kind of conservatism expressed in a radical language only because the editors of the *Partisan* lacked a conservative vocabulary.[15]

For Macdonald politics was also an extension and elaboration of the views that he expressed in the *Partisan* and the *New International*, but the progress of his thought was more circuitous. He continued to expose the conduct of the war and to fight for social change in his new magazine, *Politics*, which he and his wife began in February 1944. But as the world war ended and then shifted into the low, faltering gear of cold war, his political premises changed. Although he had rejected a good deal of Trotskyism by 1944 (he had, after all, begun a piecemeal reevaluation of it in 1939), events such as the dropping of the atomic bomb on Hiroshima loosened his faith in scientific progress and Marxism until by 1946 it had slipped away completely. In the postwar period he decided that pacifism, not active revolution, was the most practical political stance, and he joined a left-wing group with such views called the Peacemakers. But once again world events touched off a radical change in his theoretical assumptions. After the Berlin blockade, he relates, he gave up pacifism, deciding that the Russians did not respect the moral beliefs on which pacifist strategy depended for its effectiveness.[16]

The use of the atomic bomb, he wrote, made him seriously doubt progress and especially the beneficence of scientific progress: "The bursting of the atomic bomb over Hiroshima was thus merely the catalyst which precipitated, in my own thinking, a reaction which my experience in editing *Politics* had long prepared, a reaction against Marxism and scientific socialism." Ghandi's assassination provoked a deeper pessimism in Macdonald; to him Ghandi had been the last of the world's great political leaders who functioned on a human scale, yet he and Trotsky, Macdonald's other hero, were both destroyed by the

---

[15] Macdonald, "Memoirs of a Revolutionist," *Memoirs of a Revolutionist*, p. 25.
[16] Dwight Macdonald, "The Waldorf Conference," Special Insert, *Politics*, VI (Winter 1949), p. 32-b.

very processes that they had set into motion.[17] History to Macdonald operated not in a line of automatic progress or advance; rather, it seemed determined to consume its most remarkable offspring.

As Macdonald slowly turned away from the politics of the exposé, from a belief in progress, mass movements, and scientific history, he concentrated more on making man rather than social change the center of his views. In two articles, "The Root is Man," later compiled into a book by the same name, he argued that the radical must now think of the intellectuals as an audience and not the masses. One of the premises of his opposition to World War II became an argument for giving up Marxism: political action must be reduced to a personal level. Instead of asserting that socialism could aid in the struggle to make politics a meeting place for human values, he insisted that Marxism stood in the dominant stream of Western culture, a culture whose primary ideas, progress and science, he now rejected. To him, a fundamental questioning of Marxism meant that "a break with a whole cultural tradition is involved, and Marxism looms up as the last and greatest systematic defense of that tradition."

Macdonald's denial of the certainties in liberalism and Marxism left him ultimately without a basis for radical politics. He now felt that man, not history or movements, was the center of political interest. By the late 1940s and early 1950s he even rejected the meaningfulness of a "third camp" position. Exhausted by the demands of *Politics* and by the erosion of his faith in radicalism, he stopped publishing the magazine in 1949. Three years later, in a debate with Norman Mailer at Mt. Holyoke College, he reluctantly asserted: "I choose the West."[18] All the political alternatives to this decision—pacifism, socialism, and anarchism—had seemed ineffective. Macdonald's choice actually meant giving up politics, for his writings had from the beginning been premised upon his uncompromising belief in a third way. His choice was a sign that he no longer believed in

[17] Dwight Macdonald, "The Bomb," *Politics,* II (September 1945), p. 259. Dwight Macdonald, "Ghandi's Death," *Politics,* V (Winter 1948), p. 6.
[18] Dwight Macdonald, *The Root is Man* (Alhambra, California: Cunningham Press, 1963), pp. 22, 59.

such a commitment. What had begun during World War II as revolutionary isolation ended by the 1950s merely as isolation; when no alternatives appeared feasible, politics to Macdonald seemed less important.

Unable or reluctant to make his peace with the "West" complete, Macdonald still pictured himself writing in cultural matters, "against the American grain." As before, he was appalled by perversions of high culture and by what he called at one point the middlebrow counterrevolution, which he traced back to the Brooks–MacLeish thesis.[19] He remained opposed to the distortion of high culture. After *Politics* closed down in 1949, he expounded his views from the pages of the *New Yorker*, beginning in 1952. His career thus has a symmetry, for he had ended his radicalism almost where he began it—with the organ of humor for the urban intelligentsia. Despite his choice of the West, he remained critical of popular journalism, but it was a criticism no longer anchored to a belief in change. Macdonald wrote of a class-ridden cultural system, yet he proposed no alternative. He criticized middle-class culture, but proposed no specific changes. His unique faith in rationality—from Marxism to anarchism, from Trotskyism to pacifism—had once deepened and sharpened his writings, transforming politics into a struggle between ideas. Now, although he still opposed the degeneration of journalism and the low quality of intellectual art, he did so from a new position defined by his loss of faith. Thus Macdonald's choice of the West entailed, for him, an end to politics, just as he had once argued that the *Partisan Review*'s implicit alliance with America early in the cold war would lead to an end of politics. Six years later he had reached almost the same point, with one exception: the threat of Stalinism did not dominate the cultural horizon; to him it was not the central issue of culture and politics. Instead, Macdonald's retirement from politics was more complete, and he ended in much the same way as he had begun, by writing exposures of middle-class control and distortion of art.

A revealing sign of the *Partisan Review*'s abandonment of its old political orientation, its turning away from socialism as a

[19] Macdonald, *Against the American Grain*, p. 208.

practical social alternative for America, was the symposium "The Future of Socialism" published in 1947. In one sense, the symposium finally answered the question, long in the minds of the editors, of what was living and what was dead in Marxism. An editorial statement was sent to Arthur Koestler, George Orwell, James Burnham, Granville Hicks, Arthur Schlesinger, Jr., Victor Serge, and others to serve as the basis for a discussion. The statement itself was a series of challenges to traditional socialist doctrine. "Historical experience," Rahv and Phillips wrote, "since 1917 has put the entire socialist perspective into question." Faith in the advance of science and rationality had been unrewarded; the working class had failed in its historic mission; the Soviet Union had degenerated into totalitarianism—all of these surprises had made the future of socialism uncertain.[20]

To Sidney Hook, the first contributor in the series, the answers to doubts raised by the symposium were very clear. Orthodox Marxism, either as social democracy or what he called its "grotesque distortions" Leninism, Trotskyism and Stalinism, seemed "confused in idea and vicious in consequence." Socialism as originally conceived was bankrupt; intellectuals must now fight for democracy: "In this defense of democracy and its extension we should be willing to accept allies from any group or class." Hook called for a movement of purification to purge American culture of the "totalitarian liberals." But he warned, much as earlier editorials in the *Partisan* had done, that this task should be undertaken by genuine democrats, not reactionaries who did not know the difference between Stalinists and other leftists. Hook's answer, constructed almost entirely on the absolute and singular necessity to struggle against Stalinism, failed to find any place for orthodox socialism in the future; rather, he proposed that its bad effects emanating from Russia should occupy the interest of intellectuals.

Granville Hicks, formerly an enemy of the *Partisan* but long having discarded his allegiance to the Communist movement, argued that the failure of the Soviet Union required a reexami-

---

[20] William Phillips and Philip Rahv, "The Future of Socialism," *Partisan Review*, XIV (January-February 1947), pp. 23-24. Authors supplied by Philip Rahv; Rahv to Author, March 22, 1966.

nation of Marxism, its official ideology, to determine the source
of its failure. He proposed a reconsideration of the old tenets
of socialist and liberal thought: "To begin with, we had better
get rid of any remnants of belief in progress."[21]

Other contributors were also skeptical of the future of socialism, although George Orwell raised the possibility of a socialist
Europe, despite obstacles presented by the Soviet Union, the
Catholic Church, and imperialism. Arthur Schlesinger's response allowed no future at all for orthodox socialism. Rather,
he hoped that through a series of "New Deals" America would
become a more equitable society. Internally, industry and government, he felt, were basic evils of life, for they institutional-
ized "pride and greed" and "sadism and masochism," which he
assumed to be the causes of the world's problems. Thus any
government, such as a socialist government which meant more
government and more control over industry, was inherently
worse than a capitalist state which to some extent was self-
regulating. This very old argument in a new guise was employed
to explain the reality of the world that had emerged from the
world war. But like most of the other contributors to the symposium Schlesinger was primarily concerned with socialism
abroad, particularly in the Soviet Union. He, too, picked up the
attack on the *Nation* and the *New Republic*, on the "fellow
travellers" speaking of Communism as a fifth-column ideology
for the Russians. He, too, attacked the bourgeoisie, particularly
the business community, for its "cowardice" in foreign policy.
Within the context of a foreign policy of containing the Soviet
Union, he concluded, the United States could continue to develop its democratic institutions.[22] Schlesinger's new conservatism, which was based on the idealization of existing institutions as the limits of ideology, which rejected any sort of utopian
state, and which used in some instances the language of the left
to denounce other liberals and the more insular portions of the

---

[21] Sidney Hook, "The Future of Socialism," *Partisan Review*, XIV (Jan-
uary-February 1947), pp. 25, 29, and Granville Hicks, "On Attitudes and
Ideas," *Partisan Review*, XIV (March-April 1947), p. 123.
[22] George Orwell, "Toward European Unity," *Partisan Review*, XIV (July-
August 1947), p. 348. Arthur Schlesinger, Jr., "The Future of Socialism,"
Partisan Review, XIV (May-June 1947), pp. 229-242.

bourgeoisie, was too much a glorification of the New Deal ever to satisfy the editors of the *Partisan Review*. But if the editors were unwilling to draw the conclusions of a Schlesinger or of a Burnham, their assumptions nonetheless pointed in this general direction. One noteworthy aspect of the symposium was that no politically active socialist participated in it: the question of the future of socialism was left in the hands of men who had been deeply disillusioned by the failures of the 1930s. In a letter to managing editor Catherine Carver, Irving Howe, who wrote frequent reviews for the magazine, asked rhetorically: "Don't you think the list of people you have in your future of socialism symposium rather one-sided: That is most of them have for one reason or another abandoned active participation in the socialist movement, as well as orthodox Marxism."[23]

Rahv's comments on the future of socialism came almost a year after the *Partisan Review* symposium in an article criticizing strains of thought that had developed out of the failure of the left. One, represented by John Dos Passos, was the abandonment of socialism for "free enterprise"; the other, by Dwight Macdonald, was the switch from socialism to pacifism, from Trotsky as mentor to Ghandi. Rahv called for a hardheaded approach to the present, for an end to ideology and utopian dreams. The hopes of the 1930s, he felt, had been forever destroyed; the vision of a "kingdom of freedom" must now be replaced by a "higher level of necessity." Rahv's desire for a *"disenchanted socialism,"* his rejection of automatic progress, yet his refusal to give up a faith in science, represented an attempt to reaffirm ideas that he had long held in the midst of a world of disintegrating choices. "After all," he asked, "what other ideas are there?" Rahv's portrait of the homeless radical, an intellectual without a country because of his rejection of Communism, seemed a man who was required somehow to relate to the world in which he lived, somehow to use the institutions of society to further his cause, somehow to take sides, however reluctantly, in a world badly divided. Again, Rahv scolded liberals who tried to "take a balanced view of total evil." Those who attempted to compromise with Soviet desires

---

[23] Irving Howe to Catherine Carver, March, 1947, *Partisan* MSS.

acted to justify this evil: "Collaborationist liberalism has thus fallen heir to the broken ideology of the Bolsheviks—an ideology so degenerated that in Soviet Russia it has become an alibi for mass-murder."

But most striking in Rahv's disillusioned appraisal of the future of radicalism was his rejection of the radical past, his search and partial discovery of a heritage quite different from orthodox Marxism and his reconsideration even of the early Bolshevik Revolution: "Lenin, particularly, despite the brilliance of his strategic concepts, was historically speaking, at once the master and the martyr of utopian illusions. . . . From this point of view his thought was far inferior to that of Dostoevski, who was acute enough to discern that to start with a theory of unlimited freedom is to end up with unlimited despotism in practice."[24]

Rahv's political radicalism after the war was indeed homeless. It attached itself to no movement, although he called for a temporary alliance with capitalism. It envisioned no great advance in human society, proposing instead a higher level of necessity as the goal of socialism. It found no radical heritage except in the lessons of socialist thinkers now tempered by despair. Rahv remained true to his early style of thought: liberalism was no more attractive in 1948 than it had been in 1938. Yet when confronted with a vision of "total evil" in the Soviet Union, it seemed necessary to make peace with society. The revolution that failed, the revolution that was betrayed, was now the revolution to be feared. It was unthinkable for him to terminate his own involvement in socialism, just as it was impossible for him to relinquish his radical vocabulary, but the categories

---

[24] Philip Rahv, "Disillusionment and Partial Answers," *Partisan Review,* XV (May 1948), pp. 528-529. What Leslie Fiedler called a "final irony" in an article on the *Partisan Review,* that is, the identification of the magazine with John Dewey through his disciples Ernest Nagel and Sidney Hook, is really no irony at all. See Leslie Fiedler, "Partisan Review: Phoenix or Dodo?" *Perspectives USA,* XVI (Spring 1956), p. 96. Dewey's philosophy, particularly as employed by Hook, supplied philosophic insights into the dangers of a detached, idealistic philosophic system—one could see Marxism in this way—which complimented the immense distrust of utopianism that runs through the later writings of Rahv and Phillips and many of the *Partisan's* contributors.

of his political ideas were structured by disenchantment. Nice-
ties of logic and modifications of judgment were swept away by
the harshness of formulations such as "total evil" and by such
characterizations as "collaborationist liberalism." In a world
presenting two choices, evil and partial evil, he picked the latter, still believing in democratic socialism. And for him, after
all, what other ideas were there? In his political writings he
used a vocabulary and a style of thought that did not always
fit the meaning of his judgments. Politics became as intricate
as metaphor and as ambiguous as literature; thus it was that
Rahv could avoid the implications of a complete identification
with the West and his radical identity was preserved.

William Phillips's politics were also dominated by an obsession with Stalinism. In an article, "The Politics of Desperation,"
he prefaced his remarks with this justification for writing on
politics: "In the last few decades politics has made greater
claims on intellectual life than ever before in modern history."[25]
The primary duty of the intellectual, he proposed, was to fight
Stalinism, yet at the same time remain careful not to succumb
to the reactionary tradition of the West. He attacked liberalism,
calling it a "political canard" that ultimately worked in the
favor of Stalinism. In a world ruled by necessity it seemed imperative for the intellectual, if he were at all concerned with
existing freedoms, to struggle against Russia.

It is highly significant that Phillips also used fiction to expand his political ideas. In a short story, "Sleep No More,"
which he published in the *Partisan Review* in 1949, he discussed elements of moral sentiment and implications of political
decisions that illuminate his other writings. In an almost sur-
realistic, or perhaps Kafkaesque, atmosphere he examined the
feelings of a man asked by a government agency to discuss the
political views of a neighbor. As the main character is put on
the spot to make a decision about cooperating, his involvement
with the problem of intellectual Communism flashes through
his mind; at one point he thinks that a witch-hunt means that
innocent people are being charged. And yet, he counters, some

---

[25] William Phillips, "The Politics of Desperation," *Partisan Review*, XV
(April 1948), p. 449.

people are guilty. Should someone ask if he were against witches, he would reply: "I am unequivocally opposed to them." Unwilling to commit himself, the character again weighs arguments for and against cooperating. What is the nature of the accused person's guilt? Is Miss C—— an enemy agent or does she merely hold dissident views? Within its own terms, the story illustrates perfectly the moral trap set by Phillips's own political position, by his own politics of desperation. But the story also raised another issue—the nature of the struggle against Communism. Some years earlier Phillips, Hook, and others had warned of letting the task of purging culture of Stalinism slip into the hands of reactionaries; this too was a dilemma in "Sleep No More."[26]

In December 1948 Phillips wrote to Whittaker Chambers, asking him to write an article on his political experiences of the last decade. Phillips noted that the editors of the *Partisan* were well aware of Chambers's position: "We think it valuable for a magazine like *Partisan Review* to explain to its public that behind the sensational headlines lies a human and political story involving the tragedy of a lost cause—a tragedy that has moral, political and personal repercussions."[27] This is one thing that Phillips's short story sought to do.

Phillips's ambiguity about politics was more fully revealed in a series of reviews that he wrote for the *American Mercury*. During a short period in 1952 and early 1953 Phillips was a regular contributor to the magazine and for one month was listed as an associate editor. In his reviews, many of them dealing with Communism, Phillips struck sometimes directly, sometimes obliquely at the problem that had come to obsess American culture: how to deal with American Communists. On the one hand, he was deeply disturbed that some intellectuals had failed to believe in the guilt of Alger Hiss. And he felt that even if the Communist party was not a national threat, "I, for one, see no reason to countenance these activities."[28] On the

26 William Phillips, "Sleep No More," *Partisan Review*, XVI (March 1949), pp. 237, 241.
27 William Phillips to Whittaker Chambers, December 16, 1948, p. 1, *Partisan MSS.*
28 William Phillips, "In and Out of the Underground," *American Mercury*,

other hand, he argued, one must not give in to the reactionary
politicians. To Phillips, politics, when it did not center in the
threat of Communism, was directed toward preserving the intellectual's critical stance toward society, an exploration of the
problems raised by his own political position of commitment to
the West.

The issue of McCarthyism in 1952 and 1953 fulfilled a warn-
ing that the editors had made immediately after World War II:
their own struggle against Communism was being expropriated
by McCarthy, "a political bum," as Rahv bitterly described him.
Despite its own anti-Communism, the *Partisan* opposed the Mc-
Carthy campaign. James Burnham, a long-time friend of the
magazine and a member of the advisory board, could not accept
the magazine's stand on the Senator from Wisconsin and resigned from the board in late 1953. If he was perhaps more
logical than the *Partisan* in supporting McCarthy, Burnham
overlooked everything but logic: the tactics, the anti-intellectualism, and the suspicion of all dissent purveyed as opposition
to Communism. Burnham's letter of resignation, printed in December 1953, argued that McCarthyism as pictured in the press
was an invention of the Communists; therefore he could not
oppose it. The editors' reply was a brief, general statement on
the issue of McCarthy and politics: "We have always been opposed to the anti-anti-Communist attitude that prevails in some
intellectual circles, and we are equally opposed to the new anti-
anti-McCarthy attitude advocated by Burnham. It seems to us
that anti-Communism is strengthened rather than weakened by
outright opposition to McCarthy and his methods."[29] The lack
of creative thought is apparent even in the language of this
reply. Here, as elsewhere, political ideas were wound and

LXXIV (June 1952), pp. 92-99, and "Changing Fathers in Midstream,"
American Mercury, LXXVI (January 1953), p. 108. See also Diana Trill-
ing, "A Memorandum on the Hiss Case," *Partisan Review,* XVII (May-
June 1950), pp. 499-500. Mrs. Trilling attacks liberals who do not accept
Hiss's guilt. Implied in this article is a very ambiguous attitude toward
McCarthyism, because of her notion that political ideas are political acts;
hence no toleration of Communism is possible.
[29] Philip Rahv, "Our Country and Our Culture," *Partisan Review,* XIX
(May-June 1952), p. 307, and "Reply by the Editors," *Partisan Review,*
XX (November-December 1953), p. 717.

tangled in negatives. No positive cause, no commitment to change seemed to have any relevance.

The political position of the *Partisan Review*, noted for its anti-Communism and yet its continued discussion of socialism, enhanced its position as a cultural center. Writers such as Jean Paul Sartre, who might not be expected to do so, continued to write for the magazine. Its reputation abroad seemed to match its aspirations: "To such English intellectuals as critic George Orwell and Editor Cyril Connolly," noted one American journal, "the bi-monthly *Partisan Review* is the voice of the U.S. intellectual left." And, significantly, the *Partisan* was the second major American magazine to appear in postwar England. From Germany, Melvin Lasky, who became the magazine's German correspondent, wrote to Rahv in the fall of 1947 that the reception accorded the *Partisan* in that country had been tremendous. In addition to its prestige abroad, the magazine attained a degree of stability at home that it had never had when Allan Dowling, a New York poet, became an "angel" and agreed to contribute enough funds to enable the *Partisan* to become a monthly for the first time since 1938.[30] Beginning in 1948, the magazine was published with an advisory board that included Dowling, Burnham, Hook, Lionel Trilling, and James Johnson Sweeney.[31]

---

[30] "Light up in London," *Time*, XLIX (March 30, 1947), p. 58, and "Angel with a Red Beard," *Time*, XLIX (June 1947), p. 64. *Time* cited the support as $50,000 a year.

[31] The relationship of the Central Intelligence Agency to individuals who wrote for the *Partisan Review* and the sponsorship of the magazine after 1959 by the American Committee for Cultural Freedom raise the possibility that everything I have said in this book is misleading or irrelevant. It might further suggest the complicity (as yet undisclosed) of the magazine itself in the thought control exercised by America's supersecret and best publicized spy agency. Concrete evidence of anything of this sort has not appeared. Moreover, the discussion of intellectuals (to extend and broaden the problem) and their participation in government institutions belongs in another place and perhaps in different hands. The issue goes well beyond the C.I.A. and any conscious or unconscious acceptance of its stipends. Men and their ideas must be considered for what they are and what they mean, not for who pays their bills. Views are most often engendered historically, and only very rarely may we catch them wearing a price tag. The important thing is that a good many intellectuals and America's leading spy agency came to the same conclusions at much the same

The *Partisan* continued, however, to be controversial among intellectuals. James Farrell, an old ally, wrote that the literature of the magazine, particularly a short story of Lionel Trilling's, "The Other Margaret," published in 1945, was an expression of the general retreat from radicalism and a sign of the "growing moral snobbery of the advanced and cultivated New Yorker," typical of the "Partisan Review intellectual." Later other critics joined in to argue that the magazine had succumbed to conformism, that it had retreated into the protective boundaries of American culture: "The formerly liberal journal *Partisan Review*," wrote critic John Aldridge, "has lately become the chief organ of a new intellectual orthodoxy."[32]

Lionel Trilling in his preface to *The Partisan Reader*, a collection of stories, poems, and articles published in the magazine in 1944, praised the magazine for attempting to fill the ideological gap between traditional liberal ideas and the writings of the great twentieth-century authors Proust, Gide, Lawrence, Kafka, and others. "We can say," he wrote, "that no connection exists between our liberal educated class and the best literary minds of our time." There seemed to be no intercourse between "the political ideas of our educated class and the deep places of the imagination." Later Trilling stated at length his argument about the distinctness of the self in relation to culture and society, a primary idea of the avant-garde. It was Freud, he argued, who "made the idea of culture real for a great many of us." "The function of literature," he concluded, ". . . has been to make us aware of the particularity of selves

time about America's role in world society. That event is fraught enough with historical questions to keep historians away from the pitfalls of easy explanations for a long time. See Dwight Macdonald, "Politics," *Esquire*, LXVII (June 1967), p. 72, Jason Epstein, "The CIA and the Intellectuals," *London Magazine*, VII (July 1967), pp. 5-19, and Christopher Lasch, "Cultural Cold War," *Nation*, CCV (September 11, 1967), pp. 198-212.
[32] James T. Farrell, *Literature and Morality* (New York: Vanguard Press, 1947), p. 14, and John Aldridge, *In Search of Heresy: American Literature in an Age of Conformity* (New York: McGraw-Hill, 1956), p. 38. This is one of the more intelligent criticisms. See also Mark Schorer, "Art and Dogma," *New Republic*, CXV (November 11, 1946), pp. 634-635; Paul Bixler, "Little Magazines, What Now?" *Antioch Review*, VIII (March 1948), pp. 63-77; and Seymour Krim, "Our Middle-Aged 'Young Writers,'" *Commentary*, XIV (October 1952), pp. 339-344.

and the high authority of the self in its quarrel with its society and its culture."[33] The *Partisan Review* modulated radical politics and avant-garde literature in the sense that it focused on the intellectual as a member of a separate class and on the subversiveness of his ideas to traditional culture, fostered in estrangement from middle-class society. But from its modulation between two originally distinct and perhaps even contradictory elements, political liberalism and advanced art, the magazine had gradually asserted a new combination of art and politics. Under the impact of the politics of the postwar period the editors of the *Partisan* and many of its contributors conceived of a new liberalism—no longer defined by a faith in progress or change, no longer inspired by utopia, but made temperate by the experience of the 1930s and moderate in the sweep of its hopes for the future. It was a liberalism defined by its opposition to optimistic liberalism and a politics of radical rhetoric suited to the conception that the intelligentsia was a radical class and that its literature was subversive. But a strong undercurrent in the history of the *Partisan Review* after World War II also revealed a growing suspicion on the part of its editors of the necessity to be radical at all.

One hint of this suspicion was revealed in the frequent discussion of the intellectual and the writer as a neurotic during 1944 and 1945. The distinction between the estranged intellectual and the neurotic intellectual is an important one. The estranged intellectual may be neurotic, but his inability to adjust to society and his subsequent introspection are the results of the inhospitability of his culture. Estrangement, as originally used by the *Partisan* editors, depended on a social and not a psychological analysis, largely Marxian in origin. The neurotic intellectual, however, could be unadjusted for a variety of reasons, some of which have little to do with the social or political structure. Although the editors of the *Partisan* never ceased to write of the intellectual's estrangement, the importance given to the thesis that the writer was neurotic and, most

---

[33] Lionel Trilling, "The Function of the Little Magazine," *Liberal Imagination* (New York: Viking Press, 1950), p. 98, and Lionel Trilling, *Freud and the Crisis of Our Culture* (Boston: Beacon Press, 1955), pp. 33, 36.

of all, the interchangeability of the two concepts are primary indications that the older class analysis of the intelligentsia was being discarded.

In 1944 William Phillips wrote that by definition, an artist who attempted to express new ideas was a "young man at war with the existing gods and disposed to nurse his disaffection and sense of alienation—a zealot, we might say, of the advance guard."[34] Contrasted with this formulation was an important reassessment by Arthur Koestler two issues later of the meaning of estrangement. The article on the intelligentsia printed in the *Partisan* in the summer of 1944 was at once a step in Koestler's abandonment of orthodox radicalism and an historical and psychological examination of the fundamental attributes of this elite. Koestler's analysis brushed aside the Marxist hypothesis that the economic process by itself created its own superstructure. Historically, he asserted, the intelligentsia had been characterized by its inherent neurosis: "To quarrel with society means to quarrel with its projections in one's self, and produces the classical neurotic split patterns." Because of their psychological state, frustrated "not too much and not too little," the intelligentsia performed the function for society of introspection and self-interpretation; they were the creators of ideology.[35] The distance between the nonconformist and the crank, he concluded, was short, and hostile pressures from society might narrow that gap.

Koestler's conclusion that neurosis was the key to understanding the intelligentsia was important, but it did not entirely please the editors of the *Partisan*. Moreover, his amateurish use of psychology—for example, his attempt to characterize Marx as a "pathologically quarrelsome old sponger"—was clearly not a very fruitful line of analysis. Yet the general direction of his article helped to broaden the magazine's discussion of the relation of psychology and art and extended, in some ways, the original argument that the intelligentsia was a class possessing certain

---

[34] Phillips, "Portrait of the Artist as a Middle-Aged Man," *Partisan Review,* XI (Winter 1944), p. 121.
[35] Arthur Koestler, "The Intelligentsia," *Partisan Review,* XI (Summer 1944), pp. 267, 275.

recognizable behavior. In 1946 Koestler replaced George Orwell as the London correspondent of the magazine.

Delmore Schwartz, a young writer from New York who was brought to the editorial board of the *Partisan Review* in late 1943, was also concerned with the alienation of the modern poet. Schwartz, like many writers for the magazine, had attended Columbia University and had published one early article in the *Marxist Quarterly*, the organ of independent Trotskyist intellectuals in 1937. Both a poet and a teacher, Schwartz had sent some of his most important early writing to the *Partisan*.[36] In his article, "The Isolation of Modern Poetry," for *Kenyon Review* in 1944 he wrote that it was not merely the modern poet who felt alienated, but that culture as well as sensibility and imagination were also alienated. The artist felt himself a stranger and an alien separated from society by his values as an artist. His reaction consequently was to cultivate his own sensibility, to write about himself.

Of the editorial staff of the *Partisan* it was particularly William Barrett, a young philosopher from Columbia University who became an associate editor in early 1947, who developed the concept of the writer as a neurotic. In 1944, reviewing a work by Santayana, Barrett had discussed that philosopher's dislike of history: the ingredient Santayana lacked, he concluded, which might have made him a great thinker, was "intellectual *anxiety*." Later, in "Writers and Madness," he discussed Jonathan Swift as a psychic type who, he hypothesized, had foreshadowed writers to come for two centuries. The loneliness of the writer seemed to be the central fact of his existence: "Out of the ravages of his experience, his desperate loneliness, he must put forth these works which look back into his gaze with conviction and authenticity and wear about them the gleams of interest—cathectic charges, in the technical term. . . ."[37] To Barrett, the peculiar alienation of the writer was the sort of "madness" that could be traced back to the ancient Greeks, the madness of a

---

36 Kunitz, "Delmore Schwartz," *Authors*, 1st Supplement, p. 885. George Orwell was awarded the first *Partisan Review* Award in 1949.
37 William Barrett, "Writers and Madness," *Partisan Review*, XIV (January-February 1947), p. 22. Barrett received his Ph.D. at Columbia and worked with the State Department in Italy during World War II.

Swift or a Joyce. But the neurosis of the artist could be explained less by examining the class structure than the artist himself. The most useful intellectual breakthrough in America, he wrote in 1952, was the permeation of the culture by psychiatry, which was more important than the "social consciousness in the thirties, literary academicism in the forties, and neoconservatism in the fifties."[38]

In Phillips's later writing, too, the problem of neurosis seemed to replace the problem of alienation. In 1952, in a review of current French literature, he wrote that "Only Camus appears to be carrying on the earlier tradition of European fiction, in his two brooding novels, *The Stranger* and *The Plague*, whose subject is man's moral loneliness." In a longer discussion of the relation between art and neurosis he wrote that there was little direct relation between neurosis and art in the sense of neurosis explaining art, but "there is the fact that many, if not most, writers, painters, and musicians in the modern period have been neurotic." And it was this coincidence that seemed most interesting to the critic.[39]

The seminal discussion of alienation came in a long symposium, "Our Country and Our Culture," in 1952. The editorial statement observed that American intellectuals had begun to regard America in a new way; they no longer felt alienated as had Henry James, or Ezra Pound, or Van Wyck Brooks. "For better or worse, most writers no longer accept alienation as the artist's fate in America; on the contrary, they want very much to be part of American life," it concluded.[40] The results of the war—the polarization of the world between America and Russia and the cultural refuge offered by the United States—called for a more appropriate image of American society. Although most writers wished to feel a part of America and to work out their values in terms of its institutions, there were serious complica-

---

[38] William Barrett, "Our Country and Our Culture," *Partisan Review*, XIX (July-August 1952), p. 422.
[39] William Phillips, "European Fiction," *American Mercury*, LXXV (July 1952), p. 103. Phillips, "Art and Neurosis," *Art and Psychoanalysis*, p. xvii.
[40] "Our Country and Our Culture," *Partisan Review*, XIX (May-June 1952), pp. 282-284.

tions, the most important of which was the domination of culture by mass art. The editorial statement made little pretense to examine alienation as a political phenomenon; rather, it seemed a state of culture, of mass culture versus elite culture. The fading of the political element in alienation, first embodied in the post-war importance of a psychological interpretation of the intelligentsia, resulted from a practical end of opposition to American politics, from the choice of the West. The necessity of being alienated—once assumed—now seemed less obvious. As James Burnham put it in his reply, "These relationships were not so clear or so desperate a generation ago. What has happened is not that American culture has become better in that time, but the world much worse."[41] Moreover, the old belief that European culture was more advanced and more complex than American civilization was no longer an automatic reflex of the editors. Rather, European culture now seemed confused and still influenced by Communism, even though America had largely shed its beliefs in this variant of Marxism.

Philip Rahv wrote in remarks on the change in American culture that to his mind the principal reason for this development was the "exposure of the Soviet myth and the consequent resolve . . . to be done with Utopian illusions and heady expectations." Whatever one might say of American democracy, "it actually exists." Rahv argued that the society itself had become more receptive to the intellectual; thus the phenomenon of the *embourgeoisement* of the American intelligentsia was apparent. Because of this, some eager anti-Stalinist intellectuals had swallowed the American reality whole. They had become supporters of McCarthy and their philosophy was sterile and negative. Rahv did not reject anti-Communism, but merely argued against the unintelligent, ineffective way in which these rigid dogmatists conducted themselves. If Rahv deplored Mc-Carthy as a kind of kitsch demagogue, he also rejected kitsch as a meaningful culture. It was true, he argued, that alienation was a characteristic of the avant-garde. This was neither good nor bad in itself, but one must admit that it had produced great

[41] James Burnham, "Our Country and Our Culture," *Partisan Review*, XIX (May-June 1952), p. 291.

art. Ultimately, he concluded, one cannot accept America completely, but one must give up the struggle to change it: "If under present conditions we cannot stop the ruthless expansion of mass culture, the least we can do is to keep apart and refuse its favors."

William Phillips also found the origins for the new sense of Americanism in the political experiences of the 1930s: "More recently, with the threat of Soviet totalitarianism and with the exhaustion and political confusion of Europe, American artists and intellectuals have acquired a new sense of belonging to their native land. . . ." Despite the political origins of the rediscovery of America, Phillips felt that there were depths of an artistic rediscovery that must also be marked. These new attitudes must not be allowed to degenerate into chauvinism or into mere anti-Communism. To Phillips the artist was no longer the alienated man, but the suspended man, "suspended between tradition and revolt, nationalism and internationalism, the aesthetic and the civic, and between belonging and alienation."[42] He must go to his native roots, yet remain an internationalist.

The notion of the end of Bohemia, the end of alienation and independence, and in a sense the end of any desire for alternatives suffuses this symposium. In the editorial statement the responses of Rahv and Phillips and to some extent of the other editors show a distinct awareness of the end of an era. The never-ending cycle of the rediscovery of America, so much a part of the literary and political movements of the twentieth century and so heartily resisted by the editors of the *Partisan Review* in the late 1930s, now pervaded their thinking, however they might fight it. The distinctive combination of politics and avant-garde art, developed through the convolutions of the 1930s and revolving about the changing view of the intellectual, the writer, and the critic, had now become static. The unique relation of radical art and politics had ultimately come to rest on a theory of the intelligentsia that by 1952 no longer seemed applicable. The long and complicated history of literary radi-

---

[42] Rahv, "Our Country and Our Culture," *Partisan Review*, pp. 304, 310, and William Phillips, "Our Country and Our Culture," *Partisan Review*, XIX (September-October 1952), pp. 586, 589.

calism ended in irrelevance. It seemed wisest to face the future with whatever ideas of the past could be salvaged. Old assumptions from before World War I—the carefree faith in the experimental life, in science, radicalism, and progress, the automatic belief in the affinity of radical politics and radical art—had disappeared.

The pressure of politics, the politics of desperation, forced the *Partisan Review* out of its alienation and, as William Phillips put it, into a suspended state. The belief in independence from government institutions and universities—once a strong sentiment that gave special meaning to the existence of the little magazine—had evaporated. The politics of negativism dissolved any real alternatives, and radicalism became more a style of thought, a rhetorical device, than any deep-rooted, positive response to the need for political change in America. The old union of radical politics and radical art became past history. The old dynamism was depleted. Political radicalism was negative, and radical art, the avant-garde, was a language of dead writers. But if history swept in upon the *Partisan Review* and caught it in a dilemma of its own making, the past perhaps would also save it from sterility, for its tradition of radicalism, of naysaying, kept it from succumbing entirely to the logic of its own premises and saved it from total commitment to any cause.

Bibliographic Essay

Personal Papers and Manuscript Collections

Randolph Bourne Papers, Columbia University.

Malcolm Cowley Papers, Newberry Library, Chicago, Illinois.

Jack Conroy Papers, Private Collection.

Floyd Dell Papers, Newberry Library, Chicago, Illinois (includes extensive correspondence with Joseph Freeman).

League of American Writers Papers, Private Collection of Franklin Folsom, Roosevelt, New Jersey.

Partisan Review Papers, Rutgers University.

The sources for the history of literary radicalism are so diverse that I shall discuss only certain special topics that are of particular interest to the subject. Literary radicalism has at least one foot in literary history, a subject in which a number of important and extensive bibliographies already exist. Perhaps the best-known and extensive of these is Robert E. Spiller et al., *Literary History of the United States* (New York, 1963). Biographical material can be located by using volumes of *Current Biography* (1940-1965, New York), although the two volumes of *Twentieth Century Authors* by Stanley Kunitz and Howard Haycraft (New York, 1942 and 1955) are very useful. Often biographical material is also available in the "Notes on Our Contributors" sections of little magazines. Interviews have been another source of such information.

Interviews have also provided an important supplement to the essays and creative works of literary radicalism. I am indebted to Jack Conroy, F. W. Dupee, Franklin Folsom, Dwight Macdonald, Nancy Macdonald, George Novack, William Phillips, Philip Rahv, and Alexander Trachtenberg for discussing with me the immensely complicated history of literary radicalism.

The greatest source material is of course the publications of literary groups and political parties. Many of the articles that I have used, while they provided useful information, are not important enough in themselves to be mentioned here. One characteristic of the writings of the group of literary radicals that I have discussed should be noted here: the tendency to be frank, to wear one's intellectual ideas openly, to attempt persuasion. Because of this quality, the articles written for obscure journals are often important documents in cultural history.

Published Memoirs and Periodicals

Published memoirs for the period covered by this book are extensive and often very useful. The two volumes of Van Wyck Brooks's autobiography *Days of the Phoenix* (New York, 1957) and *From the Shadow of the Mountain* (New York, 1961) provide important insights into the development of this central figure. Malcolm Cowley's *Exile's Return* (New York, 1934) is a well-known work which has been influential in interpreting the 1920s. Floyd Dell's *Homecoming* (New York, 1933) is an important recollection of early Greenwich Village and the publication of the *Masses*. Several articles for the *American Mercury* (1947 and 1949) and *Century Magazine* (1925) relate his attitude toward the Village in the 1920s. Max Eastman's three important memoirs, *Enjoyment of Living* (New York, 1948), *Heroes I Have Known* (New York, 1942), and *Love and Revolution: My Journey Through an Epoch* (New York, 1964), are often defensive, but remain important sources. James T. Farrell's *Reflections at Fifty* (New York, 1954) is useful for the 1930s and 1940s. The autobiography of Joseph Freeman, *An American Testament* (New York, 1936), is a charming and important account of the 1920s and early 1930s. Ernest Hemingway's *A Moveable Feast* (New York, 1964) is occasionally useful, but often peevish. Granville Hicks's *Part of the Truth* (New York, 1964) is valuable for the 1920s and early 1930s. His earlier book, *Where We Came Out* (New York, 1954), is part memoir and part polemic. Morris Hillquit's *Loose Leaves From a Busy Life* (New York, 1934) recounts the career of this important American socialist. Matthew Josephson's *Life Among the Surrealists* (New York, 1962) is an important corrective to the view that expatriates were all alienated or sought to make their art conform to aesthetic criterion alone. Alfred Kazin's *Starting Out in the Thirties* (Boston, 1965) is a very personal memoir. Mable Dodge Luhan's *Movers and Shakers* (New York, 1936) is interesting for its accounts of the famous evenings in the Village's most famous salon. An amusing and perceptive memoir is Dwight Macdonald's short *Memoirs of a Revolutionist: Essays in Political Criticism* (New York, 1957). Harry Roskolenko provides an interesting discussion of Trotskyist intellectuals in his book *When I Was Last on Cherry Street* (New York, 1965). The

Autobiography of Lincoln Steffens (New York, 1931), an influential book among young intellectuals in the early 1930s, relates the fascinating life of this important figure. Art Young, in *On My Way* (New York, 1928), recounts the *Masses* period.

One of the most important sources for the history of literary radicalism is the little magazine. Recently several secondary accounts have been published which deal with the history of specific magazines. The standard work is Fred Hoffman, Charles Allen, and Carolyn F. Ulrich's *The Little Magazine* (Princeton, 1947), which catalogues most of the important little magazines and in a long introductory essay discusses the history of this specialized publication. Useful also is Walter Goldwater's bibliography of *Radical Periodicals in America, 1890-1950* (New Haven, Conn., 1964). Numerous articles have also been published discussing little magazines such as Leslie Fiedler's "Partisan Review: Phoenix or Dodo?" in *Perspectives USA* (1956), which is a sympathetic but critical account. Max Eastman, Michael Gold, Floyd Dell, and Joseph North have all discussed and argued over the meaning of the *Masses* tradition. Of special interest for the *Seven Arts* is James Oppenheim's "The Story of the Seven Arts," *American Mercury* (1930). Nicholas Joost's *Scofield Thayer and THE DIAL* (Carbondale, Ill., 1964) is not as useful as William Wasserstrom's more complete *The Time of the Dial* (Syracuse, 1963). One of the best works on the history of a little magazine is Susan J. Turner's *A History of The Freeman* (New York, 1963).

The principal little magazines contain the literature, the critical essays, and often the memories of literary radicalism in America. For the earliest period the most important magazines were *The Comrade*, edited by John Spargo and in 1905 absorbed into the *International Socialist Review*, Upton Sinclair's short-lived *Upton Sinclair's Magazine*, *Wilshire's Magazine*, and the *Intercollegiate Socialist*. Some of these, such as *Wilshire's Magazine* and the *International Socialist Review*, achieved an impressive circulation level.

The two most important magazines of the Greenwich Village renaissance were of course the *Seven Arts* and the *Masses*. Important too, however, were the *New Republic*, the *New Review*, a socialist publication absorbed by the *Masses*, and such publications as *Mother Earth*, edited by Emma Goldman, and the *Blast*, edited by Alexander Beckman. Beyond the radical Village intellectuals, other Americans expressed an important new view toward America. Two publications in particular illustrate this—the *Soil* magazine, which in some ways anticipated important attitudes of the 1920s, and the

Little Review, edited by Margaret Anderson, which reflected the per-vasiveness of anarchism and the movement for women's rights.

Post-World War I magazines were in general less optimistic about political and cultural change. One important exception to this was *Broom,* edited in Europe by Harold Loeb and Matthew Josephson. The *Dial,* located in New York, did much to introduce current Euro-pean literature to the America intelligentsia, as did the much more commercial *Vanity Fair.* The short-lived *Freeman* brought the tradi-tion of the *Seven Arts* into the 1920s, but did not achieve the bril-liance of its predecessor. The *Liberator* was a recreation but a less successful version of the *Masses,* which was combined with *Labor Herald* and *Soviet Russia Pictorial* in 1924. Somewhat later the *Modern Quarterly,* edited by V. F. Calverton, promoted cultural radicalism, and throughout the 1920s and 1930s the publication printed essays by a number of important radical intellectuals. The *New Masses,* founded in 1926, attempted to recapture the mood of prewar days while remaining much less independent from partisan politics. During the 1930s the magazine was the principal intellectual organ of the Communist party. Other Communist publications such as the *New Magazine,* the Sunday Supplement of the *Daily Worker,* and, to a limited extent, the *Communist* developed and refined theo-ries of proletarian literature in the late 1920s. *The Road to Freedom* is an interesting anarchist publication for the 1920s. The *Menorah Journal,* from the early 1920s to the 1930s, is important for two reasons. It illustrates the shift at the end of the 1920s among many intellectuals to favor the Russian Revolution. But the magazine also was the organ that printed the early works of the group that later became an important segment of Trotskyist opinion in the United States and included Herbert Solow and Lionel Trilling. Less political avant-garde publications such as *Broom, Transition, The Hound and Horn, This Quarter,* and others featured the experimental work of writers during the 1920s, many of whom were attracted to the Com-munist literary movements of the next decade.

A number of little magazines in the late 1920s and early 1930s were dedicated to proletarian literature. The *New Masses* was of course the center of this movement. Jack Conroy's *The Rebel Poet* was one of the first of these. After 1933 the John Reed Clubs spon-sored a number of publications such as the *Blast, The Partisan, Dy-namo,* and, most importantly, the *Partisan Review.* The *Little Maga-zine* and the *Anvil* (another Conroy magazine) also became part of the proletarian movement. During this period figures who would be important in the radical movement somewhat later began publishing

in little magazines. Two of these, *Miscellany*, edited by Dwight Macdonald and others, and the *Symposium*, edited by James Burnham
and Philip Wheelwright, are of special importance to the later history of the *Partisan Review*.

The mid-1930s saw the disappearance of most of the radical little
magazines; only the *New Masses* and the *Partisan Review* survived.
Two new publications began at this time: The *Marxist Quarterly*,
a short-lived organ of Trotskyist intellectuals, and *Science and Society*, which was a pro-Communist publication.

For the end of the 1930s and early 1940s a number of magazines
are important to the history of literary radicalism, including the *Nation*, the *New International* (Trotskyist), and *Politics*, edited by
Dwight Macdonald beginning in 1944. During this period also, cultural magazines such as the *Kenyon Review*, the *Sewanee Review*,
and the *Southern Review* among others printed the works of radical
intellectuals. Moreover, *Fortune* magazine provided the literary left
with a number of important writers during this period, including
James Agee and Dwight Macdonald.

Another important source for the history of literary radicalism
during the entire period covered is contained in the official publications and newspapers of the various left-wing groups, including the
Daily Worker, the *New Leader* (socialist), the *Militant* (Trotskyist),
and *Labor Action* (American Workers' party).

Secondary Accounts

The most influential account of literary radicalism in America is
Daniel Aaron's *Writers on the Left* (New York, 1961), an exhaustive
treatment of the politics of the radical intelligentsia from 1912 to
the end of the 1930s. V. F. Calverton's *The Liberation of American
Literature* (New York, 1932) was a relatively early attempt the make
a case for radical literature. Harold Clurman's the *Fervent Years:
The Story of the Group Theatre and the Thirties* (New York, 1957)
is an excellent account of the theater during the Depression decade.
James T. Farrell's *A Note on Literary Criticism* (New York, 1936)
is an important summary of the effects of the proletarian movement
at midpassage. Philip Foner's *Jack London: American Rebel* (New
York, 1947) is a sketchy discussion of London as an early literary
radical. Granville Hicks in his important *Great Tradition* (New York,
1935) argues that the great tradition of American literature is a
combination of realism and naturalism and optimism, which combined embody most of the premises of proletarian literature. Morgan
Himelstein's *Drama Was a Weapon: The Left-wing Theatre in New*

York; 1929-1941 (New Brunswick, 1963) recounts the extent of the radical theater movement. Alfred Kazin's excellent *On Native Grounds* (New York, 1942) is very important for understanding the literary issues of the period. A brilliant, but uneasy essay on radical intellectuals is Christopher Lasch's *The New Radicalism in America, 1889-1963: The Intellectual as a Social Type* (New York, 1965). David Lifson's *The Yiddish Theatre in America* (New York, 1965) provides a number of insights into the little-known radical tradition of the Yiddish theater. Henry May's *The End of American Innocence: A Study of the First Years of Our Own Time* (New York, 1959) is useful if overly schematic. Walter Rideout's *The Radical Novel in the United States, 1900-1954* (Cambridge, Massachusetts, 1956) is a helpful early discussion of radical literary movements. Lillian Symes and Travers Clement in their book *Rebel America* (New York, 1934) discuss the early history of literary radicalism. *Liberals and Communism* (Bloomington, Ind., 1966) by Frank Warren, III attempts to gauge the impact on liberal intellectuals of the widespread radicalism in the 1930s. Edmund Wilson's several collections of essays, including *The Shores of Light* (New York, 1952) and *The American Earthquake* (Garden City, 1958), contain a number of perceptive essays that contribute to the history of literary radicalism. Despite the large number of excellent books on the issues of radicalism among intellectuals, too many of them have been polemical, or occasionally romanticized, and too little attention has been paid to the fundamental intellectual and literary issues at stake.

One of the peculiarities of American history is that it has devoted much time to minor political movements such as the Communist or Socialist parties. Often, in such cases, when little influence can be attributed to such third party movements, there is a dramatic unity, a rise and decline, and a comprehensible story which is much less apparent in the history of major political parties. Little need be said about the very large bibliography of works on socialism. This has been adequately compiled in the second volume of Donald Drew Egbert and Stow Person's *Socialism and American Life* (Princeton, 1952). Important supplements to the history of the party are David Shannon's *The Socialist Party of America* (New York, 1955), Howard Quint's *The Forging of American Socialism: Origins of the Modern Movement* (Columbia, South Carolina, 1953), and particularly James Weinstein's *The Decline of American Socialism, 1912-1924* (New York, 1967) which challenges many of the standard interpretations of the movement.

The history of American Communism has also been broadly, but unsympathetically treated by scholars. Exceptions to this are generally by participants in the movement. One such book is James P. Cannon's *The First Ten Years of American Communism* (New York, 1962). An early activist in the party, Cannon went on to help found the Trotskyist opposition in the late 1920s. Theodore Draper's *American Communism and Soviet Russia: The Formative Period* (New York, 1960) and *The Roots of American Communism* (New York, 1957), both written for the series *Communism in American Life* edited by Clinton Rossiter, are extremely useful. William Z. Foster's *History of the Communist Party of the United States* (New York, 1952) reveals a number of important attitudes of the party toward its own past. Irving Howe and Lewis Coser's *The American Communist Party* (New York, 1962) is useful particularly for the 1920s and early 1930s.

The two most important books on American Trotskyism are James P. Cannon's *History of American Trotskyism; a Report of a Participant* (New York, 1944) and the relevant sections of Isaac Deutscher's *The Prophet Outcast, Trotsky: 1929-1940* (London, 1963). An important article, which takes the view that the Trotskyists entered the Socialist party in 1935 largely to protect Trotsky from attacks on him in the Soviet Union and to use the Socialists to gain access to the American masses, is M. S. Venkataramani, "Leon Trotsky's Adventure in American Radical Politics, 1935-7," *International Review of Social History* (Part 1, 1964).

Histories of Greenwich Village and the Bohemian life in America are particularly relevant to the story of literary radicalism. Aside from the extensive memoirs that recount the exploits of Village residents, a number of books have discussed the phenomenon of Bohemianism. Allen Churchill's *The Improper Bohemians* (New York, 1959) and Albert Parry's *Garrets and Pretenders* (New York, 1933) are two standard, but often superficial accounts. Soloman Fishman's *The Disinherited of Art* (Berkeley, 1953) is a fascinating study of alienation among American artists, a characteristic of many Village intellectuals. An extremely useful book, which discusses the art of the Village, is Frederick J. Hoffman's *The Twenties: American Writing in the Postwar Decade* (New York, 1955). Henry May's *End of American Innocence* has an extensive discussion of the intellectual climate of the prewar Village. Caroline Ware's *Greenwich Village, 1920-1930* (Boston, 1935), a sociological study of this New York district, provides a wealth of useful information.

Much of the history of the Village is contained in nostalgic articles by figures as diverse as William Barrett, Floyd Dell, Max Eastman, and many of the participants in the various Village cultural movements. During the 1930s many critical articles appeared, written by Mike Gold and Joseph Freeman. Many memoirs of writers and artists touch on life in the Village, including Matthew Josephson, Mable Dodge Luhan, Lincoln Steffens, Max Eastman, Malcolm Cowley, Harold Loeb, Joseph Freeman, and Granville Hicks.

One important subject that is related to American Bohemianism has been little discussed. This is the tradition of vagabondage and the figure of the hobo. The most useful book on this subject by Nels Anderson, *The Hobo: Sociology of the Homeless Man* (Chicago, 1923), is, unfortunately, dated.

One of the most important subjects of American literary life is the expatriation of intellectuals during the 1920s. Here memoirs are once again very useful—by Cowley, Freeman, Hemingway, Josephson, Loeb, and others. The best discussion of expatriation is in Warren Susman's unpublished "The Pilgrimage to Paris" (University of Wisconsin, 1958). A model of its kind, this thesis discusses the great variety of reasons for exile and the factors that made possible the creation of the American colony of artists in France. Another important discussion of exile is R. P. Blackmur's "The American Literary Expatriate," in *Foreign Influences in American Life*, edited by David F. Bowers (New York, 1952). Expatriation is also touched on by almost every general literary history of the twentieth century and by more specialized studies of the 1920s. The movement of American writers and artists to Europe during this decade was the center of a good deal of contemporary discussion. Mass-circulation magazines as well as the literary journals and radical periodicals were all concerned with exile and debated its meaning widely.

Related to what Americans discovered in Paris are two important movements: dada and surrealism. A number of books are informative on these topics. One of the best accounts is in Matthew Josephson's *Life Among the Surrealists*. An interesting compilation of articles and documents of dada is Robert Motherwell's *The Dada Painters and Poets: An Anthology* (New York, 1951). Several books on surrealism have been helpful, including Ferdinand Alquie's *The Philosophy of Surrealism*, translated by Bernard Waldrop (Ann Arbor, 1965), Yves Duplessis's *Surrealism*, translated by Paul Capon (New York, 1962), and Wallace Fowlie's *The Age of Surrealism* (Bloomington, Ind., 1950). Two books by one of the leaders of surrealism are useful in understanding the connections between art and Marxism that developed in the late 1920s: André Breton's *La Clé des Champs* (Paris, 1953) and *Position Politique du Surrealisme* (Paris, 1935).

Index

James Burkhart Gilbert
is now Associate Professor of
History at the University of Maryland. He received a B.A. in English from Carleton College (1961)
and holds an M.A. (1963) and a
Ph.D. (1966) in American History
from the University of Wisconsin.

DATE DUE

JAN 6 '70			